# HAWAII

**First Edition**
**1992**

# *TABLE OF CONTENTS*

## *FEATURES*

## *GUIDELINES*

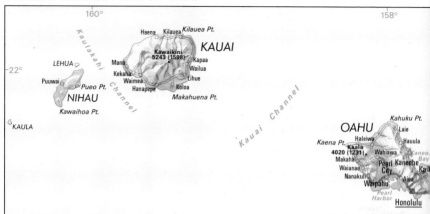

# LIST OF MAPS

156°

22°—

H A W A I I A N

ISLANDS

*kapuu*
*ad*

*Kaiwi Channel*

MOLOKAI
Hoolehua  Kalaupapa  Halawa
Maunaloa
Laau Pt.  Kaunakakai  Kamalo  **Kamakou**
**4970 (1515)**
*Kalohi Channel*  Honokahua  *Pailolo Channel*
Nakalele Pt.

*Kahului Bay*

Keanapapa Pt.  **Puu Kukui**
**5788 (1764)**  Wailuku
LANAI  Lanai City  *Auau Channel*  Lahaina  Kahului  Pukalani  Keanae
MAUI
Kaumalapau  **Lanaihale**
**3370 (1027)**  Kihei  Waiakoa  Hana
Palaoa Pt.  *Maalaea Bay*  **Puu Ulaula**  Kauiki Head
**10023 (3055)**
*Kealaikahiki Channel*  *Alalakeiki Channel*

Kealaikahiki Pt.  KAHOOLAWE  Kaka Pt.

*Alenuihaha Channel*

Upolu Pt.
Hawi  Halawa
KOHALA MTS.  HAWAII
Kawaihae  Honokaa
*Kaiwaihae Bay*  Waimea  Paauilo

O C E A N  Honomu
**Mauna Kea**
**13796 (4205)**  Papaikou
Keahole Pt.  *Hilo Bay*
Hilo  Leleiwi Pt.
Kailua  Keaau
**Mauna Loa**
**13679**  Pahoa
Captain  **(4169)**  Cape
Cook  Volcano  Kumukahi
KONA  **Kilauea**
**Caldera**  Kalapana
**4078 (1247)**
KONA COAST

*Honuapo Bay*
Naalehu

Ka Lae

20°

## HAWAIIAN ISLANDS

| 0 | 20 | 40 | 60 km |

| 0 | 20 | 40 miles |

156°

# A HISTORY
# OF HAWAII

For millions of years, the islands of the Hawaiian archipelago remained unsettled. No one saw the volcanoes pour their lava into the sea. No one heard the birds with colorful plumage singing in the rainforests. No skilled fishermen's nets or spears endangered the fish in the seas. The islands, unseen, unheard, unknown, retained their primal dignity – unchallenged by discovery, empowered by the magnitude of the forces of creation.

People were latecomers to these islands, isolated in all directions by thousands of miles of open sea. It was not until the Huns were at the gates of Rome that seafaring Polynesians set sail from the Marquesas Islands, nearly 2,000 miles (3,200 km) to the south, on a voyage of exploration and settlement that would take them to Hawaii.

These Polynesians navigated the vastness of the mid-Pacific Ocean, following the sun by day and the stars by night, taking note of winds, currents and migrating birds, and carefully eyeing the shapes and sizes of clouds and waves. So they charted a celestial course that allowed them to return home and make repeated voyages to Hawaii, carrying the food, supplies and people that would enable them to settle the islands. Some 500 to 1,000 years later, long after contact between Hawaii and the Marquesas had ceased, a second wave of migrations began. This time, it brought settlers from the Society Islands, the archipelago west of the Marquesas that includes Tahiti.

*Preceding pages: A native of Maui with the spirit of aloha. Vacationers on Waikiki's beach. A hula dancer in traditional garb. Viscous molten lava flows into the sea at Kalapana. A tender Hawaiian mix. Left: Lava hardens in distinctive braided patterns.*

Duplicating the navigational feat of the Marquesans, the Tahitians too made repeated voyages to Hawaii, gradually establishing themselves on all the main islands. In time, the voyages from Tahiti also ceased. Hawaii, the most magnificent of all Pacific archipelagoes, would have 1,000 years to evolve a culture of its own. The world beyond the horizon existed only in tales and chants.

It remains uncertain whether the Marquesans and Tahitians lived together peacefully. Hawaiian legends tell of an elfin people called *menehunes* who already inhabited Hawaii when the Society Islanders arrived. To them are ascribed magical powers and superhuman building skills. Perhaps the Marquesans were the source of the *menehune* legends. Some have also linked the Marquesans to the *kuawa,* outcasts at the bottom of Hawaii's rigidly stratified social order.

What little has been established as fact about the early Hawaiians comes from archaeological sites around the islands, from artifacts collected, and from sketches made by the first European crews to reach Hawaiian shores in the late seventeenth and early eighteenth centuries. The balance of knowledge has its origin in the chants, legends and genealogies that link the people to their history and their gods.

**Enter the Gods**

The gods played a very crucial role in the lives of all Polynesian peoples, and the Hawaiians were no exception. The gods were attached to all things spiritual and physical. Of all the Hawaiian gods, goddesses and demigods, the most revered were Ku, Lono, Kane and Kanaloa – all of whom had many personae. Lono, for example, honored as god of peace, agriculture and fertility, might appear as a tree, a fish, or in a half-man, half-hog form. Kanaloa, god of the ocean and ocean winds, might appear either as an octopus or as a man.

Ku, as god of war, was manifest as Kukailimoku, "the snatcher of land." As Kunuiakea, "Ku of the great expanse," he was unseen, living in the highest heavens as protector of all the Ku gods. Ku also appeared as the rising sun, confirming his role as the god of masculine power.

Kane, the procreator, was provider of sunlight, fresh water and nature's life-sustaining power. As Kanenuiakea, he was creator of heaven and earth, and of the things that filled them. He was called "the many gods in one god" by the Hawaiians – an indication of the universality of all life that was at the root of Hawaiian consciousness and belief.

Even the creation of mankind was linked directly to the gods, who lent their assistance in transforming a mud figure into the first man and his shadow into the first woman. The high chiefs claimed the right to rule on the basis of their god-linked genealogies that empowered them with the spiritual force called *mana*. The most honored, those possessing the most *mana*, traced family origins all the way back to the beginning, the point in time when the islands themselves were given life by the gods.

By Hawaiian tradition, the islands were born of the gods. Therefore, if not for its beauty, the land, the *aina*, was considered sacred. The gods were everywhere, residing in rocks, mountains, and the molten lava being the domain of impetuous Pele, the goddess of the awesome volcanic fires. For the Hawaiians there were no boundaries between the physical and the spiritual world: the gods, the people and the islands were all part of one great continuum.

## A Trail of Migrations

As contemporary research reveals it, Hawaii was one of the last of many stops the Polynesians made in their travels from the Asian mainland across the Paci-

*Above left: A wooden temple image. Above right: The god Ku. Right: The arrival of the first Polynesians by artist Herb Kane.*

fic. Those migrations, measured in the span of thousands of years, are confirmed not only by Hawaiian memory. Scientific research has traced the Polynesian dispersion by carbon-dating artifacts, tracing the origins of foods favored by the Hawaiians, and searching for similarities between Hawaiian and other languages of Polynesia and Southeast Asia.

It is likely that the migrations began somewhere in India at the dawn of human history. The progenitors of the Hawaiians eventually made their way down the Malay Peninsula and across coastal seas to the islands of Indonesia and Micronesia. Here they perfected the seafaring skills that would allow them to cross the vastness of the south and central Pacific.

Eventually, they settled in an area now called the Polynesian Triangle – delimited by New Zealand in the southwest, Easter Island in the southeast, and Hawaii in the north. In total, the Polynesian homeland was more than twice the size of Europe measured from the Ural Mountains to the Atlantic Ocean. Tonga, Samoa and the Tokelaus – westernmost of the islands that would later be called Polynesia ("many islands") by the outside world, were the first to be discovered and settled. The Society and Marquesas Islands followed some centuries later.

Later, the migrants headed southwest to the Cook Islands and New Zealand; and southeast to the Austral and Tuamotu archipelagoes and isolated Easter Island. Some say they continued on from here to South America. Others disagree, but there seems little reason to doubt that such a voyage might have occured.

What is certain is that in heading north they came upon the islands of Hawaii, where they settled and prospered.

Less certain is what motivated the Polynesians to uproot themselves and repeatedly risk their lives in search of new islands to settle. They had begun their migrations at a time when most of humanity was still nomadic, gathering plants, hunting animals and catching fish. Farming and animal husbandry were skills that had not yet evolved.

Whatever the reason, the carefully planned voyages were made in large double-hulled canoes fashioned from great trees that were hollowed by fire, then skilfully carved and sanded with stone tools. Measuring 60 to 80 ft (18 to 25 m) in length, they were securely lashed together by rope made of coconut fiber, and were powered by sails of hand-beaten *tapa,* a cloth made from the inner bark of a variety of trees.

A thatched hut, large enough to shelter 20 to 40 people, was built on the central platform between the two hulls. It offered protection from sun and storm for people and provisions. Proper provisioning was critical, especially for crews heading into unknown seas on voyages that might last a month or longer. Stocks included dried fruits and vegetables, chicken, and coconuts for meat and water.

### A New Life Begins

It is not known whether the first settlers reached Hawaii by design or by chance. Whichever, they came well prepared for life in a new land, bringing with them chickens, pigs and dogs, and more than two dozen species of plants – including coconut, taro, breadfruit, sweet potato, banana and sugar cane, all staples of the Polynesian diet. Other plants included varieties with medicinal, cosmetic and domestic uses. The Polynesians were well aware of the value of the plants that surrounded them, using their awareness of nature's bounty to full advantage.

Farming and fishing were the two primary occupations and the first settlements were founded along the coast and in valleys whose rivers offered a steady supply of fresh water. Taro was the most important crop; it was usually grown in terraced fields that were fed river water by a system of irrigation ditches. The

*Right: A turn-of-the-century postcard showing a Maui couple pounding taro.*

dark root, cooked and fermented, provided *poi,* a nutritious, slightly sour pudding that accompanied most meals.

Food was stored in hollowed gourds, and hung from posts in beautifully woven baskets. Although a small fire was usually maintained within the house, most cooking was done outside in an underground oven called an *imu.* Foods were wrapped in leaves and steamed in it.

The sea proved a third dietary resource for the Hawaiian people. It provided seaweed, shellfish, turtles, and standards like *ama'ama* (mullet) and *mahimahi* (dolphin fish). Since all the needs of the chiefs were expected to be met, great fish ponds were built for the *ali'i,* providing them with a perpetual abundance.

Houses were typically built of thatch atop a carefully constructed framework of wood. Some were entirely thatched, others had thatched roofs and stone walls. Thatching was made from fragrant *pili* grass, *hala* (pandanus), *ti* and *ku* (sugar cane). Many houses were surrounded by walls of tightly lashed sticks.

While a chief's house might measure 15 by 70 ft (4.5 by 21 m), commoners lived on a far less grandiose scale: A room no more than 20 or 30 ft (6 to 9 m) long and 8 to 10 ft (2.4 to 3 m) wide often accommodated a large family. Children were numerous and were treated as a blessing; they were often raised not only by their parents, but also by grandparents, aunts, uncles, cousins and non-relatives, all of whom were part of the typical extended family.

Most homes had no windows and were entered through a small door covered by a piece of *tapa* or a woven mat. Oil-rich *kukui* nuts provided light. Furnishings were simple, usually consisting of no more than a few sleeping mats of woven pandanus or coconut leaves, and some woven-leaf pillows.

Clothing was likewise simple, well-suited to the mildness of the climate. *Tapa,* beaten from the inner bark of the

mulberry tree, provided an all-purpose fabric, the natural off-white color often dyed or imprinted with geometrical designs. Men typically wore a *tapa* loincloth called a *malo,* while women wore a long cloth skirt called a *pa'u.* Long *tapa* capes, tied over a single shoulder, were worn when it was cold. Sandals were woven of *ti* leaves and *hau* tree bark. *Ti* leaves were also woven into thick capes as protection against rain and cold.

Thousands of brightly colored feathers, collected with much effort from rainforest birds, were woven into capes that were perhaps the most elaborate example of Hawaiian aesthetic sensibilities and skill. Red, yellow and black feathers were preferred. Hunters studied birds' habits and roosting places in order to become more proficient at catching their feathery prey. Some birds were released after a few selected feathers had been taken.

Feathers were sewn to fabric or mesh backing with thread made from the *olona* vine. The resulting capes were worn only by the highest chiefs or by warriors of great ability. Leis, masks, helmets and sacred objects were also meticulously sewn with feathers, confirming Hawaiian featherwork as some of the most sophisticated ever produced.

### Chiefs, Priests and Gods

Politically, Polynesian Hawaii was a feudal theocracy. A hierarchy of chiefs, headed by the *moi,* or king, ruled with help from the priestly class, the *kahunas.* Since rank was based on ancestry and on the *mana* generated by exalted ancestry, it is not surprising that the power of the *moi* was absolute: In his veins flowed the blood of the gods. Few dared challenge the sacred rights of chiefly descent.

The *kahuna nui,* or high priest, advised the *moi* on all matters of significance, while the spiritual well-being of the lesser chiefs was attended to by a hierarchy of priests. From the practice of medicine to the building of a canoe, from birth to death to marriage and war, benedictions were offered and ceremonies performed.

*Above: The Ahuena Heiau (temple), in the compound of Kamehameha the Great.*

Sorcery and divination were widely practiced by *kahuna* who developed "supernatural" skills. The *kahuna kaula* was a prophet who foretold future events: The spirit of a god spoke through this priest, causing him to speak out fearlessly, even if that meant revealing a turn of events that his chief did not want to hear. The *kahuna kuhikuhilani* read omens in the skies, while the *kahuna kilo hoku* studied the movement of the stars. The *kahuna po'i'uhane* was able to capture the souls of the living and the dead. Greatly feared were the *kahuna 'ana 'ana,* who were able to pray their victims to death. The belief in such powers persisted well into the nineteenth century, long after Hawaii had been Christianized and the priesthood disbanded.

There were many *heiau* (temples) in the land, some dedicated to peaceful gods, some to gods who demanded human sacrifice. Usually built atop large rock platforms, the *heiau* housed sacred figures and provided priests and chiefs with a place to pray and seek the approval of the gods. For their part, the commoners, called *maka'ainana,* had their own, simpler means of communing with the gods, worshipping and making offerings at family shrines and altars.

The *ali'i,* or chiefs, were all in service to the *moi.* The *kalaimoku* was selected by the *moi* from the ranks of the *ali'i* to serve in an advisory capacity equal to that of the high priest. *Mana* was of critical importance in establishing chiefly rank. The highest chiefs could trace their history back 100 generations and more, linking themselves to the gods well before the migrations from the Marquesas and Society Islands. With no written language to record the past, people of well-trained memory were selected by chiefly families to memorize genealogies that were many hours in the telling.

These genealogies, as well as stories of creation and the gods, were presented in powerfully lyrical chants *(mele)* accompanied by rattles, flutes, mouth bows and drums – music of hypnotic simplicity. *Hula* accompanied some chants; the sensual movements of this dance provided an image that would become synonymous with Hawaii. All of the entertainment reaffirmed chiefly authority.

With *mana* based upon ancestry, the marriages of ruling chiefs were as much a matter of state importance in Hawaii as they were when royal Europe was in its prime. Producing offspring of high *mana* was a primary consideration to chiefs. If a high chief could not find a spouse of suitable *mana,* a sister or brother, uncle or niece might be chosen as a mate. Once children were born and the continuation of the line was assured, the high-ranking husband or wife might take a second or third partner, a reality that changed only with the conversion of the Hawaiians to Christianity in the nineteenth century.

The land was the property of the *moi,* who provided for his people by making grants of land to a select bureaucracy of lesser chiefs. They distributed land to those who would work it and who would pay for the right with up to two-thirds of all that was grown or produced. Taxes might be paid in taro and hogs, or fishnets and feathers. With economically sound judgment, the land under a chief's control usually ranged from mountains to the sea, providing a degree of self-sufficiency to each chiefly district.

When a high chief died, all the lands he had granted were forfeited – surrendered to the new high chief to be redivided in grants to chiefs of his preference. Only in the nineteenth century, when Western influence began to predominate, was the private land ownership introduced.

### The Powerful *kapu*

No matter what one's class, however, rights were rigidly defined by *kapu,* regulations that were enforced with lethal seriousness. *Kapu* regulated all aspects of

life, imposing strict limits on the behavior of chiefs and commoners alike.

Some *kapu* were long-standing laws of the land, like those prohibiting women from eating with men and barring women from enjoying foods like coconut and pork. Some *kapu* were pragmatic, such as the prohibition against war during the *makahiki,* when taxes were collected. Some *kapu* were just and far-sighted, such as those regulating the use of natural resources; others were severe and unjust, especially those formulated by the priests to keep society under control. For instance, should a commoner break the *kapu* against his shadow touching a ranking chief, the penalty might well be death – instantaneous and unmourned. It was the rigidity of the *kapu* system, which had grown powerful from unquestioned belief in the gods, that gave Hawaiian culture its cohesiveness and continuity. When times of change were forced upon Hawaii early in the nineteenth century, it was that same rigidity that led to the rapid collapse of the *kapu* system and the society it had perpetuated.

### Makahiki and War

In feudal fashion, tribute was paid each year during the sacred *makahiki* festival that ran from the middle of October to the middle of February. Held in honor of Lono, the god of peace, agriculture and fertility, *makahiki* was the main festive event of the Hawaiian calendar, complete with its own Olympiad of sports, for Lono was also patron of sporting games. During the *makahiki,* a *kapu* was placed on war, ceremonies in the temple ceased, and all unnecessary work was stopped.

Just as the best spear throwers, wrestlers and tug-of-war teams were honored at the *makahiki,* so too were the chiefs. At *makahiki,* the high chief traversed his domain in ceremonial procession to collect tribute paid in the form of produce, handicrafts and services.

Many of the events performed at the *makahiki* in honor of Lono were also dedicated to Ku, the fearsome god of war. Wars were a frequent occurrence in Polynesian Hawaii. Mock battles, in which competing troops used blunted weapons and stopped short of killing their foes, provided training for real wars that were played for the fullest of stakes, in battles in which casualties were numerous and mercy was in limited supply.

Chiefs spent a great deal of time training their warriors for battle. Before war was declared, a chief would consult his advisors and priests, seeking reassurance that the time was right for victory. If the gods deemed the time propitious, mobilization orders were sent to the lesser chiefs. Hand-to-hand combat with clubs and daggers was the norm, although slings and spears were used when armies were at long range. On occasion, opposing champions would fight proxy battles for the armies that backed them.

War was the natural consequence of an expanding population, for by the seventeenth century, once-unpopulated Hawaii was home to an estimated 250,000 to 400,000. Fertile land and the resources of forest and sea had once been available for the taking, but as the population grew, conflicting territorial claims led to centuries of increasingly commonplace and brutal warfare. By the late-eighteenth century, four chiefs ruled the eight main islands of the archipelago.

The process culminated in the late-eighteenth century when a Big Island chief named Kamehameha laid claim to a united archipelago. Ironically, this consolidation coincided with the arrival of the first European explorers and American trade ships.

**Enter Captain Cook**

Even as the Hawaiians loved and fought, lived and died, unaware of the

*Above: An early depiction of hula dancers.*
*Right: A chief in regalia. Far right: Captain Cook being received on Kauai in 1778.*

ILES SANDWICH, UN OFFICIER DU ROI EN GRAND COSTUME.

immense world beyond the limits of their island realm, that world was closing in on them. With matchless irony, it was from their ancestral islands to the south that two great ships on a voyage of discovery set sail, laden with marvels and strange men from places unimagined.

The British captain, James Cook, was aboard the *HMS Resolution* when it departed Bora Bora, in the Society Islands, into uncharted seas. Islanders had told him of inhabited islands far to the north, but none had made the voyage for centuries, and it remained for Cook to learn whether their stories were fact or fiction.

On January 18, 1778, Cook's crew sighted Oahu, confirming the existence of a new archipelago. Due to strong winds, Oahu remained out of reach, as did Kauai when it was sighted later in the day. It was not until the following evening that the *Resolution* and the *Discovery* were able to drop anchor off south Kauai's Waimea coast.

*Makahiki* was underway. This was Lono's festival, and stories said that Lono, long gone from Hawaii, would one day return on what would appear to be a moving island. Lono's symbol – tapa cloth hung on a crossbar – looked much like the lowered sails aboard Cook's two vessels. Hawaiian historian Samuel Kamakau told of the impact on the Hawaiians at Waimea that day:

"The next morning (Jan. 20) chiefs and commoners marveled at it (the ship). Some were terrified and shrieked with fear. One told another, 'They are trees moving about on the sea.' A certain *kahuna* named Kuohu declared: 'That can be nothing else than the *heiau* of Lono and the place of sacrifice at the altar.' The excitement grew stronger, and louder grew the shouting. Thus the name of Lono spread from Kauai to Hawaii."

That same morning, Cook and some of his men were rowed to shore. The meeting would impress all concerned, Cook not the least. Realizing the racial links between the people of New Zealand, Tahiti, Easter Island and Hawaii, Cook declared them "the most extensive nation upon earth." The Kauaians he found "frank and of cheerful disposition," their villages clean, their fields tilled and well kept, their feather cloaks and helmets of the finest workmanship. Naming the islands after his patron, the Earl of Sandwich, he would later declare them "in many respects the most important discovery made by Europeans throughout the extent of the Pacific Ocean."

Charged with discovering a northern passage between Europe and Asia, Cook soon set sail for Alaska, returning to Hawaii in November 1778 to escape the arctic winter. For eight frustrating weeks, his ships circled the islands in search of a harbor. They finally made port on January 16, 1779, in Kealakekua Bay on the Big Island of Hawaii.

Kealakekua was sacred to Lono, and again *makahiki* was underway, with high chief Kalaniopuu in residence in honor of the god. When word spread of Lono's return, thousands came to share in the welcome, which impressed Cook with its spectacle.

Feasts and exhibitions were held in Cook's honor and the ships were given all manner of provisions in exchange for iron and trinkets, weapons and clothing. Despite the royal treatment, by February Cook was once again ready to depart for arctic waters. A first attempt was foiled when a storm damaged the *Resolution*'s foremast, forcing Cook to return to Kealakekua to make repairs.

By the time Cook returned, *makahiki* was over. The bay, put off-limits by a *kapu* decreed by Kalaniopuu, was deserted. It soon became evident that this unexpected return reduced Cook and his crew to more human proportions. As the ships prepared to depart a second time, the proper repairs having been made, a cutter tied to the *Discovery* was stolen.

*Right: Kamehameha speaks to his oldest son, Liholiho, a twentieth-century depiction by Hawaiian artist Herb Kane.*

Cook, accompanied by nine marines, went ashore to recover the cutter or take Kalaniopuu hostage until it was returned. The king's warriors took up their weapons when word spread that Kalaniopuu was in danger, attacking with stones, clubs and daggers – and quickly taking Cook's life. Shooting muskets into the crowd, five marines escaped, making their way back to their ship.

Later, two delegations of Hawaiians made their way to Cook's ship, returning the parts of his body that had not been taken for ceremonial use. On February 22, the British ships, without their captain, set out on the long journey back to Great Britain.

## Kamehameha and the Hawaiian Kingdom

It is said that on the night of Kamehameha's birth, a comet streaked across the Hawaiian sky announcing the birth of a high chief. Born at some time between 1753 and 1758 in the North Kohala district of the Big Island, Kamehameha was the grandnephew of Alapai, high chief of the Big Island. The chiefess Kekuipoiwa was his mother, and although the chief Keoua was accepted as his father, there were many who believed that he was in fact the son of Kahekili, high chief of Maui, against whom he would be compelled to fight many battles in his effort to unify the islands under his rule.

A unified Hawaii had been the goal of more than one high chief in the course of Hawaii's history, but it had not yet been accomplished when Kamehameha set out to fulfil his destiny. Taken into Alapai's court at the age of five, and later accepted as a member of the court of Kalaniopuu, Alapai's successor, he received the rigorous training then usual for a high-ranking and important Hawaiian warrior.

From the beginning, the gods seemed to favor Kamehameha, though he was not the highest ranking *ali'i* of his genera-

tion. In his teens, he was said to have moved the great Naha stone, of which it was prophesied that anyone who moved it would rule the Hawaiian islands. Other stories contributed to his reputation that was confirmed more than once on the battlefield.

Kamehameha was in his twenties when Captain James Cook made his second Hawaiian landfall at Kealakekua Bay in 1779. Taken aboard *HMS Resolution* for Cook's rendezvous with the Big Island's royal court, he quickly realized that the weapons and technology he saw were the key to successfully unifying the islands. Ambitious enough to care, smart enough to accurately judge the future, the young Kamehameha was able to absorb change and use it to his own great advantage.

In 1785, he married the beautiful teenage chiefess Kaahumanu in a love match that would last a lifetime, and would eventually see her named regent for Kamehameha's heirs. At 6 ft (1.82 m) tall, she was a match for her 6-ft, 6-in (1.98 m) husband, who was then in the midst of

establishing his claim to Kalaniopuu's Big Island kingdom.

Kalaniopuu had died in 1781, naming his son Kiwalao heir and Kamehameha as guardian of the war god, Kukailimoku. Renowned as a warrior in battles fought at Kalaniopuu's side, Kamehameha soon defied his uncle's wish and claimed the chieftaincy as his own.

Having seen the Western arsenal first hand, Kamehameha took advantage of the first opportunity to put that weaponry, and the expertise behind it, to use in fighting his cause. In 1788, he acquired a field cannon and some British navy-issue muskets. Two years later, the capture of the trader *Fair American* and an encounter with her sister ship, the *Eleanora,* provided a more significant haul, adding cannon, muskets and, most importantly, the knowledge of several crewmen who accepted his offer to settle on the Big Island and serve his cause.

In 1790, Kamehameha invaded Maui, overwhelming the forces of Maui high chief Kahekili. The man rumored to be

Kamehameha's father also hoped to unite the islands, and this battle was the first of several between them. Other chiefs pursued the same goal, and no sooner had victory on Maui been achieved than rebellion flared on the Big Island as Kalaniopuu's second son, Keoua, declared his right to the Big Island's chieftaincy.

Returning to the Big Island, Kamehameha engaged Keoua in two inconclusive battles along the Hamakua coast. Then Pele made an appearance, further enhancing Kamehameha's chances for victory when a large contingent of Keoua's forces was overwhelmed by a volcanic eruption. To the Hawaiians, the message was clear: The goddess favored Kamehameha's claim.

Returning to Kawaihae, on the advice of his priests, Kamehameha began work on a great temple dedicated to Kukailimoku, the war god who was his patron. Work on the temple was well underway

*Above: A woman offering sacrifices to goddess Pele on the Kilauea volcano.*

when Kahekili attacked from the Waimanu Valley with a large armada of war canoes. Kamehameha responded with an equally large fleet. Both sides made use of death-dealing cannon mounted on double-hulled canoes. Kamehameha was again victorious.

Disheartened by Kamehameha's victories and Pele's disfavor, Keoua agreed to attend the dedication ceremony at the temple that Kamehameha's men were now completing at Puukohola. Keoua arrived by canoe, attended by his court, resplendent in chiefly regalia. Kamehameha waited on shore with an equally impressive retinue. It was one of Kamehameha's men who threw the first spear, killing Keoua on the spot. His body was taken to the temple altar, presented as an offering to Kukailimoku. His position as *moi* of the Big Island confirmed, Kamehameha awaited the approval of the gods before his next move.

The death of Kahekili in 1794 provided the opportunity for which Kamehameha had been waiting: the two sons

Kahekili had named as his heirs were soon involved in a no-holds-barred war. The victor, Kalanikupule, seized control of the British ships that had been acting as his allies, demanding that they carry his troops to the Big Island to do battle with Kamehameha.

Off Waikiki, the British sailors regained control of the commandeered vessels. Setting Kalanikupule ashore, they sailed to the Big Island to warn Kamehameha. Gathering a force of 16,000 warriors, Kamehameha carried the war to Oahu, destroying Lahaina and despoiling the West Maui coast en route. He reached Waikiki in the middle of April 1795. Kalanikupule's troops were routed, their defeat made legendary when they were forced over a cliff's edge at the Nuuanu *pali*. All of the islands, except Kauai and Niihau, ruled by high chief Kaumualii, now belonged to Kamehameha.

While Kauai twice escaped Kamehameha's efforts at conquest, the momentum of his victories elsewhere eventually drew that most isolated of the islands under his control. In 1810, Kaumualii acknowledged Kamehameha's authority and willed him his kingdom.

With the kingdom for which he'd fought united and at peace, the warrior king, soon to be 60, retired to Kailua on the Big Island's Kona coast. Kauileauoli and Liholiho, sons he had sired by the high-born chiefess Keopuolani, stood ready to inherit his lands, acknowledged as the highest born of all the *ali'i*.

Kamehameha had not only realized his wildest dreams; he had established a kingdom whose legitimacy would survive for nearly a century. More than a chief, he was the embodiment of a way of life, the culmination of 1,000 years of Polynesian history. When he died in 1819, few understood how soon that world would collapse, brought to surrender by the impact of new ideas, foreign diseases, and the politics of a world that would find Hawaii a tempting prize.

## Liholiho and the End of *kapu*

It was one thing for the legendary Kamehameha to maintain the old order despite the end of Hawaii's hermetic reality. It was quite another thing for his son, the high-born Liholiho, to do the same. Only when his august father died, did it become obvious just how much was irrevocably lost with the king's passing.

The pressures for change were not only external, for by 1819, 40 years had passed since the first foreigners had reached Hawaii's shores. Now each year saw increasing numbers of foreign ships, mostly British, French and American, heading to Hawaii to reprovision after long months at sea.

No one mistook this increasing flow of foreigners for returning gods, and their very invulnerability to the once inviolate *kapu* undermined Hawaiian belief both in the gods and in the system perpetuated in their name by *ali'i* and priests. There were already signs of a spiritual and cultural uncertainty, brought on by the immorality of the rough-edged seamen who spent their money on whisky and women when they were in port.

Increasingly indebted to the foreign traders, who sold them all manner of goods, the chiefs began to demand more labor from the commoners under their control: time to harvest *pelu,* used as a stuffing for mattresses and pillows, from tree ferns; time to harvest sandalwood from upcountry forests for shipment to China; time to grow the crops that the chiefs would use to pay their rapidly accumulating debts.

Caught between his native past and an alien present, Liholiho was in his early twenties when he succeeded his father as Kamehameha II. Pampered by a doting mother and treated as sacred by those who respected his *mana,* the young king succumbed to the pleasures of his rank without understanding its responsibilities. Under the influence of his high-born

mother, Keopuolani, and of Kaahumanu, the imperious queen named regent for the youthful heir, Liholiho surrenderred the Polynesian past and its heritage to the uncertainties of change within several months of his father's death.

For quick-witted and wilful women like Keopuolani and Kaahumanu, contact with the outside world would give recurring proof that the ancient *kapu* no longer applied. Pursuing the end of a system they considered spiritually discredited and inconsistent with their dignity and rights, they brought about change by challenging the *ai kapu* that forbade men and women to have meals together. Kaahumanu set things in motion on the day of Liholiho's investiture as Kamehameha II by stating her opposition to the *kapu* system and eating a banana, a food *kapu* to women, in the king's presence. Keopuolani followed suit several days later, lunching on pork and bananas in the

*Above: Kamehameha I. Right: Lot Kamehameha, A. Liholiho and adviser G. Judd.*

presence of Liholiho and his younger brother, Kauikeauoli.

Pressured by priests and chiefs to punish the offending queens and reaffirm the validity of ancient tradition, Liholiho withdrew to the upcountry remoteness of Waimea, on the Big Island. It was November, and *makahiki* was underway. On the night of *kukahi,* sacred to the war god Ku, Kaahumanu hosted a lavish dinner, setting the tables without regard to *kapu* foods, without even a *kapu* screen for separation. Dressed in a British naval uniform, Liholiho took his place at the head of the men's table. Kaahumanu, Keopuolani and several of Liholiho's wives presided over the women's table. Traditional chants were sung, in revealing contrast to attire and ceremony. Suddenly, Liholiho rose, made his way to the women's table, and in full view of the expectant crowd, sat down and began to eat. With a simple act the power of the *kapu* was suddenly ended.

Within months, the ancient temples were pulled down and abandoned, the priestly class disbanded, the icons of gods destroyed or hidden by those who still believed in the old ways. As if fated, a new spiritual message was already on its way to fill the spiritual void that followed the collapse of *kapu*.

### The Missionaries Arrive

The first missionaries reached Hawaii aboard the brigantine *Thaddeus* in April 1820. Eight months out of New Bedford, Massachusetts, they did not know of the changes being already underway when they set sail, but they were prepared to "convert the heathens" at any cost.

Armed with stern, disciplined New England Protestantism, they brought their message of sin and salvation to commoners and *ali'i* alike. The high-born Keopuolani, mother of the king, was the first *ali'i* to convert, followed soon by Queen Regent Kaahumanu.

Although their message was stern, the missionaries also taught the Hawaiians the skills they would require to become "civilized." Schools were set up to teach farming and animal husbandry. An alphabet was chosen, transforming Hawaiian into a written language. The Bible was quickly translated, and the schools taught the Hawaiians to read and write a language whose most beautiful aspect had been its oral tradition.

In the four decades that followed the arrival of the *Thaddeus,* missionaries would become a significant power behind the throne. They taught Hawaii's future kings, advising them both in the faith and in ways to handle the demands for commercial advantage being made by the ever-increasing number of foreign ships in Hawaiian waters. In later generations, the missionary families would produce the businessmen and landowners who would plot a course for statehood in the American Union.

### A Young King Dies

In 1823, aged 28, Kamehameha II decided to head for England, hoping for a meeting with King George V. He set sail aboard the British whaling ship *L'Aigle* accompanied by the lovely Kamamalu, his half-sister and most favored of his five wives, the missionary Hiram Bingham and members of the royal court.

Some six and a half months later, the *Aigle* docked at Portsmouth, with the royal party transferring to London. At first all went well, with the royal couple receiving considerable attention. Then, in July 1824, both Liholiho and his queen took sick with measles. In a preview of a tragedy that was to almost annihilate the Hawaiian people, neither was able to fight off this foreign illness. Kamamalu died on July 8, followed six days later by the grief-stricken king.

*HMS Blonde,* a British naval vessel, was put at the disposal of the Hawaiians.

The bodies of the dead royalty were placed on board, reaching Oahu on May 6, 1825. Great was the grief in the islands, but with Kaahumanu as regent and Kauikeauoli, Liholiho's equally high-born brother, to provide continuity, the transition was peacefully made.

### Kamehameha III

Born to Kamehameha and Keopuolani in 1814, Kauikeauoli was only 11 when his brother's body was brought back to Honolulu from London and he was named Kamehameha III. Too young to remember much of his father or of Hawaii without foreign influence, he was far more westernized than Liholiho, as much a product of the new age as the old.

Kauikeauoli was caught in a web of irreconcilable beliefs, a victim of misdirected energies and conflicting priorities. The 30 years of his reign started with youthful indiscretion and rebellion and ended with demoralization brought about by the unrelenting demands of tightrope

diplomacy. That his reign accomplished the transition with the monarchy intact seemed nothing short of miraculous.

Although he would never join a church, Kauikeauoli ultimately came to rely upon the advice of several missionaries who left their churches to play ministerial roles in his government. They helped establish a system of schools, provide a constitution and parliamentary government, and deal with the demands of foreign governments and of Americans and Europeans, who were settling in the islands in increasing numbers.

Year to year, the king was confronted with challenges to his reign over what were now more regularly called the Sandwich Islands than Hawaii. In 1843, the arrogant British commander George Paulet coerced Kamehameha III into surrendering his kingdom to the British crown. Five months later the deed was undone

*Above: Preaching on Kauai. Right: King Kamehameha III as a child. Far right: Saint Benedict's Church on the way to Napoopoo.*

when Britain refused the transfer – most likely in consideration of the watchful presence of the French and Americans.

Americans, the largest foreign community settled in the islands, also had partisans of annexation, and the matter was openly discussed in the Hawaiian and American press. The issue of Hawaiian independence was seemingly settled in 1849 when, after more than a decade of negotiations, treaties accepting that fact were signed by Great Britain, France and the United States.

For most of the rest of the nineteenth century, that guarantee remained secure. But time was playing to the disadvantage of the Hawaiians. Measles, chicken pox, smallpox, tuberculosis, syphilis and other diseases, against which the natives had no immunity, were visited upon the defenseless Hawaiians one after another, so quickly reducing the population that by 1854, when Kamehameha III's reign came to an end, the native population had fallen to 70,000 from an estimated 300,000 to 400,000 at the time of Cook's

arrival. In the decades that followed, the problem only worsened. By the turn of the twentieth century, fewer than 20,000 Hawaiians of pure Polynesian blood remained, a consequence of disease and growing infertility. Kauikeauoli himself died childless. His two children by Princess Kalama died in infancy, an event increasingly frequent among *ali'i* and commoners alike. But the kingdom he left behind, though still vulnerable, was better prepared to deal with the colonial powers vying for advantage.

Internally as well, Kamehameha III had moved his kingdom along a road of change that seemed inevitable. Through the Great Mahele of 1848, he had divided the lands of his kingdom, providing separately for the government, the royal family, and all of Hawaiian ancestry. He had overhauled the system of taxation, nurtured the seedlings of plantation agriculture, and expanded the system of missionary schools. Yet by 1854, the once-rebellious young man had become a hardened fatalist. His authority com-

promised by realities he could not always control, he had more than once declared himself "a dead man" in relation to the course of events. On December 15, 1854, the point proved true.

### Kamehameha IV

Within an hour of Kauikeauoli's passing, his nephew, Alexander Liholiho, had been named Kamehameha IV. Grandson of the first Kamehameha king, he came to the throne, aged 20, in a Christian ceremony at Kawaiahao Church in Honolulu, where the royal capital had been moved in the 1840s. Honolulu's deep-water harbor was considered the best in the Pacific by the hundreds of whalers and trade ships making port calls each year. By the mid 1850s, Hawaii's largest business was the reprovisioning of whalers and the providing of in-port recreation for their crews. Honolulu and Lahaina, on Maui, were the primary ports of call.

Taken to America and Europe by his missionary teacher Gerritt Judd, Kamehameha IV practiced a form of royalty more in the style of a British monarch than a traditional Hawaiian chief. His advisors were primarily Anglophiles, as was his wife and true love, the high-born chiefess Emma. Both preferred the more formal regal style of British democracy to the freewheeling individualism of Hawaii's resident Americans.

Seeing the rapid decline of his people and moved by their plight, Kamehameha IV and his queen helped found the first hospital dedicated to aiding the Hawaiians in their struggle against the various diseases to which they had been exposed. Recognizing the necessity of immediately stabilizing the population if Hawaii was to preserve its independence, the king also brought the first foreign contract laborers to the islands, starting with a shipload of Chinese in 1852.

Five years into his reign, the birth of a son, named Albert Edward, provided the inspiration the king needed to tackle the problems of governing in times of change. But *auwe noho'i e,* the ancient cry of mourning, would soon be heard, as death shattered his dreams for the future. On August 27, 1862, the Prince of Hawaii died of a brain fever that was likely meningitis. Plagued by depression, the 29-year-old king, weakened by asthma and grief, died.

### Kamehameha V

Prince Lot Kamehameha came to the Hawaiian throne by default. Although older than his brother Alexander Liholiho, circumstances had placed him second in line for the throne. Withdrawn, pragmatic, and not particularly well liked, he would prove an admirable standard bearer for the Kamehameha line. He reigned for nine years, providing careful leadership and political will.

*Right: Chinese contract laborers and immigrants arrived in the nineteenth century.*

Working tirelessly to secure the rights of the crown, Kamehameha V fought for and secured a new constitution (1864) that reasserted royal prerogatives – in keeping with the king's belief that his rule was divinely inspired, and with the paternal responsibility of a high chief to his people. With these responsibilities in mind, he sought Pacific Islanders to settle in the islands as a "cognitive race" to supplement the still-dwindling native population. When his efforts in Oceania failed, he looked toward Japan.

Labor was increasingly in short supply, and the need was fueled by the demands of Hawaii's growing number of sugar plantations. By the middle of Kamehameha V's reign, in fact, sugar and plantation agriculture had replaced whaling in the number one slot of the Hawaiian economy. But sugar created its own problems, tying the Hawaiian economy closely to that of the United States, where most of Hawaii's sugar was sold.

As celebrations were being prepared for his 42nd birthday, the enigmatic king suddenly took ill. Within days, he was dead. Little more than 80 years after the first Kamehameha had claimed Hawaii's throne, his last successor left the kingdom without an heir.

With the death of Kamehameha V, no clear-cut claimants remained for the Kamehameha throne. On his deathbed, Kamehameha V had finally chosen his cousin, Beatrice Pauahi, last of the descendants of the first Kamehameha; but she had refused. In the election that followed, Prince William Charles Lunalilo, grandson of Kaahumanu's sister and Kamehameha's half-brother, was elected to the throne: He was deemed the highest born of the remaining *ali'i,* proof of how few Hawaiians had survived.

A well-liked bon vivant, Lunalilo took his new position seriously, surprising those who believed Lunalilo to be too irresponsible to lead the nation. But by August, barely six months into his reign,

Lunalilo was taken ill, the result of too many years of heavy drinking and self-indulgence. By February 1873, it was all over. One year and 25 days after it began, the Lunalilo dynasty came to an end.

## Monarch for a New Dynasty

David Kalakaua, Lunalilo's rival in the royal election of 1872, once again ran for king in the 1873 election. Now, his rival was Queen Emma, the widow of Kamehameha IV. Kalakaua, then 38, won. Throughout his 17-year reign, he was in mortal combat with the annexationists, a powerful opposition. For the annexationist party, the monarchy was becoming anachronistic. Sugar plantations covered the landscape, and the United States was the logical market for their output. Even after a reciprocity treaty had been signed, allowing Hawaiian growers easy access to the American market, the monarchy retained its enemies.

Plantation agriculture had not only tied Hawaii closer economically to the United States; it had brought about a demographic transformation. As the number of Hawaiians declined, thousands immigrated from Japan as contract laborers. By the 1880s, there were also settlements of Portuguese and Chinese, not to mention a large community of Americans. The Hawaiian component was an increasingly smaller and more fragile percentage of the whole.

Despite the pressures of his reign, Kalakaua did much to reestablish what was Hawaiian about his kingdom. The *hula*, long banned by missionary sensibilities, was revived, as were the traditional music and chants that accompanied it. Also, a man of his times, Kalakaua appreciated Victorian elegance and royal ceremony, seeing them as consistent with his role as a nineteenth century monarch and traditional high chief. He became known as "the Merrie Monarch."

Sophisticated, sensitive, intelligent, observant (he was trained as a lawyer and was admitted to the bar in 1870) and politically active, having served the ad-

33

ministrations of the last two Kamehameha kings, Kalakaua well understood Hawaii's vulnerability. Concerned with establishing a secure dynasty that would provide future stability for the kingdom, he had named his younger brother, Leleiohoku, as his heir. But when rheumatic fever claimed Leleiohoku in 1877, his sister, Lydia, became heir apparent.

To undercut the influence of the annexationist lobby in Hawaii, Kalakaua visited the United States to secure American recognition of Hawaiian independence, obtaining a reciprocity treaty for the free export of sugar to the U.S. in the process. Further good news came with the birth of a niece, the princess Kaiulani, born to his other sister, Likelike.

In 1878, Kalakaua ordered work to begin on a large, Victorian-style palace designed to enhance the prestige of the monarchy. Completed in 1882, Iolani

*Above: Kalakaua (r) and Lunalilo (second from left), Hawaii's first elected kings. Right: Liliuokalani, Hawaii's last queen.*

Palace served as a backdrop for a European-style coronation to coincide with the ninth anniversary of Kalakaua's ascension to the throne. Those hostile to the monarchy quickly condemned the king's extravagance, as they did his efforts at establishing himself as king of a federation of the Pacific's Polynesian islands.

By 1887, opposition to Kalakaua's rule grew more organized. The Hawaiian League formed to seek constitutional changes that would limit the king's power, or lead to the overthrow of the monarchy. Before the year was out, the Bayonet Constitution, so called because forced upon Kalakaua under threat of insurrection, had been promulgated, limiting the rights of the crown.

In July, a force of 80 men under the leadership of Robert Wilcox, a quixotic half-Hawaiian whose loyalities were to the monarchy, gained access to the palace grounds and tried to remove the antimonarchical government from power. The effort failed, and Wilcox was arrested and acquitted after a lengthy trial.

The legislative elections scheduled for 1890 provided Kalakaua with his only hope of restoring royal authority. The election took place in February under the watchful eye of American and British warships anchored offshore. With the king's partisans victorious, the ground was laid for a restoration of royal prerogatives. But the hope proved futile when the king suffered a mild stroke, followed by an attack of cirrhosis, while he was visiting California. He died on February 20, 1891, aged 54.

## The Overthrow of the Monarchy

Liliuokalani came to the throne in 1891. She had been born in 1838, when memories of ancient ways were still intact. Immediately confronting the constitutional crisis seemingly resolved by the elections of 1890, Liliuokalani shared Kalakaua's commitment to a strong monarchy. Although she was married to an American businessman, John Dominis, Liliuokalani shared both her brother's wilful personality and his love for things Hawaiian. Even before she was named queen, she had composed songs like *Aloha O'e (Farewell to Thee)* that were widely recognized as classics.

Taking advantage of Kalakaua's death to reassert themselves politically, the annexationist forces, led by the arrogant, self-serving Lorrin Thurston, quite overtly discussed Liliuokalani's overthrow and renewed the sense of crisis that plagued Kalakaua's reign. Even the more benign of her opponents, like the diplomatic Sanford Dole, pursued goals incompatible with those of the new queen.

Having named Princess Kaiulani as her heir, Liliuokalani made an extensive tour of her island kingdom to determine her position and to gauge the support she might get in doing away with the Bayonet Constitution of 1887. As she awaited elections scheduled for 1892, the queen weathered the attacks of an increasingly

vocal opposition. But the royal government was unsure of how far it should go in suppressing dissent. Even when arrests were made of the rabidly anti-monarchist leaders of a secret society called the Hawaiian Patriotic League, the government chose not to press charges. Liliuokalani's position, already seen as weak, continued to deteriorate.

Later in 1892, another, more aggressive secret society, the Annexationist Club, was formed by Lorrin Thurston. While on government business in the United States, Thurston made a side trip to Washington to seek support from President Benjamin Harrison's administration. Upon returning to Hawaii, he used the Bayonet Constitution to openly attack the queen. Within six months, the cabinet had to be changed four times.

On January 13, 1893, Liliuokalani appointed yet another cabinet for legislative approval, informing its members of her plan to unilaterally declare a new constitution when the legislative session came to an end.

Her intentions were quickly revealed to Thurston, who advised the attorney general and the commander of the *USS Boston,* anchored offshore. Confronted with her cabinet's refusal to legitimatize her new constitution, the frustrated queen was forced to retreat.

Events were moving beyond Liliuokalani's control. On January 16, American troops landed, ostensibly to assure public order should the queen's position further deteriorate. That same day, with the monarchy paralyzed, a Committee of Safety formed by the Annexationist Club proclaimed a provisional government, having refused a compromise proposal that the teenage Kaiulani replace Liliuokalani as queen.

Having secured several government buildings not far from the palace, the revolutionaries – with the support of American troops – were declared the *de facto*

*Above: Wrecked battleships following the Japanese attack on Pearl Harbor. Right: The U.S. and Hawaiian flags.*

government by American resident minister John L. Stevens. Inside Iolani Palace, wishing mainly to avoid blood shed, Liliuokalani acknowledged "... the superior force of the United States ... until such time as the Government of the United States shall, upon the facts being presented to it, undo the action of its representatives and reinstate me in the authority which I claim as the constitutional sovereign of the Hawaiian Islands."

For several years the deposed queen, in residence at Washington Place (now the governor's mansion), pursued restitution. Even after the Republic of Hawaii had been declared, with Sanford Dole as president, her representatives were in Washington trying to restore her throne. But events, it seemed, had gone too far, with the issue more a matter of whether Hawaii would remain an independent republic or be annexed as a territory of the United States.

Fearing a native uprising, the republican government waited until 1895 to arrest Liliuokalani and try her for treason. Placed under house arrest in a wing of Iolani Palace, now the headquarters of the republican government, Liliuokalani was found guilty, fined $5,000, and sentenced to five years' hard labor – although the latter portion was commuted by a respectful President Dole. In September, after being released from her Iolani Palace quarantine, she returned to Washington Place, receiving a full pardon the following year.

In 1900, seven years after her overthrow, Liliuokalani was presented with annexation as a *fait accompli,* and the American flag was raised over what had once been her palace. The independent Kingdom of Hawaii was now officially a territory of the United States. Adjusted to the inevitability of fate, Liliuokalani died on August 21, 1917, frail and forgiving of those who had altered the course of Hawaii's history.

### Pearl Harbor ... and Statehood

By the turn of the twentieth century, plantation agriculture – with sugar and pineapple the primary crops had emerged as the mainstay of the Hawaiian economy. Immigration continued at a rapid pace, with Filipinos and Puerto Ricans added to the continuing influx of Japanese and Chinese. The decades that followed were a quiet time, politically and socially, for the islands. Trade, primarily with the United States, prospered as Hawaii became increasingly Americanized. By the 1940s, it had emerged as a unique hybrid with elements of Polynesian, Oriental and American culture. The military, long interested in Hawaii's mid-Pacific location, established itself at Pearl Harbor, which became the headquarters of America's Pacific fleet. With tensions building as Japan pursued imperialistic goals, Washington was relying heavily on Pearl Harbor's strategic importance. Japanese planes attacked on the morning of December 7, 1941, killing over 1,200 and drawing isolationist America – and Hawaii – into World War II. The war years would familiarize America with its mid-Pacific outpost, as thousands of American servicemen were stationed in the islands or spent time in Hawaii traveling to or from Pacific battlegrounds.

Familiarity with the islands revived interest in statehood once the war had ended, although the ultimate outcome was delayed by political wheeling and dealing in Washington. Finally, in March 1959, Congress voted to admit Hawaii and Alaska to the American Union, and the former officially became the fiftieth state. That same year, the first commercial jets landed at Honolulu International Airport, ushering in an era in which tourism would replace sugar and the military as Hawaii's economic bulwark.

Today, liberal and firmly in the camp of the Democratic Party, Hawaii continues to grow. Tourism and trade are vital elements in the state's emerging role as a cultural and commercial bridge between North America and Asia.

37

# HAWAIIAN CULTURE
# AND CUSTOMS

*In the beginning was the ocean, and
the long canoes and the men who were
part of the ocean and the sky and the islands. These islands of the mind are re-
membered from the time before and connected by great waters. You descend from
the time before and the water and the
land are one, sought by the* kama'aina,
*the children of the islands.* – The Kumulipo

The Polynesians – and the Hawaiians
in particular - maintain a firm belief in the
nobility of their origin as one spanning
the time all the way back to the legendary, mystical haze of time since before
Earth was created. In the *mele* chant of
*The Kumulipo*, Hawaii's song of creation,
with no written language before the
nineteenth century, they have kept alive
the names of more than 180 generations,
a period of time covering some 3,600
years. The chants speak of great voyages
from a distant land to the west, the land of
"the birth of man." Hawaii, according to
*The Kumulipo*, was named for Hawaii
Loa, a great explorer who "came from the
night and the moving space."

Centuries ago, the Polynesians created
what is today recognized as the fastest of
the world's sailing craft – the catamaran.
They were technologically advanced for
their time. Only now are Western boat
builders discovering the safety and tremendous speed of the "double hull."

The ancient Polynesian sailors needed
no radar, compass, sextant or chrono-
graph to travel vast distances. They
needed only a navigator. Through long
study and the knowledge of his predeces-

*Left: The Aloha Festival king in a traditional
feather helmet and cape of Hawaii's high
chiefs. Above: Flower leis and warm smiles
are both part of Hawaiian tradition.*

sors, he read the directions of ocean currents and waves, sometimes using peb-
bles and shells strung on bamboo splints
for a "map." He knew the prevailing
storms and winds at each time of year. He
watched the flights of sea birds and the
white teeth of coral reefs. He saw the pale
green of islands reflected on distant
clouds and he could smell land.

The last of the Polynesians to seek and
settle new land, the Hawaiians, lived in
isolation for more than 1,000 years. Here
they developed a unique feudal civilization. They lived in open, airy houses,
bathed daily, and followed a regimen of
sports such as surfing, swimming, spear
and javelin throwing, bowling, paddling
canoes, hula and wrestling.

The Hawaiians ate on fern-adorned
*tapa* mats, spread under trees or blue
skies. Reclining on one elbow or resting
on one hand, the chiefs and nobles used
the fingers of the free hand to select foods
before them, dipping into great platters of
roast pork, whole fish, bowls of vegetables and *poi* (a paste made from the taro

root). Fruits were separated into small portions. Bowls of highly polished wood, gourds, and beautifully woven baskets set a handsome table. Gourds for relishes, half-coconut shells for cups, and finger-bowls were changed for the different courses.

In the years after Captain Cook's visits in 1778 and 1779, Hawaiian culture began to slip away. The contact-starved native people borrowed more and more from the ships arriving from other worlds, but the exchange was highly unfavorable: diseases, rum and guns for food, water and aloha.

Kamehameha I, who united the Hawaiian islands and ruled from 1795 to 1819, understood that the Hawaii of the past was no longer. He worried about his islands' role in the growing Pacific. Among the nations whose ships called at Hawaii, he leaned toward the English, even designing his little country's flag like the Union Jack, with the Cross of St. George in the upper left-hand corner and eight horizontal stripes of red, white and blue. His coat-of-arms declared his beliefs and hopes for Hawaii: *Ua mau ke ea o ka aina i ka pono,* "the life of the land is preserved in righteousness."

## "King Sugar"

After Kamehameha's death, many of the old *kapus* rapidly broke down. Formal religion and sacred rituals ceased. Fate could not have dealt a kinder hand to the morally determined band of New England missionaries and teachers who sailed into Hawaii in 1820. They found the Hawaiian people eager to accept the Protestant faith in place of the religion they had cast aside.

These Boston Congregationalists proceeded to change the lives of the Hawaiians forever. They introduced not only Christianity, a written language, three-part harmony and their missionary progeny; they also brought sugar cane, which radically changed the islands.

Hawaiians had always had a type of wild sweetgrass cane called *ko*. They used it for sweetening desserts and as children's chewing sticks. So the arrival of "King Sugar" was welcomed. Its cultivation eventually led to the mix of races that inspired author James Michener to call the modern people of Hawaii "the golden people."

The new cane was not worker-friendly. It demanded long hours of heavy work in hot dusty fields and in washing sheds, and it required the use of hot, noisy crushing and refining machinery. Sugar is an insatiable gobbler of water and workers, from planting to syrup.

Sugar was a concert master that led Hawaii immigrants into a series of musical chairs. The industry imported one foreign ethnic group after another. The newcomers, after working their contractual years, moved as quickly as possible to a better life and were soon replaced by the next group.

It wasn't that the plantation owners wanted life to be that way. But sugar was a dawn-to-midnight taskmaster, and many workers left the fields as soon as they had saved enough money to do any other kind of job.

### The Chinese

Chinese were among the earliest people to migrate to the islands, arriving even before the missionaries. They came on European and American trading vessels that decided to overwinter in Hawaii. In 1789, Chinese carpenters and crew on the *Eleanora* decided to remain in the islands. (In 1989, the modern Chinese community celebrated its 200th anniversary in Hawaii.)

By the mid-nineteenth century, sugar was Hawaii's chief export, dominating

*Right: A visitor has his palm read at a stall at Waikiki's International Marketplace.*

the economy. Planters begged for outside sources of cheap labor. The Royal Hawaiian Agricultural Society – operated by Europeans, not Hawaiians – recruited 180 men and 20 boys from Amoy, China, as the first contract laborers in 1851. On the 55-day ocean trip five died. The contract was for five years at a wage of $3 a month, plus passage money, food, clothing and lodging (frequently in flimsy grass shacks).

Not long after the first ship had unloaded its cargo of 195 new islanders, a second vessel arrived with 98 more. In a welcoming editorial published in January 1852, *The Polynesian* newspaper was quick to point out that this experiment in labor importation was, not only from the economic standpoint, "of considerable importance to the Islands."

Kamehameha V, at the instigation of Dr. William Hillebrand, authorized a Bureau of Immigration in 1865, and Hillebrand was sent to investigate sources of labor in Asia. He found that Chinese were easily obtained and worked hard. The Re-

ciprocity Treaty of 1876, allowing Hawaii sugar into the United States free of duty, created a sugar boom. The need for labor intensified. By 1884, there were 17,937 Chinese, most of them contract laborers, in Hawaii. They made up 22.3% of the islands' population of 80,509.

In 1898, U.S. exclusion laws in the newly annexed Territory of Hawaii shut off further Chinese immigration, except for upper-echelon merchants, students and diplomats. The number of laborers dwindled. By 1922, there were 1,500 Chinese plantation workers; at statehood in 1959, fewer than 300 remained on sugar plantations.

Early Chinese followed traditional lifestyles in sugar camps. They set up meeting halls and *tong* houses, or triads. Most had shrines to Kuan Dai for the men; the few "picture brides" were devoted to Kuan Yin, the goddess of mercy. The lodges cared for the sick and elderly, burials, banking and socializing.

Nearly half of Chinese men married Hawaiian women, and Chinese daughters

*Above: Japanese contract sugar plantation workers, photographed circa 1880.*

married Hawaiian men. They left the plantations to start their own businesses and shops. In the subsequent decades, they took increasingly significant roles in banking, medicine, education and politics. In 1970, the three richest men in Honolulu were Chinese, as was the first elected U.S. senator, Hiram Fong, in 1959, the publisher of the *Honolulu Star-Bulletin* newspaper, a rear admiral and a three-star general.

### The Japanese

For the Japanese, as for other ethnic groups, the original reason to immigrate to Hawaii was to work on the plantations. The first 148 sponsored immigrants came in 1869 under contracts permitted by the Masters and Servants Act of 1850. They arrived in the first year of the Meiji Restoration, the freer Japanese regime which had replaced samurai-enforced feudalism. Serious disagreements between Japanese and Hawaiian government agents over working conditions turned off the tap on Japanese workers until 1885. But then the floodgates opened.

In the 22 years until a 1907 agreement curtailing the flow, more than 18,800 Japanese arrived to take plantation jobs. By 1910, resident Japanese, still mostly associated with plantations, made up 40% of Hawaii's population – a source of concern to the same businessmen who had first sought them.

Most of the early immigrants were young men from rural Japan. After the agreement of 1907, more than 15,000 "picture brides" followed the men, until immigration from Asia was stopped altogether by Congress in 1924.

With a more equal distribution of men and women than most immigrants, Japanese family numbers grew rapidly. In 1940 the Japanese population stood at 158,000, more than any other ethnic group.

The 1941 attack on Pearl Harbor by imperial Japan, and the ensuing war in the Pacific, left Hawaii's Japanese suspect. But in 1943, a special all-Japanese regiment, the 442nd "Go For Broke," was formed. It fought with distinction, suffering heavy casualties in Europe along with the 100th Infantry Battalion of *nisei* draftees.

G.I. Bill benefits enabled many Japanese-American veterans to climb the economic ladder in Hawaii and elsewhere in the United States. Today, Hawaii residents of Japanese ancestry have farms and plantations of their own, are professors and doctors, and dominate all branches of the state and county governments. A governor (George Ariyoshi), two U.S. senators (Daniel Inouye, a 442nd vet, and Spark Matsunaga), a U.S. representative (Patsy Mink) and the president of the University of Hawaii have come from their ranks.

## The Portuguese

As doors closed against the recruitment of Chinese and Japanese immigrants, Hawaii began to look toward Portugal. Economic problems in their Iberian homeland had made Portuguese citizens look elsewhere for opportunities.

Experience with single Chinese and Japanese men had finally moved the Hawaii government to work toward attracting families. The first Portuguese immigrants – 60 men, 22 women and 38 children – arrived on the *Pricilla* from Funchal, Madeira, in 1878. They did not envisage becoming field workers. Many were hired as mechanics, *luna* (foremen), drivers and middle-echelon managers in the refineries.

Over the next ten years, 17 ships brought 10,998 Portuguese to Hawaii. A single ship in 1895 brought 657 more. Since then, all immigrants from Portugal, Madeira and the Azores have come as individuals or single families.

The Portuguese were already politically active in Hawaii by the time the islands were annexed by the United States. Between 1885 and 1927, there were a dozen Portuguese-language newspapers in Honolulu and Hilo. Many people of Portuguese descent have become mayors of the individual islands, served on city councils and in the state legislature. They have added priests, novelists, musicians, entertainers and sportsmen of note to the Hawaiian scene.

Almost as important, the Portuguese brought with them to Hawaii the *braguinha*, a small, versatile, five-string ukulele. Without this little instrument, Hollywood might never have made a "Hawaiian" musical.

## The Koreans

The Koreans, throughout their nearly 90-year presence on the islands, have formed only 1% to 2% of the islands' population. Most reside in the city and county of Honolulu and are particularly well represented in the professions as architects, doctors, pharmacists, chemists, social workers and judges.

Although some arrived as plantation laborers after the 1882 Treaty of Amity and Commerce with their country, Koreans never really performed the duties of contract workers as other immigrants did. Most arrived to become students, government clerks, policemen, artisans and a few Buddhist monks.

Until the end of World War II during the hard years of Korea's domination by Japan, Korean independence was the critical and paramount issue that united the community.

Urbanites, they quickly lost many of their outward national characteristics, although they retained a strong hold on family groups, food, culture and dance. Koreans took easily to intermarriage. More tolerant than assertive, they were able to assimilate with the multi-cultural

43

groups living all around them, with no loss of their own cultural and artistic identity. Koreans' ties to their homeland have helped to enrich the cultural experience of the Honolulu community. To them goes the honor of Hawaii's favorite side dish, the ubiquitous, flaming hot, pickled cabbage known as *kim chee*.

### The Filipinos

Hawaii has the largest population of Filipinos outside the Philippine Islands.

The U.S. acquisition of the Philippine Islands after the Spanish-American War of 1898 eased immigration restrictions for their citizens. In 1900, large numbers of them were allowed to enter the Territory of Hawaii as nationals, taking jobs as unskilled workers on sugar, pineapple and coffee plantations. Managers en-

*Above: A Japanese cemetery, one of many found in the Islands. Right: Smiling Samoan faces, part of the cultural mix at Oahu's Polynesian Cultural Center.*

couraged immigration by Filipinos to counteract the expanding military power of the Japanese.

Some 100,000 Filipinos had entered Hawaii by 1930. More than 90% were Ilocanos from northern Luzon; others were Tagalog-speaking Visayans. Nearly all were men.

The Depression of the 1930s spurred half of the emigrants to head to the U.S. mainland or back to the Philippines. But the 1965 Origin Quota Act permitted a larger number of immigrants to enter from Asia. Throughout the 1970s and 1980s, the number of Filipinos in Hawaii increased rapidly.

There are a larger proportion of Filipino children under 15 than any other racial group in the state. The 1990 census indicated that Filipinos are one of the state's largest ethnic groups – and among its most disadvantaged. Many of the young, as soon as they are old enough, seek jobs rather than high school degrees, and go into food-service or hotel work at the lowest levels.

Those who have gone on to college contribute much to medicine, nursing, education, law, politics and the military. Many have entered real estate. Increased involvement is expected when diplomas received in the Philippines are more widely recognized.

Recent immigrants from other southeast Asian nations, especially Thailand and Vietnam, though still few in number, have added to the ambience of Hawaii. Their influence is particularly felt in Honolulu, where their popular small restaurants and grocery stores offer tastes of unique cuisines.

### The Samoans

The largest group of Polynesian "cousins" in Hawaii are Samoans. Because American Samoa, 2,500 miles (4,000 km) to the southwest, is an unincorporated territory of the U.S., its citizens are free to travel to and from Hawaii and take up residence and work without visa restrictions.

The greatest number of Samoans live on Oahu's North Shore and Windward Coast. About 4,000 live in the Mormon enclave of Laie/Hauula, where they work at Brigham Young University Hawaii and the Polynesian Cultural Center.

Contact between Hawaiians and Samoans has been constant since about 1850. Samoan dance teams toured the U.S. in the 1920s and then settled in Hawaii. Many came during World War II to serve in the National Guard and then stayed.

The extended family remains the foundation of the Samoan life-style. American homes and economic patterns do not readily fit this exemplar. One of American Samoa's most important source of income consists of remittances from families living in Hawaii.

Several Samoan high chiefs, known as *matai*, have been installed in the Laie area and all family anniversaries are celebrated with great feasts. One of the largest is held in Ala Moana Park on Samoan Flag Day.

Samoans have contributed widely to Polynesian entertainment. Organized dance bands perform in New York, London and Tokyo. Every Samoan church has large family choirs of exquisite voice and harmony. Children are learning about their culture through art, music and crafts. Samoans are the only Polynesian race that has retained the skill of making *tapa*, a mulberry cloth.

Athletics are a means of upward social mobility for many Samoans. Local and national football teams have their quota of outstanding Samoan players, whose names remain stumbling blocks for TV announcers. Longtime New England Patriots fullback Mosi Tatupu, who was schooled in Hawaii, is among the best known. In business, Samoans have organized moving, catering and tree-trimming companies.

## A "Tossed Salad" of Races

Many people speak of Hawaii as a melting pot. It really isn't. A tossed salad is more like it.

Ethnic and cultural minorities in the 50th state coexist without consuming one another. There is no pressure to conform to a dominant majority culture, because there is no majority. According to the 1980 census, Hawaii's 1 million population – 90% of it on Oahu – is 29% Caucasian, 23.5% Japanese, 21.9% Filipino, 12.1% Hawaiian and part Hawaiian, 4.5% Chinese, 1% each Korean, Samoan and Black, and 6% miscellaneous mixed.

Nearly 38% of the people in Hawaii are of mixed ethnicity. This is a by-product of the closeness of the races in the islands – their assimilation of American lifestyles, and their exchange of customs, etiquette and celebrations. Along the way, a common "local" way of life has

*Right: Dancers perform kahiko-style (ancient) hula at Hilo's annual Merrie Monarch Festival, named after King David Kalakaua.*

developed, some times referred to as "pidgin culture" because pidgin English is its only common denominator.

Names are often mind-boggling. Prizes are awarded during college football and basketball season to mainland TV announcers who can pronounce island names like Clesson Chikasuji, Yok Sung Kwock, Kells Tenbruggencate, Kauhane Kahaleholeho or Tavana Fahailoatonga.

Hawaii has one of the highest rates of inter-ethnic marriage in the world. The resultant cross-culture produces a people who identify easily with Hawaiians, Asians and Caucasians alike.

Today only a few hundred pure Hawaiians live in the islands, including some 200 on the privately owned island of Niihau who do not mix with the people of the other islands. But part-Hawaiians are probably the islands' fastest growing group, and as they marry the proportion of Hawaiian blood in certain families is again on the increase.

## The Hula

From the advent of the missionaries to the coronation of King Kalakaua, the last king of Hawaii, the Hawaiian people were forbidden to take part in hula and traditional chants. These activities were condemned as immoral.

But the "Merrie Monarch," as Kalakaua was known around the world, had different ideas. "Let there be hula!" he declared in anticipation of his coronation, and there was. Although the male and female dancers were circumspectly clad from head to toe, they joyously moved their hips and arms to the rhythms of *olapa* and chants unheard in public for 20 years. (It was obvious that some clandestine practice had taken place.)

In the 1920s, Hollywood discovered the hula, and it became associated with cellophane skirts, plastic leis, and such distinctly non-Hawaiian songs as "Hula Moons," "Blue Lagoons" and "Yakka

Hula Hicky Doola." A degree of authenticity returned after World War II with real *ti*-leaf skirts, natural flower leis and songs written in Kalakaua's day – like *Beyond the Reef, Here in This Enchanted Place*, and *Waikiki*, often sung in the Hawaiian language.

By the 1970s, Hawaiians had returned to their roots and were once again teaching the old dances and composing new ones in their spirit. *Hula halau* (dance schools) are now filled with enthusiastic pupils. Many grandmothers have dusted off their memories and reproduced the powerful rhythms and movements of the *hula kahiko*, while young men and women search legends and songs to tell stories through exciting *hula' auana*, or modern hula.

Three main events throughout the year, and several small events, perpetuate the beauty and power of the hula. Every April, the Merrie Monarch Festival in Hilo, on the Big Island, is a return to the days of Hawaiian prehistory when 100 dancers, both men and women, and 100 drummers and chanters danced in tribute to the goddess Laka before the king, *kahunas* (high priests) and *ali'i* (nobility). Hula teams come not only from throughout the islands, but also from Hawaiian communities in Los Angeles, San Francisco and Seattle.

Two other major events, both in Honolulu, are The Kamehameha Schools Hula and Song Competition at the Neal Blaisdell Arena in April or May, and the Prince Lot Hula Festival at Moanalua Gardens in July. These presentations are as exquisite and finished in their own way as are those of the Bolshoi Ballet, but they last only one or a few days, and are not easily accessible to the public.

### The Festival Calendar

Hawaii has a joyous potpourri of holidays throughout the state that keep the months rushing happily from one special event to the next.

It all starts with blazing skies over Honolulu and a cacophony of firecrack-

ers from Koko Head to Pearl Harbor as the **New Year** is welcomed by the entire population.

Next is the lunar Chinese New Year, lasting about a week in early to mid February. A block-long row of green-satin dragons leads a parade from Chinatown to the State Capitol. The lions, with their long eyelashes and many colors, dance throughout Chinatown and nearby business sections to beg for *li-see*, good-luck money for the coming year. Musicians and dancers entertain, and special Chinese dishes are served at the district restaurants. Afterwards, a glamorous ball is held to introduce the Narcissus Queen.

In March and early April the Restaurant Row Mardi Gras comes to downtown Honolulu. Modeled on Latin American carnivals, it features performances by reggae and South American musicians. The ubiquitous Shrove Tuesday

treats are hot *malasadas*, Portuguese doughnuts-without-a-hole, served freshly cooked and rolled in crystalline sugar. They make for an appropriately indulgent meal prior to the austere weeks of the upcoming Lenten season.

April also brings **Ching Ming**, the Chinese celebration of ancestors. Specially cooked dishes are taken to cemeteries, to the ancestors' graves, and enjoyed with friends amid the popping of firecrackers.

May Day is **Lei Day**, Hawaii's celebration of flowers and the lovely garlands given so joyously in the island state. Lei contests, music and dancing fill every city park in all the islands.

Flowers are an integral part of life in Hawaii. Rare is the island home that does not have colorful flowers and plants blossoming in the yard or on the lanai. Appearing in both legend and song, their names are often bestowed upon beloved children. They adorn the shoulders and hair of Hawaii's women, and are motifs for fabrics from evening gowns to aloha

*Above: Hula dancers perform, accompanied by gourd drums called ipu. Right: A farmer in Hanalei holds a harvested taro corm.*

shirts and sports wear. At festive occasions and to welcome visitors, leis are presented along with hugs or soft kisses on both cheeks.

The birthday of King Kamehameha I is celebrated on **Kamehameha Day** in June, as leis adorn his statue across from Iolani Palace. The 18-ft (5.5 m) likeness is draped from head to toe in a myriad garlands of every color and scent. Each island has its own Kamehameha Day Parade with the usual floats, marching bands and drill teams as well as a princess and her royal court mounted on handsome horses. The young women wear *pa'u*, flowing-silk riding dresses, with crowns and leis of blossoms of their island's official flower; the steeds are bedecked with huge leis and flower trappings.

In September and October, the all-island celebration is known as **Aloha Week**. It starts on Oahu with parades, ethnic performances at the Waikiki Shell, *ho'olauea* (street parties and dancing) in Waikiki and downtown Honolulu, and special events in all hotels and resorts. In subsequent weeks, holiday activities move from island to island like a traveling medicine show.

Although the festival in its present form was organized by the Waikiki Jaycees in 1946 to attract visitors, perpetuate Hawaii's rich traditions, and boost the islands' spirits and economy in the years after World War II, the celebration actually has its roots in the ancient Hawaiian *makahiki*.

This harvest festival, discontinued after the arrival of the missionaries in 1820, was dedicated to Lono, god of cultivation and growth. It began with processions of *ali'i* in their feather capes and commoners (*maka ainani*) in *tapa* skirts. The paraders, bedecked with ferns and flowers, chanted and moved to the beat of drums as they carried gifts to the *heiau* and their king. The tall crossbar symbol of Lono, draped with the whitest of *tapa*, was carried at the head of the parade.

Today, Aloha Week is the most significant annual festival in Hawaii, involving all of its many ethnic groups.

### Special Observances

Sometimes, events celebrated by one ethnic group inspire others to adopt them as their own. That's the case with two very personal observances in Hawaii.

The "baby *luau*" that every group typically stages for a child's first birthday was originally just a Hawaiian festivity hosted by the infant's *tutus* (grandparents). A feast of traditional food, from fish and *poi* to kalua pig, was served, along with a special-occasion dessert called *kulolo*, made with coconut, taro, sweet potato and breadfruit. Everyone from family friends to distant relatives was entertained by music, dancing and singing; and the guests ensured a happier baby with gifts of toys, games, clothes, money, bonds, even insurance policies.

**Yakudoshi**, "The Crucial Year," began as a Japanese 40th birthday observance.

Now this mid-life crisis – if you will – is an occasion enjoyed by a cross-section of all ethnic groups. Friends and relatives are invited to a party at home or a restaurant, where they tease, console, joke, eat and drink, and bring presents, funny or fancy. A master of ceremonies calls upon guests for toasts for the honoree.

Summer is the time of *bon* dances and **Bon Odori**, the Japanese "Festival of the Dead." Despite its name, this is a joyous occasion. Most Japanese in Hawaii today are *sansei* and *yonsei*, third- and fourth-generation immigrants, who may lack the deep spiritual connection their forebears had to departed ancestors, whose "return to earth" is celebrated in these dances. But if young Japanese are not in attendance, they have been replaced by Caucasians, Koreans, Portuguese and others who find a warm summer evening reason enough for ritual dancing.

*Above: Hula is performed on boats in the canals of the Polynesian Cultural Center. Right: Harvesting pineapple on Lanai.*

Visitors are invited to join in the dances. The simple steps around the drum towers, the strong drumbeat, the rhythmic singing, the charm of the old women and their willingness to teach the dance, the glowing paper lanterns and the festoons of flowers make a Bon Dance an occasion to remember.

Newspapers carry weekly schedules during the season, which kicks off on the last weekend in June at Honpa Hongwanji Temple in Honolulu. Particularly outstanding is the early August Floating Lantern Ceremony, when 2,000 paper lanterns bearing candles and the names of departed beloved are floated the length of the Ala Wai Canal and out to sea in Waikiki. Held on the anniversary of the end of World War II, the celebration begins with a Bon Dance at Ala Wai Park.

Hawaii residents of all ethnic backgrounds are proud of their athletic prowess and stamina. One way in which they display this is in many running events throughout the year. The **Honolulu Marathon**, held each January, is one of

the world's best-known marathons. Runners come from North and South America, Europe, Asia, Africa and Australia.

Then there's the **Jingle Bell Run**, a spirited holiday event in mid-December. The 5-mile (8 km) fun run incorporates midway stops for song contests, costume judging and awards. Hundreds enter. Entertainment and a party follow in downtown Honolulu.

### Speaking Hawaiian ... and "Pidgin"

In the late twentieth century, there has been a tremendous renaissance of all things Hawaiian. Many grade schools on all islands, for instance, now teach the mellifluous Hawaiian language. The language, transliterated, has five vowels but just seven consonants (h, k, l, m, n, p and w). But even before this renewed interest, visitors quickly discovered the startling number of Hawaiian words that creep into daily conversations.

Most commonly heard are *aloha*, "I offer you love," used for greetings and farewells; and *mahalo*, thank you. *Haole* is a slang term for a Caucasian, especially a visitor; lifelong residents of the state are *kamaainas*. Directions are not usually given as north or south, but as *mauka* (toward the mountains) and *makai* (seaward). Public restroom doors typically are labeled *kane* (man) and *wahine* (woman). Other terms in regular use include *lanai* (porch or balcony), *puka* (hole or doorway), *lei* (flower garland), *muumuu* (a long, flowing women's gown), *pau* (finished), *pilikia* (trouble), and *kokua* (help).

Visitors, however, might get confused between the Hawaiian language and "pidgin" English. As the only state in the union in which the majority of the population has its roots in the Pacific Islands or Asia, Hawaii has bred a unique island dialect of English. "Pidgin" developed as a combination of slang, sound-alike and universal words to help the races converse. In Hawaii today, it is heard throughout the islands and even differs from one island to another.

51

True pidgin cannot really be written. Much of the meaning can depend on pronunciation, inflection and rhythm. Here are some universals:

*an'den* – And then? So what? I'm bored.

*ass wy hahd* – That's why it's hard. What can I do? It's hopeless.

*blalah* – A big, amiable Hawaiian or part-Hawaiian.

*brah* – Brother, friend.

*bumbye* – By and by, pretty soon.

*bummahs* – Bummer, too bad, that's the pits. Stronger than *auwe*.

*cockaroach* – Steal, confiscate, sneak away with.

*da kine* – Can refer to any object or idea the speaker wants it to mean. Sometimes, "that kind of ..."

*hele on* – Proceed, try something new and hip.

*howzit* – How are you? What's going on? As in, "Howzit, brah?"

*kaukau* – Food. Delicious food is *ono kaukau*.

*li'dat* – "Like that." Similar to *da kine*, but often used to explain something the speaker doesn't want to explain.

*mo'bettah* – Good *da kine*, or even great *da kine*.

*no mek menshun* – You're welcome. Don't mention it.

*pakalolo* – Cannabis, marijuana, the "green harvest."

*pau hana* – After work; especially a *pau hana* drink at the local bar.

*shaka!* – Great job. Well done. Perfect.

*tita* – Sister. Also, a down-home, country-style Hawaiian girl.

### Madame Pele

There's another powerful lady in Hawaii. Although the Hawaiian gods were thrown down when the *heiau* system crumbled in 1820, one member of a lesser pantheon remains very much a part of the Hawaiian culture and landscape – the fire queen herself, Pele, goddess of volcanoes.

Whether or not one is a devotee, one has to admire Pele's dogged determination to build. On the Big Island, she raises fortresses with her white-hot lava, only to have her sister, Namakao-Kahi, goddess of the Ocean and the West Wind, send waves to wear them down.

Hawaii's people sound a word of warning to visitors about her powers: Don't take lava rocks away from Hawaii Volcanoes National Park. Those who do frequently return them to park rangers with letters of woe, describing bad luck on their return home – broken arms or legs, unexplained fires in cars, even divorces.

Hawaiians say it's because Pele is herself a part of each volcanic eruption. A visitor may have unwittingly walked off with her eyelashes, or perhaps a little finger or toe. Of course, she wants them back.

Pele not only preserves the lava. She makes life easier for little old ladies who need to hitch rides on the Big Island. No one would fail to pick up an old woman – particularly if she is wearing a white or lavender *muumuu* and is accompanied by a white dog – because she might be Pele in her natural guise. To ignore such a person would be to risk the wrath of Pele, and who in his right mind would want to do that?

Anyone who has a drop of Hawaiian blood in his or her veins, and many who do not, pay homage to the beautiful and incendiary Pele, who so constantly reminds the islands of her presence. Devotees take offerings of leis, ohelo berries and gin to the great volcanic throat of Halemaumau Pit, her home in Kilauea Volcano in the national park on the Big Island.

Seven years ago, Kilauea Volcano lit up like a mammoth neon sign and vi-

*Right: Madame Pele, the goddess of Hawaii's volcanoes, carved in lava.*

dently pumped geysers of molten magma into Hawaii's midnight skies. Since then, Pele's fire fountains, continually bursting like Roman candles, have sent a dancing, tumbling, quarter-mile-wide stream of incandescent lava pouring down the mountainside to Kalapana, with firefalls and tidal waves covering everything in its path. The longest, largest eruption in recorded history is adding 650,000 cubic yards of lava to Hawaii daily. Even the humpback whales have gotten used to avoiding the sulfurous, boiling waters off the shores of Kalapana.

### "A State of Mind"

Why did the islands of Hawaii develop a culture all their own, and why has it remained relatively unchanged for so many centuries? Author and newspaper columnist Bob Krauss says it's because "an island is not a place in the middle of the ocean. It's a state of mind."

People on small islands such as those of Hawaii, in such a vast ocean as the Pacific, might as well be isolated in space. They can't avoid each other.

"You grit your teeth and smile, and that's the Aloha spirit!" explained one resident. "It's a way to get along which turns out to be a pretty nice way to live."

And it's when people begin to understand this and behave differently that they become islanders. They all become Hawaiians, if in name only.

People must adapt to space restrictions and alter their behavior. Each is vulnerable to the other. No one is free to put another down because of race or wealth. No one can disassociate him or herself without hurting the whole.

As the islands welcome more visitors and investors, hotel and resort management and locals alike are showing a renewed interest in Hawaiiana.

This joyous celebration of the traditions, language, music and myths of the land is in the minds of Hawaii's people. This is truly *mana* (spiritual power) and wisdom, handed down, as always, from generation to generation.

# OAHU

**HONOLULU**
**WAIKIKI**
**PEARL HARBOR**
**AND ENVIRONS**
**WINDWARD COAST**
**NORTH SHORE**
**LEEWARD COAST**

Most visitors to the Hawaiian Islands arrive first on the island of Oahu (pronounced *oh-AH-hoo*). Site of both world-famed Waikiki Beach and the city of Honolulu, perhaps the 'United States' most international city, this third largest island of the archipelago is aptly named. Oahu means "gathering place," and more than 75 % of Hawaii's population – about 805,000 residents – live here.

Vacationers arriving on Oahu for the first time may feel they have caught a glimpse of it all before, so many times have Honolulu and Waikiki Beach been depicted in television and in movies.

Vibrant, sophisticated Honolulu is a fascinating microcosm. Virtually every race, ethnic group and nationality from around the world are represented. Downtown, sleek, modern office towers reflect the major recent economic growth and development that have literally transformed the city's face within the past decade. Its industrial and financial networks span the Pacific, linking West and East.

*Preceding pages: A surfer takes to his board on Oahu's north shore where international competitions are held every year. Outrigger canoes pass the Ala Wai Yacht Harbor and Waikiki's westernmost cluster of hotels. Left: A rainbow arches over Waikiki Beach and volcanic Diamond Head crater.*

Edging Oahu's southern tip is Waikiki Beach, a series of broad, gently curving stretches of sand, framed at its eastern end by the familiar brooding profile of the long-extinct volcanic crater, Diamond Head.

But there is much more to discover than stereotypical images. The visitor who takes time to look beyond Honolulu and Waikiki Beach, appealing as they are, will experience some pleasant surprises. Around the island are fascinating historic sites; beautiful parks, gardens and natural attractions; and, on Oahu's North Shore, renowned surf challenged by only the most skilled of surfers.

Interestingly, Oahu still has more land devoted to pineapple cultivation than any other Hawaiian island. Sugar plantations also thrive, while truck farms and orchards produce nearly 20 % of Hawaii's homegrown fruits and vegetables.

Manufacturing also contributes significantly to the island's economy. Most major industries – food processing, clothing manufacturing, film production – are largely non-polluting.

The United States federal government is also a major presence on Oahu. Military installations include Hickam and Wheeler Air Force Bases, the vast Pearl Harbor Naval Reservation, and Schofield Barracks. In addition to military person-

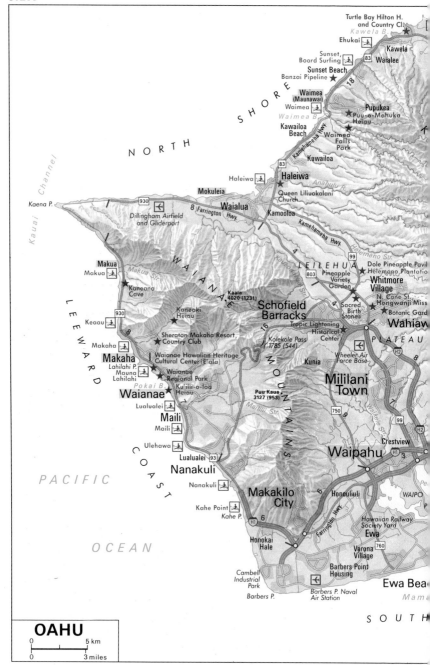

Turtle Bay Hilton H.
and Country Cl
*Kawela B.*
Ehukai
Waialee
Kawela
Sunset,
Board Surfing
Sunset Beach
Banzai Pipeline
83
18
Waimea
(Maunawai)
Waimea
*Waimea B.*
Pupukea
Puu-o-Mahuka
Heiau
Kawailoa
Beach
Waimea
Falls
Park
Kawailoa

*Anahulu R.*

Haleiwa
Haleiwa
83
Mokuleia
Queen Liliuokalani
Church
Waialua
Kamooloa
*Farrington Hwy.*
8
930
Dillingham Airfield
and Gliderport
*Kamehameha Hwy.*
4
*Helemano Str.*

*Kaena P.*
*NORTH SHORE*

*Kauai Channel*

LEILEHUA
99
Dole Pineapple Pavil
Helemano Plantatio
803
Pineapple
Variety
Garden
Whitmore
Village
N. Cane St.
Hongwanji Miss
Botanic Gard
Wahiaw
Makua
Makua
Kaneana
Cave
Kaala
4020 (1231)
Schofield
Barracks
Sacred
Birth
Stones

*Makua Str.*
930
Keeau
Kaneaki
Heiau
Tropic Lightening
Historical
Center
16
Kolekole Pass
1785 (544)
PLATEAU
H2

*LEEWARD*

*WAIANAE*
Sheraton Makaha Resort,
Country Club
Wheeler Air
Force Base
Makaha
Makaha
Lahilahi P.
Mauna
Lahilahi
Waianae Hawaiian Heritage
Cultural Center (P'ala
Ku'ilii-o-Tod
Heiau
Kunia
Mililani
Town
*Pokai B.*
Waianae
Regional Park
Waianae
Puu Kaua
3127 (953)
H2

*Kauai Channel*
Lualualei
Maili
Maili
*Kaukonahua Str.*
99
750
9
*Waikele Str.*

*COAST*
Ulehawa
Lualualei
93
Nanakuli
MOUNTAINS
*Mahili Str.*
Crestview
Waipahu
H1
3

*PACIFIC*
Nanakuli
Makakilo
City
Honouliuli
6
WAIPIO
Pe

Kahe Point
Kahe P.
H1
6
Hawaiian Railway
Society Yard
Ewa
760
Varona
Village

*OCEAN*
Honokai
Hale
Barbers Point
Housing
Ewa Bea
Cambell
Industrial
Park
Barbers P.
Barbers P. Naval
Air Station
*Mam*

SOUTH

### OAHU

0 ___ 5 km
0 ___ 3 miles

ku P.

Kahuku

83

Laie
★ Brigham Young University,
Polynesian Cultural Center

PACIFIC

Hauula

OCEAN

W I N D W A R D

Sacred Falls ★

Punaluu

83

Kahana ★

Crouching
Lion Rock

Swanzy
Kaaawa
Kaaawa

18

Puu Pauao
2685 (818)

Sugar Mill
Ruins (1864)

MOKOLII I.
(CHINAMAN'S HAT)
Kualoa P.

C O A S T

Waikane

Waiahole

Kaneohe

MOKU MANU I.

Kahaluu

Kaneohe
Marine Corps
Air Station

Pacific
Palisades

Ahuimanu
Senator Fong's
Plantations a. Gardens

83

M O K A P U

Mokapu

Bay

MOKU
O LOE I.

Heeia

PENINSULA

Valley of the
Temples

Pearl City

Kailua Bay

Haiku
Gardens

Kaneohe

Kailua

Kailua

Keaiwa Heiau
State Recr. Pk.

Aiea

99

H1

H3

Halawa Heights

78

Nuuanu Pali
Lookout

61

Foster
Village

U.S.S.
Arizona
Visitor
Center

RD I.

63

KAPALAMA
HTS.

2700
(825)

NUUANU
PALI

3

Bellows
Air Force
Station

Waimanalo

kam
using

8

Moanalua
Gardens

10

61

Maunawili

72

Bellows Field

Bellows Field

Bay

Honolulu
Internat.
Airport

H1

Keehi
Lagoon

KAMEHAMEHA
HEIGHTS

2

Fwy

NUUANU

G

Waimanalo

E

Waimanalo
Beach

MANANA I.

92

3

H1

MANOA
VALLEY

14

Sea Life Park
Pacific Whaling
Museum

Makapuu
Makapuu P.

Bay

HONOLULU

H O R E

WAIKIKI

KAHALA

Diamond Head
Crater 761 (232)

Kupikipikio P.
(Black Point)

Kalanianaole Hwy

Maunalua Bay

Koko
Head

HAWAII
KAI

Koko Head
Nat. Pk.

72

Hanauma B.

State
Underwater
Park

Kaiwi Channel

nel, nearly 25,000 civilians have found employment on the various bases.

England's Captain James Cook, sailing under the sponsorship of the Earl of Sandwich, viewed Oahu from offshore during his first Pacific voyage in January 1778. But he did not land on the island, sailing instead to Kauai. Oahu remained virtually untouched by outside influences for another 17 years, until 1795, when Kamehameha the Great invaded.

Hawaii's modern destiny was set when this "Alexander of the Pacific," the islands' greatest ruler and unifier, arrived from the Big Island of Hawaii, having already conquered Maui and Molokai. He landed at Maunalua Bay on Oahu's southern shore and, leading his armies in a famous battle, forced some of Oahu's royal defenders up the steep slopes of Nuuanu Pali, from which many of them leapt to their deaths.

*Above: The Hawaii State Capitol, one of Honolulu's interesting modern buildings. Right: A rainbow identifies Hawaiian plates.*

After the islands were united, Kamehameha's noble character came to light, as if reflecting the classic hero. Although he had been trained since birth as a warrior, and war had been his life, he turned to peace. "Return to your homes and stop fighting one another," he told his people. "Turn your spears into digging sticks and your war canoes into fishing canoes, that you may not see want."

By the middle of the nineteenth century, Hawaii's royal court had moved permanently to Honolulu. The city has since been the seat of all governments – monarchy, republic, territory and finally state. Honolulu's original Iolani Palace served five kings from 1845 to 1879. The present palace, a grand rococo structure dating from 1882, is being restored as it was in the era of King David Kalakaua, the islands' "Merrie Monarch," and his sister and successor, Queen Liliuokalani, Hawaii's last regent.

Caught at the crest of rapidly changing times, Kalakaua tried during his reign (1874-91) to unite two diverse worlds:

the slow-paced ancient Hawaiian culture, with its simple lifestyle, and the fast-moving Western world of treaties and trade, tough negotiating with covetous foreigners and pomp and ceremony. Kalakaua attempted to revive ancient practices, encouraging *kahunas* (priests) to continue their teaching and translating of the previously unwritten *Kumulipo* (Chant of Creation), which traced the long lineage of Hawaii's *ali'i* (ruling class).

Kalakaua also revived more than 300 banned hulas and created several new ones. Furthermore, he reorganized the Royal Hawaiian Band under the direction of the German musician Henry Berger, and to Berger's music wrote the words of a national anthem. "Hawaii Pono'i" is still the official state song today. Each Friday at noon, the Royal Hawaiian Band performs in the palace grounds in the charming, rococo bandstand that was originally built by Kalakaua as the coronation pavilion for himself and for his queen, Kapiolani.

The only full-time municipal band in the United States, the Royal Hawaiian Band remains a link between old and new – a link that visitors soon discover on Oahu and throughout the Hawaiian Islands.

### HONOLULU

The central area of the colorful, vibrant city of Honolulu is surprisingly compact. The waterfront and harbor section, business center, bustling Chinatown and historic Capital District may be explored in a series of leisurely walking tours. To visit some of the outlying attractions, you should plan to rent an automobile, take taxicabs, or book sightseeing tours.

And don't overlook Oahu's wide-ranging city bus system, **The Bus** (tel. 531-1611). For a nominal fare, you can take a four-hour journey around much of the island. Request a transfer, for a modest additional fee, to disembark as you choose, reboarding when another bus comes along. The buses run from 6am to

63

10:30pm. You can buy a guide booklet at virtually any Honolulu or Waikiki shop.

You can also board a jaunty **Old Town Honolulu Trolley** (tel. 526-0112) to get an overview of Waikiki, downtown Honolulu, Chinatown and the waterfront. The most inexpensive way of travelling is with an all-day pass. The red lacquer vehicles, with polished brass rails, are designed after early Honolulu streetcars. They depart from several downtown and Waikiki sites hourly 8am-3pm, making a circle tour. Stops include downtown attractions and historic sites, as well as the Hilo Hattie Garment Factory and the new Dole Cannery Square at Iwilei. When getting off the trolley, especially in outlying areas, it's a good idea to inquire when the last trolley will return. Schedules can be erratic, especially on weekend afternoons.

**Dole Cannery Square**, in the once notorious district of Iwilei, consists of an elaborate dining-shopping mall at the old Dole Cannery. One of Honolulu's best known landmarks, the pineapple water tower, is found here. Cannery tours include a fast-paced multimedia show depicting the history of the business started by James Dole at the turn of the twentieth century. There's an admission fee, but if you don't choose to take the tour, you can browse at no charge through the numerous shops and boutiques that have nested in the mall. There are also appetizing food stands serving sandwiches, snacks, luscious fresh Hawaiian fruit and such Dole delicacies as frozen juice bars and sorbets.

Dole's **Pineapple Transit** (tel. 531-8855) offers a free bus service from several downtown locations to Cannery Square. And there's a free shuttle service from the Square to **Hilo Hattie's**, which conducts free tours of its Hawaiian garment-making factory. The Transit also

*Right: Honolulu's Hawaii Maritime Center is one of the city's numerous museums.*

stops in Waikiki and other Honolulu locations, with a nominal charge on boarding.

### The Waterfront and Harbor Area

**Ala Moana Park** lies west of Waikiki, separated from that enclave by the Ala Wai Canal. With its tree-shaded ponds, broad sandy beaches and a swimming lagoon, this splendid city park is a heaven for joggers, tennis and softball players, bowlers, canoeists, anglers and sunbathers. It is, not surprisingly, usually packed on weekends.

Jutting into Mamala Bay, near the Waikiki end of the park, is **Magic Island**, the **Aina Moana State Recreation Area.** The man-made peninsula, with a beach extending from Ala Moana's, curves around a lagoon sheltered by a rock breakwater. The area is popular with fishermen and surfers alike.

At the opposite end of Ala Moana Park lies **Kewalo Basin**, a gathering place for a colorful array of vessels: charter fishing fleets, diving boats, sampans and glass-bottom, Pearl Harbor and dinner cruisers.

On Ahui Street fronting the basin, a lively, high-decibel **fish auction** is held early Monday through Saturday mornings. It's fascinating to watch vessels unload their catches, beginning about 4am. Their prizes may include *ahi* (tuna), *mahimahi* (Pacific dolphin), red snapper, and mackerel. Tuna boats also sometimes unload their catch in late afternoons or early evenings.

Across Ala Moana Boulevard from Ala Moana Park is vast **Ala Moana Center,** virtually a city within a city. The largest shopping mall in the United States when it was built in the 1960s, its restaurants, shops and boutiques still attract thousands of residents and visitors daily. It's artfully decorated with splashing fountains, ponds, sculptures and other works by Hawaiian artists.

Two later additions to the downtown shopping scene are nearby, also facing

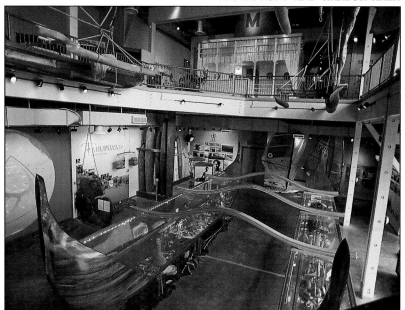

Ala Moana Boulevard across from Kewalo Basin. The attractive low-rise **Ward Centre** is a contemporary complex of interconnected stucco buildings. Adjacent **Ward Warehouse**, with its rough-hewn wooden façades, is reminiscent of the seafaring era of old Hawaii. Both include shops, restaurants, arts and crafts galleries, and souvenir stores.

West of Kewalo Basin, across the Honolulu Channel, lies the downtown waterfront. Several places of interest here are administered by the **Hawaii Maritime Center**. They include Pier 7, which served as the international steamship terminal for turn-of-the-century Honolulu, and which is now under development as Hawaii's Historic Ship Pier.

The new $6-million **Kalakaua Boathouse** is an open, light-filled structure with detailed, easy-to-follow displays. Exhibits cover Western influence on Hawaii's seagoing life, beginning with Captain Cook, the island's naval history, the old sandalwood trade, shipping, marine communications and ship tech-

nology. There's emphasis as well on the human element – sports like surfing, windsurfing and yacht racing, traditional Hawaiian and modern commercial fishing, nineteenth-century whaling and medicines of the sea. The two-story structure is designed in the style of King Kalakaua's private boathouse, which was located at the foot of Punchbowl Street during the late-nineteenth century.

The Maritime Center also includes **The Falls of Clyde,** over 100 years old and the only four-masted square-rigged ship still in existence. Here, too, when not off on an expedition, is the renowned Hokule'a, a double-hulled canoe built by the Polynesian Voyaging Society in the 1970s. Over eleven years of experimental journeys throughout the Pacific, some of them featured in the U.S. National Geographic Society films and magazine articles, Hokule'a successfully demonstrated the early Polynesians' abilities to navigate without instruments.

Also part of the complex is the landmark 1926 Art Deco **Aloha Tower** and

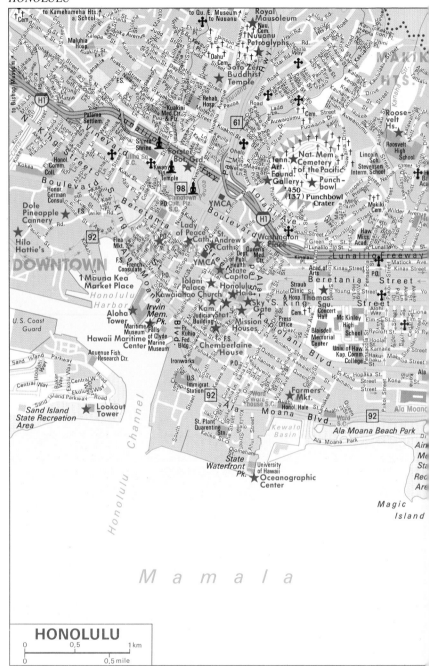

HONOLULU

0        0,5       1 km

0              0,5 mile

Maritime Museum. The tower, which still controls harbor traffic, offers superb views from its tenth-floor observation balcony. The ninth-floor museum has maritime exhibits dating from 1792.

Honolulu harbor still bustles with freighters and fishing fleets. From here, too, each Saturday night, **American Hawaii Cruises'** *Constitution* and *Independence* set sail in opposite directions on round-trip inter-island voyages. The *Constitution* calls at Kahului (Maui) Hilo and Kailua-Kona (Hawaii) and Nawiliwili (Kauai) respectively. The *Independence* first visits Nawiliwili, followed by Kailua-Kona, Hilo and Kahului. Vacationers with an extra week to spare generally find this an excellent means of exploring the islands "from the outside looking in." Shore excursions are available at all ports of call.

*Above left: Aloha Tower, once the tallest building in Hawaii. Above right: Fun in an urban setting. Right: Today high rises and traffic dominate the cityscape.*

Also from Honolulu harbor, many sightseeing excursions are available for day or evening cruises. Some offer breakfast, lunch, dinner and live entertainment.

### Legacy of the Monarchy

The internationally renowned **Bishop Museum**, founded in 1889, displays one of the world's finest Pacific collections. Its three-story **Hawaiian Hall** includes original feather capes of Hawaii's *ali'i*, bejeweled crowns and thrones of the Hawaiian monarchy, glowering *akuas* (otherwise known as *tiki* gods), musical instruments and priceless documents.

Other exhibit areas include: "The Wayfaring Art: Ocean Voyaging in Polynesia," where visitors can "sail" a computerized canoe and examine evidence of the origins of the Polynesian people; "Peoples of the Pacific: Chiefs, Bigmen and Mariners," in which ceremonial costumes and artifacts depict early Melanesian, Micronesian and Polynesian civilizations; "Hall of Discovery," where

youngsters of all ages can try their hands at playing traditional Hawaiian instruments, making their own cape design, or examining insects in the hall's specimen center, where touching is encouraged, "Life of the Land," where exhibits tell the story of Hawaii's volcanic origins, the unique plant and animal life found on these isolated islands and the effects of human habitation.

In the museum's planetarium, daily seasonal shows depict the ancient Polynesian art of celestial navigation. The new Atherton Halau is the site of daily Hawaiian musical and dance performances, and crafts demonstrations are given Monday through Saturday. The cheerful Lanai Restaurant is open daily for luncheons and snacks.

The Bishop Museum is one of the significant legacies of the Hawaiian monarchy. During the twilight of the Hawaiian kingdom, Charles Reed Bishop, a prominent Honolulu business leader, founded it as a memorial to his late wife, Princess Bernice Pauahi Bishop. She was among the last members of the illustrious Kamehameha dynasty, and was much beloved by native Hawaiians.

The Bishop Museum lies just a short taxi ride or drive from the harbor or downtown Honolulu. It's also reached via the No. 2 School Street/Middle Street city bus to Kapalama Street. Walk two short blocks toward the ocean and turn right on Bernice Street.

Nearby, you can also visit the **Kamehameha Schools** on beautifully landscaped grounds in Kapalama Heights. Established in 1887 as sole beneficiary of the vast Bishop Estate, the schools admit only boys and girls who have Hawaiian blood. Visitors, who are asked to phone ahead (tel. 842-8211), may pick up a free map at the schools' entrance.

### Early Honolulu and Chinatown

Downtown, some of Honolulu's early twentieth century buildings reflect the era when sugar barons controlled much of Hawaii's economy. Its six-block shop-

69

ping area – tree-shaded **Fort Street Mall** – is a pleasant spot for a stroll. Nearby, there's free lunchtime beer and entertainment at Davis Pacific Center Plaza on the fourth Friday of each month.

At the northern end of Fort Street Mall stands **Our Lady of Peace Cathedral.** Standing on the site of Hawaii's first Catholic church, it's downtown Honolulu's oldest structure, begun in 1843. **St. Andrew's Episcopal Cathedral,** which stands nearby, was founded by King Kamehameha IV in 1862. Across Beretania Street lies **Chinatown,** threatened a few years ago by urban blight. Today, Hawaii's largest historic district is the focus of multi-million-dollar local government and private sector efforts to restore and preserve a valued chapter of the island's heritage. Vintage structures are being restored in the 15-block area. Here Sun Yat-Sen plotted the 1911 Chinese

*Above: Iolani Palace, completed in 1887 by King David Kalakaua. Right: Tattooing is one of the businesses in Chinatown.*

revolution, and police detective Chang Apana, the real-life model for Hollywood favorite Charlie Chan, patrolled his beat and solved crimes.

Most of Chinatown's existing buildings were constructed after a 1900 fire. Today art galleries, antique stores, lei stands, herbalists and import stores line its narrow streets. Open-air markets overflow with fresh fruits and vegetables, seafoods, meats, and exotic Oriental spices. Restaurants offer everything from *dim sum* to Mandarin, Szechuan, Shanghai and Cantonese dinners. Or visitors can plan a picnic from food stalls, bakeries, groceries and noodle factories. In the heart of the district is the new **Mauna Kea Marketplace**, a five-building complex featuring Hawaiian foods and crafts.

Visitors are welcome to stroll through Chinatown on their own, or they may tour with guides from several organizations, including the **Chinese Chamber of Commerce** or **Hawaii Heritage Center.** Structures open to the public include the **Izumo Taishakyo Mission,** shrine of a

Shinto sect, and the **Kwan Yin Buddhist Temple.** Acrobats, dragon dancers and other street performers often entertain at Chinatown's **Cultural Plaza.**

Nearby on North Vineyard Street is the **Foster Botanic Garden,** a tropical haven in the heart of the city. More than 4,000 trees, ferns, orchids, exotic plants and grasses thrive in a serene green setting. The gardens are open daily, with guided tours available by reservation Monday through Wednesday.

### The Capital District

Other glimpses of Hawaii's heritage are revealed in the parklike enclave of central Honolulu's Capital District, with **Iolani Palace** as its hub. Completed in 1882 by King David Kalakaua, the imposing Victorian mansion has been painstakingly restored. Furnishings and artworks auctioned after the kingdom was overthrown are being returned, replaced, or reconstructed under the auspices of the Friends of Iolani Palace.

With its magnificent throne room, sculptured plaster, etched glass doors, carved woodwork and mirror-polished floors, the palace is a remarkable remnant from the last days of Hawaii's monarchy. Standing in the silent, soaring throne room, one may imagine how it appeared at the height of the reign of King Kalakaua and Queen Kapiolani. Then, on many occasions, it was filled with beautifully dressed, cultivated guests from many nations and was alive with laughter and small talk, cheered by the musical events which were the special joy of the "Merrie Monarch."

The only royal palace in the United States reflects varying architectural styles, and is often described as American Florentine. Kalakaua, a 33rd-degree Freemason in Scottish rite, laid the cornerstone himself and officially took up residence in late 1882, hosting a banquet for some 120 fellow Freemasons as

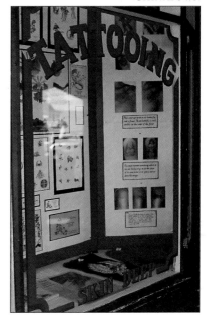

the first public festivity. After Kalakaua's death, the palace was the resident of the king's sister and Hawaii's last ruler, Queen Liliuokalani. Forced to give up her throne when the monarchy was overthrown in 1893, she was imprisoned here for nine months. She passed the time by writing songs, including the inspiring *Aloha O'e.*

Visitors tour Iolani Palace's majestic rooms in small groups, learning fascinating insights into its unique history from exceptionally well-informed guides.

Across King Street, before the restored Renaissance-style **Ali'iolani Hale** (Judiciary Building), stands a **statue of King Kamehameha I**, who unified all the Hawaiian Islands in 1810. On June 11, Kamehameha Day, the statue is draped with fragrant leis by school and civic groups. Nearby buildings span more than 150 years of island history. Among the newest is the handsome, contemporary **State Capitol,** with its volcano-shaped open crown. Visitors are welcome during office hours; the fifth-floor reception

toric Landmark, are the **Mission Houses Museum,** which includes the state's oldest frame house – built in 1821 of timber cut and fitted in Boston, and sent to the islands around Cape Horn. There's also a printing house with the Ramage press that first printed the Hawaiian language in 1822. The 1831 Chamberlain House, constructed of coral from ocean reefs, served as both a business office and residence. It has changing exhibits and an excellent gift shop.

The museum complex is open daily except on major holidays. For a small charge, knowledgeable guides lead walking tours of the Mission Houses, Iolani Palace, Kawaiahao Church, the State Capitol and other historic buildings.

Across South King Street, on the edge of the Capital District, lies the Spanish colonial-style **Honolulu Hale** (City Hall). Free art shows and concerts are frequently presented in its courtyard.

A few blocks east, on the southern edge of Thomas Square, is **Neal Blaisdell Center.** Set in landscaped grounds of coconut palms and dotted with tranquil pools and fishponds, it is home to the Honolulu Symphony, which is among the major U.S. orchestras. Classical and popular programs are presented autumn to spring in Blaisdell Concert Hall. The Hawaii Opera Theater also offers three midwinter performances in the concert hall. The Neal Blaisdell Center also includes a sports arena.

Across Thomas Square is the **Honolulu Academy of Arts.** With its slanted tiled roof, textured masonry walls, columned lanais and loggias, it's one of the city's most handsome buildings. Many galleries open onto inviting garden courtyards. The academy includes outstanding collections of Asian treasures – paintings, screens, sculptures, lacquerware, porcelain and furniture. It also has a rather remarkable collection of choice European works, donated by the Samuel H. Kress Foundation. Other exhibit areas

rooms of the governor and lieutenant-governor have excellent displays by local artists and craftsfolk.

Across South Beretania Street is another landmark – stately, colonial-style **Washington Place,** last home of Queen Liliuokalani. It's now the governor's residence and not open to visitors.

The Capital District also encompasses a U.S. National Historic Landmark complex. At Punchbowl and King Streets is **Kawaiahao Church,** the "Westminster Abbey of Hawaii." Its New England-style architecture reflects the influence of its builders, early nineteenth-century Bostonian missionaries. The church was constructed in 1842 of coral and timber by Hawaiian converts, under the direction of King Kamehameha III. The church is Congregationalist. Services are conducted partially in Hawaiian. Also on the grounds, and part of the National His-

*Above: Built in 1842, Kawaiahao Church is served by an active congregation. Right: Punchbowl National Memorial Cemetery.*

include a garden adorned with sculptures, and the Clare Boothe Luce Wing, devoted exclusively to contemporary artworks. For its part, the Academy Theatre hosts a regular schedule of concerts, films and lectures. The academy's Café Lanai, in a charming Hawaiian garden, is one of Honolulu's most delightful luncheon spots.

## Makiki Heights

The city's second major art repository, the **Contemporary Museum,** opened in October 1988 in the historic Alice Cooke Spalding House on Makiki Heights Drive. Beautifully situated in a garden setting above Honolulu, it includes the collections of museum founder Thurston Twigg-Smith, president and chief executive officer of *The Honolulu Advertiser*, who with his wife has become one of the major collectors of contemporary art in the U.S. Perhaps the museum's greatest artistic coup is David Hockney's walk-in, room-sized, environmental stage set, de-

signed for Ravel's well-known opera *L'Enfant et les Sortilèges.*

Nearby, a delightful scenic drive skirts the **Round Top Forest Reserve,** a cool, green rainforest oasis near the heart of the city. The drive winds through the lush Tantalus residential area to the **Puu Ualakaa State Park,** with a lookout more than 2,000 ft (610 m) above Honolulu's beaches. You can picnic there, take short forest walks and enjoy panoramic views of Honolulu, Waikiki and Diamond Head. There are also easy hiking trails into Tantalus State Recreation Area.

Tantalus Drive, which leads back to the center of town, passes by another important landmark of great significance: the **National Memorial Cemetery of the Pacific,** spreading over the caldera of the long-extinct Punchbowl Volcano. Eight garden Courts of the Missing line a monumental staircase leading to the Central Court of Honor and two map galleries. In the Courts of the Missing are inscribed names of more than 26,000 U.S. servicemen and women who gave their

73

lives in the First and Second World Wars, the Korean War and the Vietnam War.

On the north side of the main Court of Honor is a memorial chapel with an imposing female figure in mourning on its façade. The 30-ft (9 m) sculptured figure of Columbia, standing with a laurel branch on the stylized prow of a Navy aircraft carrier, proclaims President Abraham Lincoln's words to a bereaved mother: "The solemn pride that must be yours to have laid so costly a sacrifice upon the altar of freedom."

### Nuuanu Valley

Another scenic drive inland along Nuuanu Avenue leads to several points of interest. Nearest to downtown is the **Soto Zen Buddhist Temple,** a splendid Asian-style structure with an elaborate altar.

*Above: Three Hawaiian boys say hello with a shaka, a traditional hand greeting.Right: The tree-shaded paths of the University of Hawaii's Manoa campus.*

Though most of those who worship here are Japanese, Buddhist beliefs are explained to visitors in English.

Five blocks further is the **Royal Mausoleum State Monument,** burial place of the Kamehameha and Kalakaua.

Nuuanu Avenue merges into the Pali Highway, which leads to **Queen Emma's Summer Palace**, "Hanaikalamalama." This graceful, white-frame structure, completed in 1843, became the retreat of the popular Emma, wife of Kamehameha IV, after the king's tragic death in 1863. Maintained as a museum by the Daughters of Hawaii, it includes many of her original furnishings, including the *koa* (wooden cradle) of her son Albert, godson of England's Queen Victoria.

From the Pali Highway, a spur road leads to **Nuuanu Pali Lookout.** Here, from a concrete viewing platform in a windswept gap flanked by ragged cliffs towering hundreds of feet on either side, there are spectacular panoramic views of Oahu's Windward coast, its broad valleys extending to Kaneohe Bay.

The *pali* (cliffs) are sometimes shrouded in fog, and a strong, chilling wind seems to blow incessantly through the gap. One can almost imagine the day in 1795 when Kamehameha and his warriors marched up Nuuanu Valley, routing the forces of Oahu's King Kalanikupule. Those who were not captured or killed were driven over the precipice to their deaths on the jagged rocks below.

The scene is placid today. Beyond and below the *pali* are rich green valleys, picturesque farms and towns, and the scenic coastline of Windward Oahu. Stretches of secluded sand beach are a dramatic counterpoint to stark outcroppings of lava rock. Waikiki and Honolulu, so near, seem worlds away.

### Manoa Valley

A pair of important educational institutions are located in the eastward-lying Manoa Valley.

The **Punahou School,** one of the largest college preparatory schools in the U.S., was founded by missionaries in 1841. Its beautifully landscaped grounds include a wall adorned with night-blooming cereus, a cactus which usually blossoms around 8pm July through September. The school welcomes visitors who phone in advance (tel. 944-5714) Monday through Friday.

Nearby, the **University of Hawaii**'s main Manoa campus, east of University Avenue, is notable in many fields, including Asian and Pacific studies, oceanography, geophysics, tropical agriculture, marine biology, travel-industry management, astronomy, biomedical sciences and art. Galleries in the university Art Building feature student and faculty works. There are musical recitals in Orvis Auditorium and student productions in the John F. Kennedy Theater. Its landscaped grounds include more than 550 varieties of tropical flowers, trees and shrubs. A free campus map and a guide to its various plants can be picked up from the University Relations Office in Hawaii Hall.

Drive farther into the upper Manoa Valley to explore luxuriant tropical **Paradise Park**. (There's also a free shuttle service from Waikiki.) Here you can see exotic birds in one of the world's largest free-flight aviaries; follow winding walkways through a natural Hawaiian forest; explore gardens typical of five cultures; and visit orchid gardens and a bamboo forest. Safari rides lead through an ancient *hau* tree jungle, one of Hawaii's rare authentic rainforests. Trained macaws, cockatoos and other birds perform in shows. Guests can take part in lei-making and *poi*-pounding, or even take a hula lesson. An evening dinner show, "Magic in Paradise," is offered nightly. There's also a dining room on the grounds.

## WAIKIKI

**Waikiki Beach**, among the world's best known stretches of sand, curves eastward along Oahu's southern shore from the Ala Wai Boat Harbor almost to Diamond Head. It's actually a series of natural and man-made beaches. All are public and accessible by right-of-way, although some posh hotels do not feel inclined to publicize that fact. The surf is gentle here, the beaches protected by outlying reefs. Perhaps one of the greatest pleasures of Waikiki is – like all best things in life – free: the mesmerizing view of the Pacific, turquoise blending into cobalt, rolling endlessly in and out, capped by billowing, froth-capped breakers.

At Waikiki's western rim, the **Ala Wai Boat Harbor** lies across the Ala Wai Canal from Ala Moana Park and Magic Island. It's a haven for more than 1,000 yachts, cruisers and private boats of every description, and home of the Waikiki Yacht Club and Hawaii Yacht Club. The broad piers allow access to some of the luxurious vessels moored

*Right: A sailboat races toward Diamond Head through the blue waters of Waikiki.*

there. Some owners live all year round aboard their floating homes.

Adjacent to the harbor, the U.S. army's **Fort DeRussy Military Reservation** occupies one of Waikiki's choicest and most valuable stretches of real estate. It has long been coveted by developers, but there's no indication that the U.S. government intends to vacate the site. It's a choice R&R (rest-and-recreation) destination for American military personnel and their families.

Part of Oahu's coastal defense system, Fort DeRussy includes the **Hale Koa** hotel and recreational facilities reserved exclusively for the armed forces. Visitors are quite welcome, though, to stroll the grounds and enjoy the attractive beach.

On the property is the relatively unknown **U.S. Army Museum,** housed in Battery Randolph. With free admission, you can walk its corridors and concussion chambers and along its ramparts. The museum displays artifacts from Hawaii's military history and exhibits relating to the U.S. Army's involvement in the Pacific. The Army Corps of Engineers also shows a film on its Pacific Basin construction projects.

Nearby, fronting Waikiki's Duke Kahanamoku Beach, is Oahu's largest resort, the lavish **Hilton Hawaiian Village.** Begun by late industrialist Henry J. Kaiser in the 1950s, it now numbers 2,524 rooms and suites in several structures, including the Rainbow, Tapa and Ali'i Towers. It also has 279 residential apartments. A virtual community in itself, it has a post office as well as some of Waikiki's most elegant shops. Even if you don't stay there, be sure to visit the resort's colorful Rainbow Bazaar, with Hawaiian, Asian and Pacific wares in three themed areas – Imperial Japan, Hong Kong Alley and South Pacific. Also in the landscaped garden grounds is Buckminster Fuller's first aluminum geodesic dome, site of some of Oahu's most popular evening shows.

Greater Waikiki offers hotels, condominiums and apartments in varying price ranges. Not all, certainly, face the beach, so if that is a priority, be sure to consult with your travel agent before making reservations. The beach will often be only a short stroll away. Most accommodations will have a swimming pool.

**Gray's Beach**, adjacent to Duke Kahanamoku Beach, takes its name from an early Waikiki boarding house, Graysby-the-Sea. It's home to another historic Waikiki hotel, **The Halekulani** ("House Befitting Heaven"). Originally a private beachfront estate converted to a lodgelike resort, much of the facility gave way in 1983 to a luxurious new 456-room establishment that retains the handsomely restored old main building. It is considered Waikiki's most prestigious address, and rooms are priced accordingly.

Farther along the beach toward Diamond Head, Sheraton Hotels now manage two of Waikiki's most historic properties. The imposing **Royal Hawaiian Hotel,** known as the "Pink Palace," has been painstakingly restored to its 1927 Spanish Mission grandeur. Even though its once-expansive garden grounds are now bordered by shopping arcades, it maintains a serene, early twentieth-century elegance.

Sheraton has also restored Waikiki's first resort hotel, the **Moana Hotel,** to its original 1901 Victorian elegance. Resembling a fanciful white wedding cake, it borders a choice segment of Waikiki Beach. Its beachfront Banyan Court is home of a stately banyan tree more than a century old, under which author Robert Louis Stevenson once enjoyed resting.

Across Kalakaua Avenue, Waikiki's main thoroughfare, you'll spot two more landmarks. The sprawling **International Market Place,** a two-level shopping bazaar, includes restaurants, lounges and open-front shops selling jewelry, baskets, handicrafts and souvenirs from Hawaii, the Pacific and Asia. You won't find designer wear or fine artworks, but it's amusing to browse, and scarcely any visitor leaves without buying *something*.

Off nearby Kaiulani Avenue, behind Hemmeter Center's 1,260-room **Hyatt Regency Waikiki** with its twin 40-story towers, lies charming **King's Village**. Its attractive, upscale shops and boutiques range around three levels in structures built to resemble those of turn-of-the-century Honolulu. There's a children's hula show on Saturday afternoons, and a Changing of the Guard ceremony takes place at the entrance every evening, with participants dressed in the style of King David Kalakaua's royal guard. At night, the buildings' façades and roofs are outlined with glowing lights.

Waikiki devotees who may not have seen their favorite beach for some time are in for some agreeable surprises. The state's busiest destination has undergone a $330-million restoration. All the way from the Ala Wai Yacht Harbor to lodgings overlooking Kapiolani Park, in the

*Above: Dancers perform at the Kodak Hula Show in Kapiolani Park. Right: Weaving a basket with the long leaves of the hala tree.*

shadow of Diamond Head, hotel renovations have been wide ranging.

But the renaissance also includes office buildings, streets, sidewalks and beach parks. Major hotel chains have groomed neighborhood parks in conjunction with Honolulu's "Adopt a Park" program. Waikiki's hotel district has been the recipient of an impressive $10.5-million from the Kalakaua Avenue Safety and Beautification Project. According to an official of the Waikiki Beach Operators Association, it was all planned "to make Kalakaua one of the grandest avenues in the world."

Automobile lanes have been reduced and sidewalk widths expanded, their surfaces highlighted at wide crosswalks and intersections by earth-toned tiles. Trees, kiosks and benches offer respites for weary pedestrians to pause and absorb the passing scene amid Waikiki's hotels, restaurants, shops and entertainment centers.

Extending from the Sheraton Moana Hotel, **Kuhio Beach Park** anchors the eastern end of Waikiki, stretching all the way to Kapiolani Park. A great favorite of *kamaainas* (longtime local residents), the sheltered strand is especially popular with families. Its Waikiki Beach Center has surfboards for rent; beachboys will give you surfing lessons or take you for a ride on a surf canoe.

Near the Center, nestling in the sands, are four mysterious **kahuna stones** said to possess magical healing powers endowed by ancient priests. The beach here is tree-shaded and lined with a broad promenade. There are covered pavilions where local chess, checker and card players gather. Tables are free, but you may have to wait to find a vacant one.

In addition to Waikiki Beach Center, there are numerous concession stands along Waikiki that rent equipment and offer surfing lessons. Most are located at the hotels, including the Sheraton Moana/Surfrider, the Sheraton Royal Hawaiian, the Sheraton Waikiki, the Outrigger, the Halekulani, the Reef, the Hale Koa at Fort DeRussy and the Hilton Hawaiian Village. At some sites, you can book catamaran or sailboat rides, or even try your hand at paddling an outrigger canoe.

Local island families love to gather on Sunday afternoons in **Kapiolani Park** at the eastern end of Waikiki Beach. Given to the Hawaiian people in 1877 by King David Kalakaua, the park was named for his queen. On broad, green, tree-shaded lawns, players compete in lively softball, soccer, cricket and rugby matches. Families spread gargantuan picnics, fly kites, and run with their dogs. The park is frequented by more local residents than tourists, which makes it all the more interesting to visit and observe how typically close-knit Hawaiian families, sometimes several generations strong, enjoy each other's company.

In the park's bandstand, Honolulu's beloved Royal Hawaiian Band gives free concerts on many Sunday afternoons.

And its famed **Waikiki Shell** amphitheater is the setting for the Honolulu Symphony Orchestra's popular Summer Starlight Concerts.

Near the Waikiki Shell, on bleachers off Monsarrat Avenue, the colorful, lavishly costumed **Kodak Hula Show** is presented several times each week – Tuesday through Thursday mornings, as well as Fridays in summer. This is an excellent opportunity to take photographs of talented local dancers in brilliantly hued costumes. The show begins at 10am, but to get a good seat, come a half-hour earlier. There's a small admission charge.

Within the park, too, is the **Waikiki Aquarium,** a state-owned collection of marine life indigenous to Hawaiian waters. Again, it seems to attract more residents than tourists. But it's an excellent place to view such exotic Pacific creatures as live coral, the mysterious chambered nautilus, endangered monk seals, giant clams, live sharks and a vivid array of reef species. The aquarium and the Sea

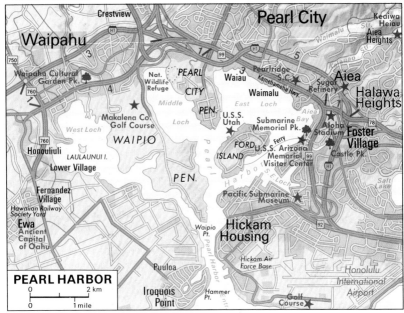

Museum depict the influence of the islands' diverse marine life on the Hawaiian culture. Popular science lectures, fishing and cooking workshops are offered frequently.

Also in the park is the **Honolulu Zoo.** It has one of the world's most complete tropical bird collections, and houses exotic animals from every continent. Here you'll find such rare species as the hoary bat, one of the few mammals known to be native to Hawaii when Polynesian settlers first arrived around A.D. 500. The array of birds includes Hawaiian owls, hawks, gallinules and the rare, endangered *nene* goose, the official state bird.

If you visit Wednesday, Saturday or Sunday, don't miss the zoo's popular Art Mart. About 100 local artists display and sell their works along the fence bordering the property in Monsarrat Avenue.

Kalakaua Avenue extends along the southern edge of Kapiolani Park and be-

comes Diamond Head Road at the crater's southern base. You're not officially in Waikiki any more, but if you're driving, it's pleasant to follow the scenic road around the side of the extinct crater, enclosed within **Diamond Head State Monument.**

An access road leads through a tunnel, open during daylight hours. Once inside the crater, you can park and follow a trail to the rim. A lookout point faces eastward toward Koko Head and Koko Crater, another extinct volcanic mass. To reach Diamond Head's summit you must follow steps, stairways and a tunnel. Most agree that the panoramic view over much of Oahu's southern shore is an ample reward for their efforts.

As another option, you may wish to join a club hike with the Diamond Head Climbers Hui. You'll be awarded a certificate if you climb the 760-ft slope (232 m), make a rubbing of the U.S. Geological Survey benchmark at the top, and present the rubbing at the New Otani Kamaaina Beach Hotel. Phone the club

*Right: A full moon rises over Diamond Head, at an open-air concert at the Waikiki Shell.*

(tel. 923-1555) for further information if you plan to do this.

After visiting Diamond Head Crater, if you're driving, you can continue along Diamond Head Road past a number of magnificent oceanfront estates. Beyond Diamond Head, **Kupikipikio** ("Black Point"), a peninsula of black lava, juts into the sea. Posh Black Point villas include that of U.S. tobacco heiress Doris Duke, a fanciful, Persian-style Shangri-La. Picturesque little **Diamond Head Lighthouse** guards the cliffs, its beacon visible far out to sea.

There are two unimproved beach parks under the cliffs lining Maunalua Bay, where Kamehameha I made his fateful landing. Local reef explorers and sunbathers flock to **Diamond Head Beach Park,** while **Kuilei Cliffs Beach Park** is more popular with surfers.

Diamond Head Road descends past these beaches, curving between more cliffside homes to intersect Kahala Avenue. You can follow it through the elegant Kahala residential neighborhood to where it ends at the **Kahala Hilton,** a luxurious hotel popular with guests who want to escape Waikiki's bustle. Visitors can stroll the hotel's public areas, explore the shops and scenic gardens, and watch regularly scheduled feedings of the hotel's resident population of dolphins and Humboldt penguins. Adjacent is the **Waialae Country Club,** site of the annual Hawaiian Open, a major event on the professional circuit, in January.

Kahala visitors can also stop at the fashionable **Kahala Mall Shopping Center.** It's air-conditioned, completely enclosed, and includes branches of popular Hawaiian emporiums, as well as one of the California-based Joseph Magnin specialty stores.

## PEARL HARBOR AND ENVIRONS

Most visitors get their first glimpse of **Pearl Harbor** as their plane comes in at **Honolulu International Airport,** which adjoins Hickam Air Force Base and the U.S. Naval Reservation.

81

The United States entered World War II immediately after the Japanese attack on the Pearl Harbor Naval Reservation, December 7, 1941. The raid is vividly recalled at the **U.S.S. Arizona Memorial,** a gleaming white monument of concrete and steel anchored above the hull of a battleship sunk on that day. Entombed beneath are the bodies of 1,177 sailors and marines.

Several commercial Pearl Harbor tours sail past the memorial, but the sensitively presented U.S. Navy tour is the only one that allows visitors to come aboard. Tours are free and leave several times daily on a first-come, first-served basis from the memorial's visitor center on the east side of the harbor. The visitor center is open from 7:30am to 5pm, but the last program starts at 3pm, and tour spaces are often depleted by early afternoon. Plan to arrive as early as possible for tickets.

*Above: The battleship USS Arizona lies beneath the Arizona Memorial. Right: Silver-green pineapple groves in central Oahu.*

The information desk is the first stop for visitors entering the center. There you receive information about the memorial, along with tickets. Within the center are a snack bar, a museum and a bookstore operated on a nonprofit basis by the Arizona Memorial Museum Association.

The interpretive program includes a talk by a National Park Service ranger, a documentary film on the Pearl Harbor attack, and a shuttle-boat trip to the memorial. (Children under 12, but over 3-ft-9 (114 cm), must be accompanied by an adult.)

The memorial has three sections open for viewing. The bell room contains one of the ship's two original bells (the other is in the state of Arizona). The shrine room has the engraved names of all servicemen killed aboard the battleship. The central assembly area comprises a viewing platform; from here the ship is visible fore and aft. Rangers are stationed aboard to provide information.

The U.S.S. Arizona Visitor Center is located off Kamehameha Highway at Pearl Harbor Naval Station, about a 20-minute drive west of downtown Honolulu. City transit buses also run from Waikiki to the base. The Arizona Memorial Shuttle (tel. 926-4747) takes visitors back and forth from Waikiki for a small charge.

Most U.S. Pacific naval commands are headquartered at **Pearl Harbor**, a huge natural harbor with 10 square miles (27 sq km) of navigable waters. It is surrounded by a 10,060-acre (4,071-hectare) naval reservation that also contains a submarine base, naval supply center and shipyard. Facilities are generally off-limits to non-military personnel.

**Submarine Memorial Park**, next to the U.S.S. Arizona Visitor Center, is a separate attraction. It displays the restored *U.S.S. Bowfin* submarine, which is credited with sinking 44 enemy vessels during World War II. The park also includes the **Pacific Submarine Museum**,

a periscope and conning tower viewing platform, and a World War II Japanese submarine. Tours are self-guiding. Admission is charged; children under six are not allowed aboard the *Bowfin*.

If you're driving, you may want to follow the H-1 Freeway to **Aiea**, just north of Pearl Harbor, to see 50,000-seat **Aloha Stadium**, site of the National Football League Pro Bowl, held annually in February. This state-of-the-art construction can change from a football to baseball configuration almost at the flick of a wrist. Its huge grandstands slide on a cushion of air, a feat that captured worldwide attention when it was completed in 1975.

Aloha Stadium is home to Hawaii's professional baseball team, the Islanders of the AAA Pacific Coast League, and the University of Hawaii Rainbow Warriors football team. It also hosts two nationally televised college football games – the Aloha Bowl in December and the Hula Bowl all-star game in January. Every Saturday and Sunday, the Aloha Swap Meet

is held in the stadium parking lot. An assortment of second-hand merchandise, along with handicrafts, fresh flowers, fruits and vegetables, is for sale at this colorful flea market variant.

Hawaii's famous "Enchanted Kingdom," **Castle Park**, is just south of Aloha Stadium. This popular amusement park's recreational facilities include miniature golf, Grand Prix auto racing, batting cages, midway rides and a water park with flume rides and river rafting. There's also an arcade with more than 200 video games.

Also in fast-growing Aiea – once a sleepy sugar-plantation town – you may want to visit huge, colorful **Pearlridge Shopping Center**. Enclosed and completely air-conditioned, its two sections are connected by monorails.

You can follow Moanalua Road to Aiea Heights Drive for glimpses of Oahu's only remaining **sugar cane refinery.** Further along this route, in a state recreation area, is **Keaiwa Heiau.** Early Hawaiians set this temple, devoted to

medicine, in a garden of herbs, plants and trees known to have healing properties. There are superb panoramic views above Aiea Heights. The park also offers a number of pleasant picnic grounds and a 5-mile (8 km), well marked hiking trail.

If you're returning to Honolulu at this stage, you may want to follow Lunalilo Freeway to **Moanalua Gardens.** It's a private estate with gardens, streams, taro patches and picnic areas open to the public. Two historic houses on the grounds were moved from other locations: Chinese Hall, a pavilion used for group parties, and a charming Victorian cottage built as a summer house for King Kamehameha V.

If you want to explore central Oahu further, turn onto the Kamehameha Highway just west of **Pearl City.** The route leads past the vast cane fields of the Oahu Sugar Company and through **Mililani**

*Above: Marines do morning exercises at the Kaneohe base on Oahu. Right: Hanauma Bay is one of Oahu's most popular beaches.*

**Town,** a planned community whose streets are lined with colorful shower trees. It's notable for its spacious green parks and a bicycle path-walkway system that encompasses virtually the whole town. Visitors are welcome to tour model homes, which are usually open for viewing off Meheula Parkway.

The Kamehameha Highway continues northward to **Wahiawa,** an old plantation town that has taken on new life as the major community servicing **Wheeler Air Force Base** and **Schofield Barracks.** Wheeler, shared by the U.S. Army and Navy, is in a lush setting south of town. It's not open to visitors, but you may want to pause at the main gate to see a replica of a P-40, the military aircraft that saw some of the action on December 7, 1941. From this base, American aviator Amelia Earhart took off in 1935 on the first flight ever made from Hawaii to the Californian mainland.

If you're interested in military sites, you can visit Schofield Barracks, a big Army installation that's home to

Hawaii's 25th Infantry Division. Established as a cavalry base in 1909, it was the United States' largest military post until World War II. Its **Tropic Lightning Historical Center** has exhibits relating to the history of Schofield and the 25th. It's interesting to drive the base's tree-shaded roads, lined by graceful quadrangular-shaped early twentieth-century structures. To enter the grounds, you only need to show proof of adequate automobile insurance.

From Schofield's Macomb Gate, you can drive 5 miles (8 km) to **Kolekole Pass**, a gap in the Waianae Mountains. Here, Japanese planes zoomed through to attack sleeping Schofield Barracks and Wheeler Air Force Base en route to Pearl Harbor. From the parking areas, paths lead up to lookouts, which offer panoramic views of Oahu's verdant central plateau.

Wahiawa has its own special attractions: the **Botanical Gardens** on California Avenue. They specialize in ferns, aroids (resembling calla lilies) and other plants native to mild, wet regions. Also on California Avenue, visitors are welcome at the **Hongwanji Mission.** The Buddha at its altar is carved from Japanese cypress and decorated with gold leaf. Nearby, colorful **North Cane Street** has attractively restored early twentieth-century wooden buildings and an early railroad depot. North of town, a turnoff leads to the **Kukaniloko Birth Stones.** Here Hawaiian *ali'i* mothers came for ceremonial royal births.

Back on the Kamehameha Highway, you'll pass along the Leilehua Plateau, burgeoning with rich green pineapple fields. In its midst, **Del Monte's Pineapple Variety Garden** displays many types of pineapples and other bromeliads. The **Dole Pineapple Pavilion** has fresh local pineapples for sale at a lower price than in stores or at the airport. You'll also find Hawaiian gifts, souvenirs and island products. The adjacent **Helemano Planta-**

**tion** includes a bakery, country store, lunchroom, and fruit, vegetable and flower gardens.

## WINDWARD COAST

From the Kahala Mall, follow Waialae Avenue as it merges into the Kalanianaole Highway and heads for **Hawaii Kai**. This popular residential community was originated by the late American industrialist Henry Kaiser. It's a self-contained area of houses, townhouses, condominiums, shopping centers and two golf courses, sprawling over 6,000 acres (2,428 hectares) of valleys and foothills.

At Oahu's southeastern tip, **Koko Head Natural Park** encompasses Koko Head, an extinct volcanic crater, and the steep-sided Koko Crater. Its interior has been developed into a home for dry-land tropical plants, including cacti. Here, the windward eastern coastline of Oahu begins to assert itself. Urban sprawl lessens. Tortured black lava-rock shores are interspersed with placid sand beaches.

Just past Koko Head lies **Hanauma Bay Beach Park.** This palm-fringed crescent, with coral reefs hidden just beneath the surface of shimmering, translucent turquoise waters, seems especially created for snorkelers. Once a popular fishing ground (until its waters were almost depleted by the fishermen), it is now protected as a state underwater park. The bay is once again a haven for parrotfish, angelfish, wrasses, sea cucumbers, sea urchins, coral and other exotic marine life. They can be viewed at various levels by snorkelers and scuba divers. Alas, popularity is again threatening the bay's once-pristine waters. Restrictions are now being placed on the frequency and times of tourist visits. Inquire locally before planning a special trip.

The coastal highway rounds southeastern Oahu at **Makapuu Point**, where **Makapuu Beach Park** is popular with body surfers. In fact, only skilled practi-

*Above: Dolphins are part of the show at Sea Life Park, on Oahu's southeast coast.*

tioners should challenge the great body-pounders here!

Near Makapuu Point is **Sea Life Park,** a fine oceanarium, run cooperatively with the nearby Oceanic Foundation Research Center. Marine exhibits rank among the world's best: they include displays of ancient Hawaiian fishing techniques, a man-made reef tank, an enormous glass-sided ocean science theater where penguins and porpoises show off their aquatic skills, and a turtle lagoon for rare, giant species from island waters.

The park recently introduced evening programs. Thursdays through Saturdays, there's a 20-minute performance featuring dolphins, Humboldt penguins and a California sea lion. Many of the 3,000 creatures in the reef tank are nocturnal and at their best after the sun sets. Nighttime guests may also stroll around the torchlit grounds and visit the new Rocky Shores exhibit, which recreates Hawaii's different tide zones and their various types of marine life. A Hawaiian buffet dinner is served in the Galley Restaurant,

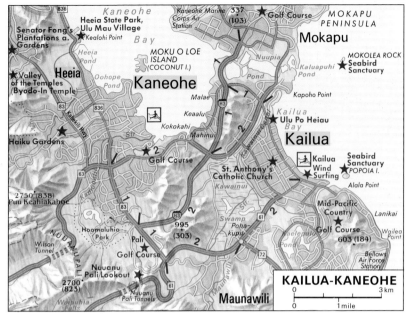

Map: KAILUA-KANEOHE

followed by a revue with island entertainers.

Outside the park's main entrance, the **Pacific Whaling Museum** displays an extensive collection of whaling artifacts.

From Makapuu Point, follow Route 72 further along the Windward Coast. Foliage-clad *pali* (cliffs) – tall, craggy, moody – rise in dramatic symmetry on the landward side of the winding road, while strangely formed, rocky islets occasionally cluster offshore.

State beach parks bordering **Waimanalo Bay** are favored for beachcombing, surfcasting, board and body surfing, swimming and snorkeling. The area's broad plains contribute much of the fruit, vegetables and flowers grown on Oahu. They are also home to some horse and cattle ranches. Another popular board and body surfing spot is **Bellows Field Beach Park,** fronting the now-inactive Bellows Air Force Base.

Next, you'll come to **Kailua Beach Park,** a fine sandy stretch edging Kailua Bay. The nearby town of **Kailua,** and neighboring **Kaneohe,** windward Oahu's two major communities, are among Honolulu's most popular "dormer" towns. In Kailua, you can turn into the Windward YMCA parking lot to visit **Ulu Po Heiau.** This ancient temple is thought to have been built by captive warriors. In Kailua also, **St. Anthony's Catholic Church** has dramatic abstract stained-glass windows. Its pews were handmade by Trappist monks.

There are some enticing options for exploring the area's scenic waters. **Windward Expeditions** offers Motomar boat trips from Kailua Beach for close up views of eight offshore islands, including the sea caves of **Moku Manu Island.** There's also snorkeling near **Manana (Rabbit) Island.** Windward Expeditions picks up from Waikiki locations; the ride to Kailua includes a stop at Nuuanu Pali Lookout, with views of Kaneohe Bay all the way from Mokolii Island to the Mokapu Peninsula.

From Kailua Bay the highway curves northward around Mokapu Peninsula,

87

site of the **Kaneohe Marine Corps Air Station,** and circles scenic **Kaneohe Bay,** a great place for sailing, boating and fishing. Drive a short distance inland along Kahekili Highway to the **Haiku Gardens,** with lily ponds, bamboo groves and tropical plants in the jungles of a large estate. There's a fine restaurant on the grounds.

Continue a bit further into the **Valley of the Temples** to reach **Byodo-In Temple,** a replica of the venerable temple of the same name in Kyoto, Japan. It houses an impressive Buddha statue and an enormous temple bell. The setting is dramatic. Majestic *pali* tower over it, and a serene reflecting lake teems with colorful *koi* (Japanese carp).

Just past the Valley of the Temples, outside Kaneohe, is a popular new Windward Coast attraction: **Senator Fong's Plantation and Gardens.** You can take a

*Above: A muscle-powered outrigger rushes toward shore. Right: Waves crash on a rocky promontory on Oahu's north shore.*

commented mini-bus tour through lush forests interspersed with landscaped gardens of exotic flowers. More than 75 different varieties of Hawaiian fruits and nuts grow in carefully tended tropical orchards. The 724-acre (293 hectare) site was developed by retired U.S. Senator Hiram Fong, the first American of Asian descent to be elected to the Senate. The former legislator still takes great delight in mingling with his visitors. Fong's Plantation offers classes in lei making and other Hawaiian crafts. The site also includes a gift shop and restaurant.

About 1,5 miles (2,4 km) north of Kaneohe, you'll come to **Heeia.** From its pier you can board a glass-bottomed boat to view underwater coral gardens and other attractions of Kaneohe Bay. The cruise sails past **Moku o Lo'e (Coconut Island)**, where a former private estate houses a division of the University of Hawaii Institute of Marine Biology (not open to visitors).

Farther off the road at Kualoa Point, the northern end of 8-mile wide (13 km)

Kaneohe Bay, is a well-known offshore landmark. It's little **Mokolii Island,** usually known as "Chinaman's Hat." When the tide is low, it's possible to walk out to explore the island or bask in the sun.

The road swings past the stone ruins of Oahu's first sugar mill (1864), then north to **Kaawa** and **Swanzy Beach Parks.** You'll see yet another landmark, the picturesque **Crouching Lion** rock formation. Beneath its leonine silhouette, the Crouching Lion Inn is a popular luncheon stop. The route then follows scenic Kahana Bay amid rich stands of banana, breadfruit and mango trees.

Past **Punaluu**, near **Hauula**, if you're feeling adventurous you may turn off at a sign pointing to **Sacred Falls.** It's a rigorous hike up a rough mountain ravine to where the falls plunge into a gorge, creating a crystal-clear mountain pool.

About 3 miles (5 km) north, this circuit brings you to **Laie.** Here, the Hawaiian Islands' most popular paid attraction, the famed **Polynesian Cultural Center,** adjoins the Hawaii campus of **Brigham Young University.** The cultural center is a project of the Church of Jesus Christ of Latter-day Saints (the Mormons), and students from throughout Polynesia help finance their education at BYUH by working part-time at the center.

At seven recreated villages, representing Samoa, Fiji, Tonga, Tahiti, the Marquesas, Maori New Zealand and Hawaii, vibrant, friendly Pacific Islanders, authentically costumed, demonstrate the arts, crafts, music and dance of their homelands. Visitors are good-naturedly encouraged to get into the spirit by learning to crack a coconut, dance a hula, play a Tahitian drum, or sample *poi* or other island foods.

Plan to arrive by early afternoon to enjoy the total experience. Colorful canoe pageants are held hourly from 1 to 4 each afternoon except Sundays, when the center is closed. Evenings, there's a performance of "This Is Polynesia," among the islands' most lavish and exciting revues. It's preceded by an extensive *luau*, featuring such traditional favorites

89

as Hawaiian-style *kalua* pig, teriyaki chicken, *lomi lomi* salmon, chicken long rice, and fresh island fish. The food is excellent. Due to the center's Mormon links, you'll sip only fresh fruit punches, unseasoned by rum or other alcoholic beverages.

## NORTH SHORE

From Laie, the highway curves inland past **Kahuku**, emerging seaward at picturesque **Kawela Bay**. The luxurious **Turtle Bay Hilton Resort** near Oahu's northernmost point is a popular base for visitors who wish to escape Waikiki's bustle. From here, you can explore the island's northern and windward coasts, glimpsing a serene, almost bucolic "other Oahu."

Past Kawela Bay, the road continues along the North Shore, renowned for its

*Above: Waterfalls and pool at the north shore's Waimea Falls Park. Right: A local family in search of some fresh seafood.*

big surf. At one of its best-known spots, **Sunset Beach Park,** winter waves soar 20 to 40 ft (6-12 m), highest in the world for board surfing. Adjacent is the notorious **Banzai Pipeline**, a dangerous surge of fast-breaking curlers that is definitely for experts only. Even during calmer winter waters, these waves should be treated with healthy respect.

Other nearby big-surf beaches include **Waimea**, **Ehukai** and **Pupukea**. It's wise to exercise caution when visiting any of Hawaii's beach parks. Don't leave valuables in an automobile, even if it is locked. Although the aloha spirit by and large abounds, crimes and unpleasant incidents can still occur in public sites.

Near Waimea Beach Park, you can turn onto Pupukea Road to the ruins of **Puu-o-Mahuka Heiau,** Oahu's largest ancient temple, once the site of human sacrifices. According to legend, a temple priest in 1780 predicted that Hawaii would be taken over by *haoles* (white outsiders) from a faraway land.

Back on the highway, near the north side of the Waimea River, is the 295-acre (728-hectare) **Waimea Falls Park.** Nestling in an idyllic setting, this is one of Oahu's most appealing natural attractions. Native Hawaiians lived for hundreds of years in this cool, verdant valley. And park management has made admirable efforts to preserve Hawaiian traditions, folklore and culture.

The **Waimea Arboretum and Botanical Garden** is a major center for propagating rare and endangered plant species endemic to Hawaii and other tropical lands.

Waimea Park's internationally acclaimed resident hula troupe, Halau o Waimea, performs the rare *kahiko* (ancient) hula several times daily. Dating back to the eleventh century, traditional hulas recount the lives and legends of the Hawaiian people through melodic *meles* (chants). Dancers wear historically authentic costumes, gathering ferns and

leaves for their construction from within the valley. Halau o Waimea members also demonstrate ancient sporting events at the state's largest permanent games site; visitors are encouraged to join them in tests of skill.

Major historical remnants, including burial and living areas, have been discovered within the valley. Others are under archaeological study. Knowledgeable guides lead tours within the sites, where preservation and reconstruction continue.

On a less erudite note, you can take a ride through the valley on a commented mini-bus tour. Guides point out tropical gardens and historic sites, and import other bits of valley lore. Jungle fowl and peacocks freely roam the park. The tram also passes beautiful Waimea Falls, where skilled divers plummet from surrounding cliffs into the pool below. ·

Visitors can picnic in a quiet meadow or dine in a park restaurant. There's a gift shop with a good selection of island bric-a-brac, including crafts, books, phonograph records or tapes.

Continuing southward along the highway, you'll pass more unprotected parks, where surf pounds incessantly. Near **Haleiwa** (pronounced *ha-lay-EE-va*), you'll see a trim dairy farm that offers a thatched-roof picnic shelter at no charge. If traveling with children, you may want to visit its farm to introduce them to some local farm creatures.

**Haleiwa Beach Park** is an excellent stop for picnicking, snorkeling and shore diving. It is considered the only North Shore beach that's safe for novice surfers.

**Haleiwa Town**, once a fashionable resort on the sugar-cane railroad, is reminiscent of the early 1920s. Many of its original wood and stone buildings have been restored and revived as restaurants, boutiques, surf shops and art galleries (including one that offers works by internationally known whale artist Wyland). Some islanders drive from Honolulu to order a hamburger or *mahi mahi* (dolphin) sandwich from the **Kua Aina Sandwich Shop** in an old wooden building on the edge of town.

91

You can follow Waialua Beach Road to **Waialua Protestant Church,** also known as Queen Liliuokalani Church for the former ruler who had a summer home nearby. The road soon connects with the Farrington Highway. This route leads to **Mokuleia** (*Mo-koo-lay-EE-yah*), where there are frequent Sunday afternoon polo matches. Beyond, at Dillingham Airstrip, the **Hawaii Soaring Club** gathers to fly gliders; visitors are welcome to watch. Members sometimes take passengers aboard their three-seater planes for a fee.

Farrington Highway leads on from here to **Kaena Point,** Oahu's westernmost point. An unmaintained dirt road rings the point, but it's difficult driving, even for a four-wheel-drive vehicle.

## LEEWARD COAST

Oahu's leeward west coast is an area less traveled than others by visitors. Typically, it's only vacationers staying at the Makaha Resort and Country Club who take the time to explore it. Yet the scenic **Waianae Coast**, lying west of the Waianae Mountains, has a distinctive appeal.

At **Makua Beach** near Oahu's northwesternmost location, just before the end of Farrington Highway, you can visit dramatic **Kaneana Cave.** This rugged rock-and-coral formation was said to be the home of a deity who could change unpredictably from a human being into a shark.

Southward on the way to **Makaha,** the entire stretch of coastal beach is a popular area for gathering *puka* shells, tiny remnants of mollusks favored by the makers of shell leis for the *puka* (hole) in the middle. Here again, don't leave valuables in your car.

South of the caves, at **Keaau Beach Park,** you'll find ancient petroglyphs on the lava rocks. Just behind, **Makaha Beach Park** is a fine, broad strand ideal

*Right: A trip into the past at the museum of the Hawaiian Railway Society in Ewa.*

for swimming and sunning. It is popular with surfers as well, although the newcomers shouldn't try the combers that may tower 20 to 30 ft (6-9 m) in winter. When the surf is up, surfers from as far away as Australia tackle the waves during the **Makaha Surfers Meets**.

The leeward coast's only major vacation resort, **Makaha Resort and Country Club,** is a pleasant enclave in an otherwise still-rustic and undeveloped area of Oahu. Here you may ask permission to walk to the restored **Kaneaki Heiau**, a seventeenth-century temple with prayer towers, grass houses, and a sacrificial altar. Originally sacred to Lono, the god of peace and fertility, the temple was rededicated by Kamehameha the Great in 1796 to his patron, the war god. The resort also encompasses residential developments, but much of the interior of Makaha Valley has been left in its natural state. It can best be explored by hikers and horseback riders.

South of Makaha, toward Waianae, lie other popular beach and surfing sites: **Mauna Lahilahi Beach Park** and **Waianae Regional Park**.

The town of **Waianae,** with a population of about 10,000, is the central settlement along Highway 93 (the Farrington Highway). It's situated on a semi-arid plain typical of the dry leeward coast.

In town, the Waianae Shopping Mall includes **E'ala,** a Hawaiian cultural center and gift shop with exhibits on the area's historic sites. The center's double-hulled voyaging canoe is moored at **Pokai Bay,** to the south, near the entrance to another major Oahu *heiau* – **Ku'ili-o-loa,** anchored by a 200-ft-long (60 m) temple.

The route leads south from Waianae past more beach parks with lyrical Hawaiian names: **Lualualei, Maili, Ulehawa, Nanakuli, Kahe Point.** Arid stretches of black lava rock divide the strands of white sand, and the landscape is dotted with twisted *kiawe* (ironwood)

trees. There are no sheltering reefs to protect the beaches from outlying currents, and the surf boils relentlessly offshore, plunging furiously onto the sand. Tourists are rarely seen on this shore; it is the playground of local residents.

U.S. military installations adjoin much of this area to the south and east. Roads traversing the reservations are not open to the public. If they were, you might see some spectacular sights: the **U.S. Navy communication towers** at Lualualei are taller than the Empire State Building in New York City.

At Kahe Point the highway turns inland, and leads past the refineries and warehouses of the vast **Campbell Industrial Park** and a new deep-draft harbor designed to accommodate some of the largest ships afloat.

The Farrington Highway merges into the H-1 Freeway near **Makakilo**, gateway to the **Barber's Point Naval Air Station.** From here, you can veer off to several inland communities of special interest. Among them is **Ewa**, a plantation

town built by Ewa Sugar Company in the 1920s and 1930s. An abandoned mill marks the company site. The attractive community features a number of restored houses, churches and company buildings. Here, too, there is a working yard of the **Hawaiian Railway Society**. It includes more than 40 pieces of rolling stock, highlighted by Waialua No. 6, a plantation engine built from spare parts.

You can also turn off the H-1 Freeway into **Waipahu**, a major gateway to the Pearl Harbor Naval Reservation. Another plantation town clustered around a sugar mill, it presents a startling contrast to the teeming military base. The **Oahu Sugar Company's mill**, one of the last operating mills on the island, is a town landmark. A village typical of early twentieth-century Waipahu is being established nearby in the **Waipahu Cultural Garden Park.** Botanical gardens blossom with an abundance of local plants, and old plantation homes have been relocated on the site. There's also a visitor center with early era exhibits.

93

## OAHU
(All area telephone codes are 808)

### Waikiki
#### Accommodation
*LUXURY:* **Halekulani,** 2199 Kalia Rd., Honolulu 96815, Tel: 923-2311, 800-367-2343. **Hilton Hawaiian Village,** 2005 Kalia Rd., Honolulu 96815, Tel: 949-4321, 800-445-8667. **Royal Hawaiian,** 2259 Kalakaua Ave., Honolulu 96815, Tel: 923-7311, 800-325-3535.
*MODERATE:* **Aston Island Colony,** 445 Seaside Ave., Honolulu 96815, Tel: 923-2345, 800-922-7866. **Miramar at Waikiki,** 2345 Kuhio Ave., Honolulu 96815, Tel: 922-2077, 800-367-2303. **Outrigger Reef Towers,** 227 Lewers St., Honolulu 96815, Tel: 924-8844, 800- 733-7777.
*BUDGET:* **Big Surf Condo,** 1690 Ala Moana Blvd., Honolulu 96815, Tel: 946-6525. **Outrigger Ala Wai Terrace,** 1547 Ala Wai Blvd., Honolulu 96815, Tel: 949-7384, 800-733-7777. **Waikiki Prince,** 2431 Prince Edward St., Honolulu 96815, Tel: 922- 1544.
#### Attractions
**Honolulu Zoo,** Kapiolani Park, 9am-5pm daily. **Kodak Hula Show,** Monsarrat Avenue near Waikiki Shell, 10am Tue-Fri. **U.S. Army Museum,** Fort DeRussy near Cinerama Reef Hotel, Tel: 543-2639, 10am-4:30pm Tue-Sun. **Waikiki Aquarium,** 2777 Kalakaua Ave., Tel: 923-9741, 10am-5pm daily.
#### Restaurants
*AMERICAN:* **Bobby McGee's,** Colony East Hotel, 2885 Kalakaua Ave., Tel: 922-1282. **Tony Roma's,** 1972 Kalakaua Ave., Tel: 942-2121. *CHINESE:* **Hee Hing,** 449 Kapahulu Ave., Tel: 735-5544. **House of Hong,** 260 Lewers St., Tel: 923-0202. *CONTINENTAL:* **Bagwells 2424,** Hyatt Regency Hotel, 2424 Kalakaua Ave., Tel: 923-1234. **Nick's Fishmarket,** Waikiki Gateway Hotel, 2070 Kalakaua Ave., Tel: 955-6333. *FRENCH:* **Michel's,** Colony Surf Hotel, 2895 Kalakaua Ave., Tel: 923-6552. **Papadore,** 3058 Monsarrat Ave., Tel: 732-9561. *GERMAN:* **Bavarian Beer Garden,** Royal Hawaiian Shopping Center, 2301 Kalakaua Ave., Tel: 922-6535. *ITALIAN:* **Matteo's,** Marine Surf Hotel, 364 Seaside Ave., Tel: 922-5551. **Trattoria,** Edgewater Hotel, 2168 Kalia Rd., Tel: 923-8415. *JAPANESE:* **Kyotaru,** 2160 Kalakaua Ave., Tel: 924-3663. **Miyako,** New Otani Kaimana Beach Hotel, 2863 Kalakaua Ave., Tel: 923-1555. *KOREAN:* **Camellia,** Waikiki Resort Hotel, 2460 Koa Ave., Tel: 922-4911. *STEAK AND SEAFOOD:* **Captain's Galley,** Sheraton Moana Surfrider Hotel, 2365 Kalakaua Ave., Tel: 922-3111. **Ray's,** Waikiki Shopping Plaza, 2250 Kalakaua Ave., Tel: 923-5717. *THAI:* **Keo's,** 625 Kapahulu Ave., Tel: 737-8240.
#### Shopping
**Eaton Square,** 444 Hobron Lane, 10am-6pm daily. **Hemmeter Center,** Kalakaua Ave. between Uluniu and Kailuani Aves., 9am-11pm daily. **International Market Place,** 2330 Kalakaua Ave., 9am-11pm daily. **King's Village,** 131 Kaiulani Ave., 9am-11pm daily. **Kuhio Mall,** Kuhio Ave. between Seaside and Kaiulani Aves., 10am-10pm daily. **Rainbow Bazaar,** Hilton Hawaiian Village, 2005 Kalia Rd., 9am-11pm daily. **Royal Hawaiian Center,** Kalakaua Ave. between Lewers St. and the Outrigger Hotel, 9am-9pm daily. **Waikiki Shopping Plaza,** Kalakaua Ave. between Royal Hawaiian and Seaside Aves., 6am-1am daily. **Weekend Art Mart,** Monsarrat Street side of Honolulu Zoo, 10am-4pm Sat-Sun.
#### Tourist Information
**Hawaii Visitors Bureau,** Suite 801, Waikiki Business Plaza, 2270 Kalakaua Ave. (P.O. Box 8527), Honolulu 96830, Tel: 923-1811.

### Honolulu (outside Waikiki)
#### Accommodation
*LUXURY:* **Kahala Hilton,** 5000 Kahala Ave., Honolulu 96816, Tel: 734-2211, 800-367-2525, on east side of Diamond Head. **Ramada Renaissance-Ala Moana,** 410 Atkinson Dr., Honolulu 96814, Tel: 955-4811, 800-367-6025, at Ala Moana center. *MODERATE:* **Plaza Hotel,** 3253 N. Nimitz Hwy., Honolulu 96819, Tel: 836-3636, 800-657-7989, near airport. **Manoa Valley Inn,** 2001 Vancouver Dr., Honolulu 96822, Tel: 947-6019, 800-634-5155, near university. **Pagoda,** 1525 Rycroft St., Honolulu 96814, Tel: 941-6611, near Ala Moana center. *BUDGET:* **Honolulu Intern. Youth Hostel,** 2323-A Seaview Ave., Honolulu 96822, Tel: 945-0591.
#### Attractions
**Aloha Tower,** Pier 9, Honolulu Harbor, 8am-9pm daily. **Bishop Museum & Planetarium,** 1355 Kalihi St., Tel: 847-1443, 9am-5pm daily. **Contemporary Arts Center of Hawaii,** News Building, 605 Kapiolani Blvd., Tel: 525-8000, 8am-5pm Mon-Fri, 8am-noon Sat. **Falls of Clyde,** Pier 7, Honolulu Harbor, Tel: 536-6373, 9:30am-4:30pm daily. **Foster Botanic Garden,** 180 N. Vineyard Blvd., Tel: 531-1939, 8:30am-4pm daily. **Honolulu Academy of Arts,** 900 S. Beretania St., Tel: 538-3693, 10am-4:30pm Tue-Wed and Fri-Sat, 2-5pm Sun. **Iolani Palace,** South King Street at Capitol Mall, Tel: 536-6185, 9am-2:15pm Wed-Sat. **Mission Houses,** 553 S. King St., Tel: 531-0481, 9am-4pm daily.

**National Memorial Cemetery of the Pacific,** Punchbowl Crater, Puowaina Drive, 8am-5:30pm daily Oct-Feb, 8am-6:30pm daily Mar-Sept. **Paradise Park,** 3737 Manoa Rd., Tel: 988-2141, 9:30am-5pm daily. **Queen Emma Summer Palace,** 2913 Pali Hwy., Tel: 595-3167, 9am-4pm daily.

### Restaurants

*AMERICAN:* **Rose City Diner,** Restaurant Row, 500 Ala Moana Blvd., Tel: 524-7673. **Yum Yum Tree,** Kahala Mall, 4211 Waialae Ave., Tel: 737-7938. *CALIFORNIA:* **Il Fresco,** Ward Centre, 1200 Ala Moana Blvd., Tel: 523-5191. *CHINESE:* **Dynasty I,** Ward Warehouse, 1050 Ala Moana Blvd., Tel: 531-0208. **Wo Fat,** 115 N. Hotel St., Tel: 533-6393. *CONTINENTAL:* **The Black Orchid,** Restaurant Row, 500 Ala Moana Blvd., Tel: 521-3111. **Maile Room,** Kahala Hilton, 5000 Kahala Ave., Tel: 734-2211. *HAWAIIAN:* **Henri Hawaii,** Paradise Park, 3737 Manoa Rd., Tel: 988-6911. **The Willows,** 901 Hausten St., Tel: 946-4808. *ITALIAN:* **Andrew's,** Ward Centre, 1200 Ala Moana Blvd., Tel: 523-8677. **Castagnola's,** Manoa Marketplace, 2752 Woodlawn Dr., Tel: 988-2969. *JAPANESE:* **Suehiro,** 1824 S. King St., Tel: 949-4584. *KOREAN:* **Kim Chee II,** Waialae Plaza, 3569 Waialae Ave., Tel: 737-0006. *MEXICAN:* **Compadres,** Ward Centre, 1200 Ala Moana Blvd., Tel: 523-1307. *SEAFOOD:* **John Dominis,** 43 Ahui St., Tel: 523-0955. **Orson's,** Ward Warehouse, 1050 Ala Moana Blvd., Tel: 521-5681. *STEAKS:* **John Richard's,** Koko Marina Shopping Center, 7192 Kalanianaole Hwy., Tel: 396-6393. **Ruth's Chris Steak House,** Restaurant Row, 500 Ala Moana Blvd., Tel: 599-3860. *THAI:* **Bangkok House,** First Interstate Building, 1314 S. King St., Tel: 537-4999. **Siam Orchid,** 638-B Keeaumoku St., Tel: 955-6161. *VIETNAMESE:* **Hale Vietnam,** 1140 12th Ave., Tel: 735-7581.

### Shopping

**Ala Moana Shopping Center,** between Ala Moana and Kapiolani Blvds. near Waikiki, 9:30am-9pm Mon-Fri, 9:30am-5:30pm Sat, 10am-4pm Sun. **New China Cultural Plaza,** 100 N. Beretania St., 8am-5pm Mon-Fri. **Ward Warehouse,** 1050 Ala Moana Blvd., 10am-9pm Mon-Fri, 10am-5pm Sat, 11am-4pm Sun. Business districts of Downtown, Chinatown, Kaimuki, Kapahulu, and University, 8am-5pm Mon-Fri.

## Oahu (outside Honolulu)
### Accommodation

*LUXURY:* **Sheraton Makaha Resort and Country Club,** 84-626 Makaha Valley Rd., Wai-

anae 96792, Tel: 695-9511, 800-325-3535, Leeward Coast. **Turtle Bay Hilton and Country Club,** 57-091 Kamehameha Hwy. (P.O. Box 187), Kahuku 96731, Tel: 293-3811, 800- 445-8667, Windward Coast. *MODERATE:* **Kuilima Estates,** (P.O. Box 399), Kahuku 96731, Tel: 293-2494, 800-367-7040, Oahu's northeast point. **Makaha Shores,** 84-265 Farrington Hwy., Makaha 96792, Tel: 696-8415, Leeward Coast. **Pat's at Punaluu,** 53-567 Kamehameha Hwy., Hauula 96717, Tel: 293-8111, Windward Coast. *BUDGET:* **Backpackers Vacation Inn & Plantation Village,** 59- 788 Kamehameha Hwy. (P.O. Box 716), Haleiwa 96712, Tel: 638-7838.

### Attractions

**Byodo-In Temple,** 47-200 Kahekili Hwy., Kaneohe, Tel: 239-8811, 9am-5pm daily. **Castle Park,** across from Aloha Stadium, Tel: 488-6822, 9:30am-10:30pm Sun-Thu, 9:30am-12:30am Fri-Sat. **Koko Head Botanic Park,** Koko Head Crater, Kalanianaole Hwy., Tel: 537-9373, 9am-4pm Mon-Fri. **Mormon Temple,** Laie, Tel: 293-8561, Mon-Sat. **Polynesian Cultural Center,** Laie, Tel: 293-8561, 11am-7pm Mon-Sat. **Sea Life Park,** Makapuu Point, Tel: 259-7933, 9:30am-5pm daily. **U.S.S. Arizona Memorial,** Kamehameha Highway, Pearl Harbor, Tel: 471-3901 or 422-2771, 8am-3pm Tue-Sun. **Waimea Falls Park,** 59-864 Kamehameha Hwy., North Shore, Tel: 638-8511, 10am-5:30 pm daily.

### Restaurants

*AMERICAN:* **Dot's in Wahiawa,** 130 Mango St., Wahiawa, Tel: 622-4115. **Proud Peacock at Waimea Falls Park,** 59-864 Kamehameha Hwy., Haleiwa, Tel: 638-8531. *CHINESE:* **Halemano Plantation Country Inn,** 64-1510 Kamehameha Hwy., Wahiawa, Tel: 622-3929. *CONTINENTAL:* **The Cove by the Bay,** Turtle Bay Hilton, 57-091 Kamehameha Hwy., Kahuku, Tel: 293-8811. **Kaala Room,** Sheraton Makaha Resort, 84-626 Makaha Valley Rd., Waianae, Tel: 695-9511. *HAWAIIAN:* **Rabbit Island Bar and Grill,** Sea Life Park, Makapuu Point, Tel: 259-9911. *STEAKS AND SEAFOOD:* **Jameson's by the Sea,** 62-540 Kamehameha Hwy., Haleiwa, Tel: 637-4336. **Stuart Anderson's Cattle Company,** Times Square Shopping Center, 98-1262 Kaahumanu St., Pearl City, Tel: 487-0054.

### Shopping

**Kamehameha Drive-In Theatre Swap Meet,** 98-850 Moanalua Rd., 7am-3pm Wed, Sat, Sun. **Pearl Ridge Shopping Center,** 98-211 Pali Momi, Pearl City, 10am-9pm Mon-Fri, 10am-5:30pm Sat, 11am- 4pm Sun.

# MAUI

**CENTRAL MAUI**

**WEST MAUI**

**KIHEI COAST**

**HANA HIGHWAY**

**HALEAKALA**

Hawaii's green, serene "Valley Island" has witnessed intensive resort development during the past two decades. But even though some purists consider its growth alarming, Maui can still coax the visitor into a state of euphoria. It is an island of contrasts, retaining areas of great natural beauty and remoteness. And it's touched as well with numerous reminders of Hawaiian prehistory.

Ancient Polynesian legend says the demigod Maui fished the Hawaiian Islands up from the sea. Originally a single catch, they broke into separate segments when his line snapped!

Maui was displeased, so goes the legend, that his namesake island – on which he made his home – was touched by the sun only a few hours each day. Determined to harness the sun as it began its morning journey above the dormant crater of Haleakala volcano, he captured its rays with a rope woven of coconut fiber. He threatened to kill it, as it had never allowed his mother sufficient time to dry the tapa cloth she made from the mulberry tree's bark. The sun begged for mercy, promising to lengthen its trip across the island's skies. And to this day,

*Preceding pages: The dramatic contours of Iao Needle, Maui. Left: An arial view of Kahului (foreground) and Wailuku.*

the island's residents boast, the sun shines brightest of all on the island of Maui. When locals proclaim *Maui no ka oi* ("Maui is the best"), many visitors fervently echo that claim.

The chiefs of old Hawaii also found west Maui a pleasant playground. Until the late eighteenth century, the island was independent, proudly autonomous. One of its greatest kings, Kahekili, established his royal court in what is now Lahaina.

About 1790, King Kamehameha the Great landed with his troops from the Big Island. Starting near Hana, on Maui's eastern coast, they advanced along the coast to the Wailuku Valley. In a bloody battle in the shadow of the towering Iao Needle, they battered the forces of Kalanikupule, son of Maui's king, into submission.

The torrential of the Iao were packed with human bodies and ran red with blood. The battle became known as *Kepaniwai*, "the damming of the waters." But King Kahekili did not concede defeat, continuing to reign in Lahaina until his death in 1794.

Following the fearsome Iao Valley slaughter, Prince Kalanikupule escaped to Oahu, where Kamehameha eventually met and defeated his forces in the decisive battle of Nuuanu Pali, definitively uniting all of the Hawaiian Islands. The

MAUI

Nakaele Pt.

Dirt Road
340

Honolua B.
Mokuleia B.
Oneloa B.
Kapalua
Napili Bay
D.T. Fleming
Honokahua
Golf Courses
Alaeloa

Honokohau
Pohaku Kani
(Bellstone)
28

Dirt Road

30

Camp
Maluhia

340

Waihee

Hookipa
Kuau
Mama
Buddhist
Mission
Lower Paia
Paia

WEST MAUI MOUNTAINS

Lahaina Kaanapali &
Pacific Railroad
Royal Lahaina
Kaanapali
Whalers Village
Museum

Crater
Village

Lahainaluna School,
Hale Pa'i
Printing House

Lahaina, Kaanapali a.
Pacific Railroad

33

Paukukalo

Kahului B.

Kanaha Bird
Sanctuary

36

Kahului
Airport

Mala

Lahaina

Puunoa
Pt.

Puu Kukui
5788 (1764)

Hale Hoikeike
VALLEY Museum

Wailuku

32

3

Kahului

Kaa

Puunene
Sugar Mill

37

7

Hali

Pukala

Auau Channel

Puanama

Launiupoko
St. Wayside

Waikapu

380

6

Kalialinui

Waikako

M

30

Mopua

Olowalu

16

Papalaua
St. Wayside
Maalaea

31

Ukumehame

30

Papawai Pt.

Humpback
Whales
Viewing

Maalaea B.

Capt. Vancouver
Monument

Kihei

350

8

Kamaoe

31

Waio

Keokea

Thompson
Ranch

37

Wailea

Wailea Golf
Courses

Po
6472

Makena

Puu Olai
360 (110)

MOLOKINI I.

Big a.
Little Beach

Makena
G.C.

Ulupalakua

Tedeschi
Winery

Dirt Road

31

Ahihi
Bay

Ahihi-Kinau
Natural Area Res.

Kanahena

Last Lava Flow
on Maui (1790)

Keoneoio

La Peruse B.

C. Hanamanoia

Alalakeiki Channel

C. Kukui

KAHOOLAWE

Lua Makua
1483 (452)

Ahupu

Kanapou
Bay

Kealaikahiki
Pt.

Waikahalulu
B.

Kamohio
B.

Kaka Pt.

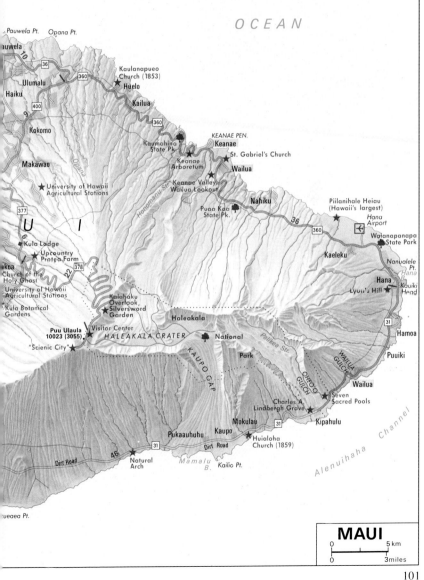

PACIFIC

OCEAN

Pauwela Pt.   Opana Pt.

auwela

10

36

Ulumalu

360

Kaulanapueo
Church (1853)

Haiku

Huelo

400

Kailua

Kokomo

360

KEANAE PEN.

Kaumahina
State Pk.

Keanae

Makawao

Keanae
Arboretum

St. Gabriel's Church

Wailua

University of Hawaii
Agricultural Stations

Keanae Valley,
Wailua Lookout

Nahiku

377

Puaa Kaa
State Pk.

Piilanihale Heiau
(Hawaii's largest)

U       I

36

360

Hana
Airport

Kula Lodge

Upcountry
Protea Farm

Waianapanapa
State Park

Nanualele
Pt.

koa
Church of the
Holy Ghost

22

378

Kaeleku

Hana
B.

University of Hawaii
Agricultural Stations

Hana

Lyon's Hill

Kauiki
Head

Kula Botanical
Gardens

Kalahaku
Overlook,
Silversword
Garden

Puu Ulaula
10023 (3055)

Visitor Center

Haleakala

HALEAKALA CRATER

National

Puu Ulaula
10023 (3055)

Pelikea Str.

Hamoa

"Scienic City"

Park

Puuiki

KAUPO GAP

OHEO
GULCH

WAILUA
GULCH

Wailua

Charles A.
Lindbergh Grave

Seven
Sacred Pools

Pukaauhuhu

Kaupo

Mokulau

31

Kipahulu

Dirt Road

46

31

Huialoha
Church (1859)

Dirt Road

Natural
Arch

Mamalu
B.

Kailio Pt.

Alenuihaha  Channel

ueaea Pt.

**MAUI**

0        5 km

0        3miles

hapless prince roamed throughout Oahu as a fugitive for several months. He was finally captured in a remote cave and brought before Kamehameha as a trophy. The conqueror ordered his head be crushed on one of his altars.

The victorious Kamehameha established a residence on Maui after the Iao Valley battle. The island's Hana coast had been the birthplace of his favorite wife, the influential Kaahumanu.

After Kamehameha's death, Kamehameha II (Liholiho) was so taken with Maui's tropical beauty that, in 1820, he made Lahaina his capital. The seat of his government was transferred from Kailua, on the west coast of the Big Island, and Lahaina remained Hawaii's capital until 1845, when that honor was awarded to Honolulu.

*Above: A Hawaiian woman at a cultural festival. Right: Getting ready for a traditional luau – a pig is removed from a typical Hawaiian imua, an underground oven after steaming for up to six hours.*

In Lahaina, it is claimed, the Great Mahele originated. This progressive reform, which was formally declared in 1848 after the move to Honolulu, finally led to the breakup of Hawaii's feudalistic society. Royal land was divided into *kuleanas* (plots) that common folk could own.

In the early nineteenth century, Lahaina was visited by two groups of voyagers that could not have been more at odds: brawling whalers and determined New England Protestant missionaries.

For more than four decades, beginning in 1819, Lahaina was one of the world's great whaling ports. The whalers spent months at sea, hunting north and south of the islands and as far away as Japan. They came to Maui to reprovision, and when in port they sought whisky and women as fervently as they had hunted whales.

It was a frenzied, violent time. Often 50 ships at a time were anchored in Lahaina Roads, and in whaling's peak year – 1859 – 549 ships visited Lahaina.

Placed bow to stern, it would have been possible to walk across their decks all the way to the neighboring island of Lanai.

By the 1860s, the Pacific whaling business had begun to collapse, victim of the rise of the petroleum industry and the disruptions of the U.S. Civil War. Maui turned to ranching, the cultivation of sugar cane and pineapples. Little Lahaina slipped into a sunny daydream that lasted well into the 20th century.

Even as late as the mid 1970s, many of the town's streets were unpaved. But with development of the vast, nearby Kaanapali Beach resort area, Lahaina has burgeoned. Maui is second only to Oahu's Waikiki Beach as Hawaii's most popular visitor destination.

Several airlines offer direct flights from the U.S. mainland to Kahului, Maui's major commercial city. And Hawaii's inter-island carriers have daily flights between Oahu and Maui.

At Kaanapali, at the Kapalua resort further north, and at the Wailea and Makena resort areas on the southwest coast, visitors will discover some of Hawaii's finest vacation hideaways. The Pacific Ocean is exceptionally clear here, ideal for snorkeling and scuba diving. Maui resorts also boast some of Hawaii's finest golf courses.

No Maui guest should miss two dramatic island excursions. A drive along the verdant northeastern coast leads to the picturesque village of Hana. The drive itself rivals the destination, winding past scenic vistas, tranquil beaches, isolated fishing villages and dense jungle growth.

One of the Pacific's most dramatic sights is the view from the rim of Haleakala, Maui's giant volcanic crater. It's as large as Manhattan Island.

Intriguing, too, is Maui's cool, green "upcountry," home of the so-called *paniolos* (Hawaiian cowboys). It's also a major retreat for Maui's growing arts community, and a favored getaway for film and television personalities. Worlds apart from the popular beach resorts, it reflects another fascinating dimension of Hawaii's second largest island.

## CENTRAL MAUI

Many visitors tend to bypass **Kahului**, the island's major seaport and site of its primary airport. The well-planned model city is perhaps best known as a starting point for the 52-mile (84 km) scenic drive to Hana.

But Kahului is well worth a brief exploration in its own right. It has several excellent shopping centers and is home of Maui Community College, a branch of the University of Hawaii.

**Kanaha Bird Sanctuary**, 1.5 miles (2.4 km) southwest of the airport, is a splendid spot for viewing migratory waterfowl during winter months. From an observation hut, it's possible to get close-up glimpses of migratory ducks, Canada geese and other birds from the North American mainland. Abutting the sanctuary is the attractive **Kanaha Beach Park**,

*Above: The Nene, a flightless goose native to Hawaii and recently saved from the edge of extinction, is the official state bird.*

a delightful, tree-shaded place to picnic and enjoy grandiose panoramic vistas across Kahului Bay.

Recently established just outside Kahului is the **Alexander and Baldwin Sugar Museum**, the first of its kind in Hawaii. Located south of town at **Puunene**, on the road leading from the airport, it's easily recognizable by the stacks of the C&H (California & Hawaii) sugar mill. The museum offers historical photographs and exhibits about the sweet crop that supported Hawaii's economy for more than 150 years.

Highway 36 leads eastward from Kahului to the rustic, colorful town of **Paia.** Many artists live and work in this area. The community has several galleries, including the prestigious **Maui Crafts Guild,** which displays the artistry of member woodworkers, leather crafters, weavers, painters, metal workers and ceramicists.

Kaahumanu Drive leads directly from Kahului into its "twin city" of **Wailuku,** seat of the Maui County government.

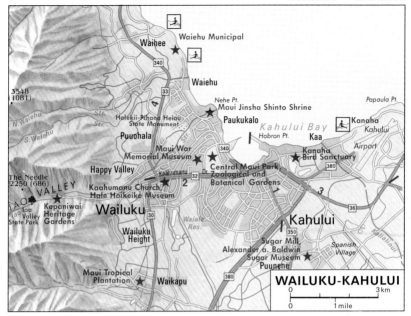

Near the harbor's western edge, and extending to the fringes of Wailuku, **Central Maui Park** has a still-developing cultural center and museum, and the compact **Maui Zoological and Botanical Gardens,** opposite Maui's **War Memorial Stadium.** You can stroll the beautifully landscaped park to acquaint yourself with intriguing plant and animal life from Hawaii and many other parts of the world. When completed, the park will also encompass the War Memorial recreational area, and will feature a variety of sports fields, bicycle trails and pleasant pedestrian walkways.

Although the two towns have virtually grown together, an aura of an earlier era pervades Wailuku with its charming provincial façades. Missionaries settled here as early as 1837, and the original section of the **Kaahumanu Church,** Maui's oldest Christian house of worship, dates from that time.

Nearby, off Iao Valley Road, stands **Hale Hoikeike,** an excellent small historical museum directed by the Maui Historical Society. Built in 1841 as a home for Edward Bailey, headmaster of the old Wailuku Female Seminary, it includes artifacts dating from the Hawaiian monarchy. Displays include *koa* wood calabashes and silver punch bowls. The Kahekili Room, dedicated to independent Maui's last ruler, includes implements from Hawaii's Stone Age. Here, too, are exhibited ancient petroglyphs, those distinctive stick-like carvings and drawings found on lava rocks and in many caves throughout the islands. The museum building is listed on the U.S. National Register of Historic Places.

About 3 miles (5 km) south of Wailuku, at **Waikupu,** an enterprising group of business and government leaders has planted a bright idea from Australia in Maui's fertile soil. Based on the Sunshine Plantation in Queensland, the **Maui Plantation** is identified by its giant windmill. Visitors can board jaunty trams for leisurely rides through coffee, ginger, guava, banana and macadamia nut groves. The wide spectrum of fruits,

vegetables, flowers and trees has attracted agriculturists from around the world. They come to see how plants that would normally require a diversity of climates and soils can coexist, even thrive, in the Waikapu Valley. There's a market and restaurant on the grounds.

From Wailuku, a winding 3-mile (5 km) road leads up Iao Stream into the **Iao Valley**. This site, where Kamehameha won his bloody victory, is tranquil now. It includes **Kepaniwai Heritage Gardens,** a picturesque park in formal style with pavilions reflecting the diverse cultures that have made Hawaii's identity.

At the road's end, **Iao Valley State Park** is dominated by the green-mantled basaltic rock pinnacle of **Iao Needle.** Hiking trails lead through exotic jungle vegetation, populated by a lyrical bird life, to the top of a ridge, for views of the Needle and the valley far below.

*Above: Evening idyll. Right: The Buddha at the Jodo Mission in Lahaina is the largest bronze Buddha in Hawaii.*

Iao Needle is surrounded by the serrated cliffs of **Puu Kukui,** a dormant volcano considerably less famous than Haleakala. But it's also reputed as being the second wettest spot in the state of Hawaii after Kauai's Mount Waialeale. More skilled climbers sometimes challenge its vertical rock walls.

### WEST MAUI

The map of Maui is often compared to the profile of a voluptuous woman – her throat is caressed by Maalaea Bay, her head consists of West Maui.

This area includes two of the island's major vacation destinations. Just outside historic Lahaina, about midway up the peninsula, is the extremely popular and well-developed Kaanapali beach resort area. To the north lie Napili Bay and Kapalua Beach, which have recently emerged as other popular hideaways.

The little town of **Maalaea**, the southern tip of the "profile," clings to the aura of a tranquil fishing village. From here, there are magnificent vistas of Mount Haleakala across the sparkling blue waters of Maalaea Bay.

Between November and April – sometimes May at the outside – this is an excellent spot for viewing **humpback whales** as they swim and spout near the shore. The arrival of the first whale each year, and the departure of the last, are events that receive island-wide publicity. In fact – although pods range from the Big Island to Kauai – the sheltered, busy **Auau Channel** between Maui, Lanai and Molokai is their favorite Hawaiian place for mating, birthing and "singing" their haunting, otherworldly love songs.

At Maalaea's harbor, and in Lahaina, you can book excursion boats to see the gentle creatures at close range. Or you can pack a picnic lunch and a pair of binoculars to enjoy a free show at any of several parks – Papalua, Ukumehame, Launuipoko and Puanamana, for instance. These well-maintained facilities front the coast from Highway 30, a quite spectacular drive that winds northward from Maalaea to Lahaina. The shore is rugged, and in winter waves sometimes surge in furiously. The beach parks are popular with board surfers.

Competing with the scenic shoreline are the jagged, picturesque West Maui Mountains, backdropping the green-gold sugarcane fields of the Olowau Plain. In an unlikely setting in the casual community of **Olowau**, you'll discover one of Hawaii's most remarkable restaurants: Tiny **Chez Paul** specializes in classic French cuisine. Dinner reservations are essential. Also near Olowau, you can explore one of Maui's best preserved petroglyph sites.

### Lovely Lahaina

Maui's primary vacation destination is **Lahaina.** Its whalers may have vanished, but the presence of the early Bostonian missionaries is still felt strongly – espe-

cially in the New England atmosphere of many of Lahaina's older buildings.

The town is compact, best discovered in leisurely strolls. It combines a genuine, slightly raffish charm with increasingly visible tones of latter-day commercialism. There has been a tremendous influx of new shops and stores in the past few years. Although this has resulted in some crowding, traffic jams and a certain contrived look, the overall ambience and appeal of the town have improved as far as most visitors are concerned. Shops sell everything from fine coral jewelry, Hawaiian designer fashions and original artworks to typical tourist items such as plastic pineapple earrings and matching *aloha* shirts and *muumuus*.

The entire old section of town is a U.S. historic landmark. With the backing of the state and federal governments, along with major efforts of the privately funded Lahaina Restoration Foundation, some areas are gradually being returned to the appearance of their mid-nineteenth-century heyday.

The best place to begin exploring Lahaina is at the **Baldwin House Museum** on Front Street. This restored residence of an early missionary-physician, Dr. Dwight Baldwin, offers many glimpses into the town's early days. Refurbished by the Lahaina Restoration Foundation, it includes many original furnishings and genuine period antiques. The well-tended grounds include a reproduction of Baldwin's gardens and grape arbor. The house served both as Baldwin's medical office and as a center for missionary activity. The guides here, some of whom are descendants of the early missionaries, are especially well trained and knowledgeable. You can pick up a free map here for a walking tour of the compact downtown area.

Adjacent to the Baldwin House is the **Masters Reading Room**. Originally a storeroom for missionaries, it was con-

*Above: The port of Lahaina has a long history, as royal capital, as a whaling center and today as a capital of tourism.*

verted in 1834 to a downtown "officers club" by the captains of whaling ships. With its coral block-and-fieldstone façade impeccably restored, it's now headquarters of the Lahaina Restoration Foundation.

Just down Front Street, on the other side of the Baldwin House, stands the **Richards House**. The first coral-stone house in the Hawaiian Islands, it was the home of William Richards, the first Protestant missionary to Lahaina. Richards left the mission in the mid 1830s to work directly for the kingdom as chaplain, teacher and translator for Kamehameha III. He helped draft the Hawaiian constitution and traveled to the United States and England as the king's envoy to seek recognition of Hawaii's independence. He also served as the kingdom's first minister of education.

The **Brick Palace** once stood across Front Street on a placid waterfront site behind the library. Built around 1800 by ex-convicts from a British penal colony in Australia, it was probably the islands' first Western-style building. Constructed at the command of Kamehameha I, it was used as a storehouse and residence. The cornerstones and foundation have been excavated; an exhibit by the Lahaina Restoration Foundation tells its history.

Nearby stands the *hauola* stone, used by the ancient Hawaiians as a healing place. On grounds just offshore here, remains of the Kapukaiao taro patch could be seen as late as the 1950s. Kamehameha III once worked there in an effort to demonstrate the dignity of labor to his subjects.

## More Historic Sites

In the center of town is the delightful, rambling **Pioneer Inn,** across Wharf Street from the harbor. It was built in the early 1900s. Its wrap-around lanais are a pleasant place to sip morning coffee or enjoy a leisurely lunch while viewing the local scene. Sooner or later, tradition says, no matter where you are from, if you sit long enough, some acquaintance will certainly walk past! Accommodation in this historic property is basic, but clean and well maintained. If you reserve Room No. 6, you'll occupy quarters once used by Queen Liliuokalani.

The **Old Courthouse** stands in the town square, across Hotel Street from the Pioneer Inn. The center of anti-smuggling activity during the whaling era, it was built of coral stone from the ruins of *Hale Piula*, the palace of Kamehameha III. It now houses the **Lahaina Art Gallery,** which stages free exhibits by local artists.

Reconstructed remains of an old fort stand beside the courthouse. Nearby, its network of branches spreading over the entire square, is a mammoth banyan tree, said to be the largest in the islands. It was planted in 1873 by William O. Smith, sheriff of Maui, to commemorate the 50th anniversary of Lahaina's first Christian mission.

A short stroll eastward along Front Street leads to the **Holy Innocents Episcopal Church.** Although the present structure dates from 1927, the Episcopal Church in the Hawaiian Islands was established in 1862. The building's distinctive paintings include a Hawaiian madonna and child. The altar design features taro, breadfruit, local fish and other specifically Hawaiian symbols.

**Maluuluolele Park,** across the street on the edge of the historic district, once included a pond said to be the home of a powerful water spirit. Maui chiefs occupied a residence on an island in the pond, and three kings of the Kamehameha dynasty later lived there.

Nearby stands **Waine'e Church**, on the site of the first stone house of worship in the islands. Built here between 1828 and 1832, it was subsequently destroyed several times. Author James Michener described it in his epic novel *Hawaii* as the "church that just wouldn't stand." It was renamed Waiola, "water of life," when it was rebuilt in 1953. In the adjacent **Waine'e Cemetery** are buried such figures as Keopuolani, wife of Kamehameha I; Nahienaena, their daughter; Kaumuali'i, a chief of Kauai; and William Richards, the noted missionary.

Many old Lahaina buildings have fallen into ruin or have been destroyed. One that has survived is **Hale Paahao,** "Struck in Irons House," Lahaina's prison from the 1850s. Built by convicts at a leisurely pace out of coral stone from the demolished waterfront fort, it had the standard wall shackles and ball-and-chain restraints for hard cases. Most of the inmates were there for desertion from ships, drunkenness, working on the Sabbath, or dangerous horseback riding! Today the restored building serves a different role in Lahaina life: It is often the scene of community celebrations.

Typifying the diversity of Hawaii's religious heritage is the nearby **Buddhist Hongwanji Mission.** Members of the

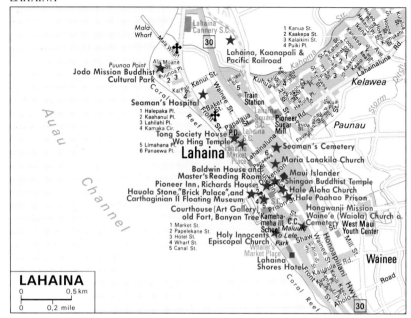

**LAHAINA**

0        0,5 km

0      0,2 mile

sect have been meeting here since 1910; the present temple was built in 1927. Visitors are welcome at special celebrations, which include the Buddha's birthday in April and the August Bon Memorial festivities.

The **Buddhist Church of the Shingon Sect**, with its green paint and simple wooden architectural style, is typical of those built all over Maui during the plantation era, when Japanese laborers were imported to work in the sugar cane fields.

The **Wo Hing Temple and Museum** on Front Street, built in 1912 as a fraternal hall for a Chinese society, has recently been restored. Its rare artifacts include the only public Taoist altar on the island. In the adjoining cookhouse, you can view priceless films of the Hawaiian Islands taken by inventor Thomas Alva Edison in 1898 and 1906.

*Right: The Lahaina-Kaanapali & Pacific Railroad runs through West Maui canefields from Lahaina to the Kaanapali Resort.*

**Lahaina Harbor**

Although the whaling era has long since passed, the harbor is still a busy place. Don't miss the **Carthaginian II Floating Museum**, a two-masted square-rigged brig of the type that brought early missionaries from New England, around Cape Horn, to Lahaina. Whaling-era artifacts are displayed, and an excellent audiovisual program, "World of the Whale," introduces visitors to the humpback whale.

The craft that anchor in the harbor today are mostly private pleasure boats, sailing cruisers, sightseeing vessels and fishing charters. Those who love to fish can depart from here to troll for marlin, along with such other coveted Hawaiian deep-sea catches as *mahi mahi* (Pacific dolphin fish), *ono* (wahoo), *ahi* (yellowfin tuna), *aku* (skipjack tuna), *kawakawa* (bonito) and *ulua* (jack cravally).

If you're not a fishing enthusiast, don't miss exploring the outlying waters anyway. Cruises aboard glass-bottomed

boats and sailboats are offered several times daily. Some include a luncheon or sunset dinner. Among them is the *Lin Na.* This jaunty 50-ft (15 m) glass-bottomed motor sailer, shaped like an original Chinese junk, leaves Lahaina harbor several times daily. Some of its enthusiastic, young crew members even make dives to feed fish and bring up coral.

Lahaina is also a major center for scuba diving. Several companies have trips for both beginners and experienced divers, with all equipment provided.

On the outskirts of town near the old Mala wharf, which inter-island ships used until 1941, stands the serene **Jodo Mission** with its temple, pagodas and bell towers. Its beautiful Japanese cultural park commemorates some of the islands' earliest immigrants, and there's a giant bronze Buddha imported from Japan.

**Lahainaluna School,** located on a hillside outside Lahaina, offers dramatic vistas of the harbor. The famed educational institution was founded by missionaries in 1831, and the brightest young

Hawaiians were enrolled here. A public institution since 1923, "L'Luna" is a remarkable combination of high school, boarding school, and vocational and agricultural academy.

On its grounds is the historic **Hale Pa'i**, the printing house of the Protestant missionaries. It turned out hundreds of thousands of pages in the Hawaiian language. Included were an early history of the islands based on accounts collected by Lahainaluna Seminary students, and a Hawaiian grammar and dictionary. The building has been restored as a printing museum; its displays include a working model of the original press.

The little steam-powered engines of the westernmost railroad in the United States chug cheerfully through the sugar-cane fields of Maui, shuttling visitors and local residents between Lahaina and the posh Kaanapali Beach resort area. Officially, it's called the **Lahaina, Kaanapali & Pacific Railroad,** though everyone knows it as "the sugar cane train." With its locomotives and coaches mod-

eled after turn-of-the-century Hawaiian passenger trains and its quaint Victorian stations, it's another of the links between old and new that are an integral part of island life.

### Kaanapali and other Beaches

**Kaanapali Beach,** one of Hawaii's most extensive resort complexes, includes modern condominiums, apartments, houses, villas and seven deluxe beachfront hotels.

In addition to a wide variety of shops and stores at these properties, Kaanapali also boasts the centrally located, multilevel **Whalers Village.** This attractive and tastefully designed dining-and-shopping complex houses a distinctive museum with authentic displays relating to the whaling industry. There's a frequent shuttle service between Whalers

*Above: An aerial view of Big Beach at Makena. Right: Snorkelers and scuba enthusiasts take to Maui's clear waters.*

Village and the various hotels and condominiums.

Kaanapali Beach Resort also has two 18-hole championship golf courses, served by their own clubhouses. Most hotels and condominiums have tennis courts. Among them, the **Royal Lahaina Resort** offers one of Hawaii's largest tennis facilities, the Royal Lahaina Tennis Ranch, which includes a practice wall. Six courts are lighted for evening play. Regulation tennis attire is required to play on these courts. If you haven't come prepared, you can buy clothes in the pro shop. North of Kaanapali, Highway 30 leads to Napili Bay and Kapalua Beach, gateways to Maui's rugged, spectacular northwest coast.

The **Napili Bay** area is a popular destination for family vacationers who prefer to rent a fully equipped condominium apartment or cottage. Many of them return year after year. The area's rate of growth has increased in recent years, bringing at times unavoidable congestion. But the beaches are among Maui's choicest, and for vacationers seeking a more informal retreat than a major resort hotel, this may be just the answer.

Neighboring Kapalua Point fronts curving **Kapalua Beach,** a gently sloping strand that offers safe, protected swimming and surfing. The complex includes Kapalua Bay Hotel and several residential communities, most of which have rental vacation villas. A Ritz-Carlton hotel is under development.

Kapalua also has two 18-hole championship golf courses and a tennis center. It offers windsurfing, scuba diving, snorkeling and sailing.

The coastal drive northward is among Maui's most dramatically beautiful. The blue Pacific rushes against rocky black cliffs, while inland the rolling green-gold meadows are somewhat reminiscent of the west of England.

Several well-maintained beach parks, including **Oneloa Beach** and **D.T. Flem-**

**ing Park,** extend beyond Kapalua Bay. **Makuleia Bay** and **Honolua Bay** are marine-life conservation districts, their diverse underwater life protected by state decree. All parks are likely to be crowded with local residents, especially on weekends. Surfing and swimming on this coast is only for experts.

The road narrows and becomes more winding as it proceeds northward, following the route of an old royal horse trail. The pavement ends at **Honokohau.** If you have a four-wheel-drive vehicle, continue along this spectacular stretch of North Maui coast, all the way around the peninsula's northern tip and back to Wailuku. It's a distance of about 10 more miles (16 km).

If you decide to turn back at Honokohau, first drive down into its jungle-like valley, where orchids cling to the slopes and residents cling to old lifestyles, cultivating taro in neat patches along the streambeds. It's so near, yet so far, from West Maui's other world of elegant vacation resorts.

## KIHEI COAST

**Wailea Resort**, the Valley Isle's newest full-scale luxury retreat, is located about 6 miles (10 km) south of the vacation town of **Kihei** on Maui's southwestern coast. Wailea's entire 1,450-acre (587 hectare) tract – three times the size of Waikiki – is being meticulously developed. Stringent zoning regulations mandate that no building be higher than 25 ft (8m) above the adjacent road.

The resort boasts a series of five perfectly scalloped, golden-sand beaches, among the finest natural beaches in the Hawaiian Islands. There are also two 18-hole championship golf courses and a large and complete tennis club, known as "Wimbledon West." Wailea offers both rental condominium apartments and villas, and five luxurious hotels. Oceanfront walkways and a free shuttle service provide easy access to all resort properties and facilities.

A shuttle service is also available between Wailea and the neighboring, 1,000-

acre (405 hectare) **Makena Resort**, a smaller, secluded, idyllically situated retreat. There are five more excellent beaches here. Snorkeling excursions can be booked to the clear waters around tiny offshore **Molokini Island**, and the resort also sports such facilities as a golf course and a tennis club.

A short drive on Old Makena Road leads to one of Maui's rare black-sand beaches. Further down the road, mansions and fishing shacks sometimes stand side by side in the live-and-let-live manner of Old Hawaii. A few remnant rock walls remain from ancient fishing villages. In the late nineteenth century, **Makena Landing** was a busy port, second on Maui only to Lahaina.

Vigorous vacationers may like to climb to the top of **Puu o Lai** volcanic cinder cone for panoramic views of Maui's southwest coast. From its summit,

*Above: Weaving baskets from hala leaves.*
*Right: The dramatic beauty of Kahokuloa Head along the rugged West Maui coast.*

December through May, the **Pacific Whale Foundation** operates a lookout station from which scientists and volunteers take inventory of migrating humpback whales. Waters off this stretch of the Maui coast shelter the giant creatures and their calves during their annual migration to Hawaii's warm waters.

From Puu o Lai's crest, you can also hike down to the aquamarine waters of **Big Beach** or **Little Beach**, favorite swimming spots of local residents.

If you intend to drive all the way south and east to La Perouse Bay, it's best to have a four-wheel-drive vehicle. The unpaved road is rough and rock-strewn. Sometimes, granted some advance notice, Makena's Maui Prince Hotel can arrange this excursion for guests.

This southern tip of Maui encompasses the **Ahihi-Kinau Natural Area Reserve**, protecting rare corals, fishes, and other marine life. The road passes by the last lava flows from Haleakala, thought to have occurred around 1790. The legend proclaims Makena became known as the "beach of mourning" after the fire goddess, Madame Pele, unleashed this fiery flow to the sea. The area it engulfed became known as *Honuaula*, "red land," after the flaming lava flows.

**La Perouse Bay** is another superb marine and land reserve. Along with Ahihi Bay, it provides the best snorkeling and diving grounds on Maui's south shore. At La Perouse Bay, Hawaiian nature is left alone to flourish as it would without the burden of human interference. Here, the ill-fated French explorer Rear Admiral Jean-François Galaup, the Count de la Perouse, anchored his two frigates on May 28, 1786 – seven years after the death of Captain James Cook. After sailing off two years later toward Australia, he journeyed into oblivion, never to be heard of again.

La Perouse Bay is a stark, rather dramatic-appearing place, where the forces of nature are not to be tempted. Waters often crash fiercely against the rocks: It's much too rough for swimming. Agile local anglers, though, favor its lava-strewn, rocky promontory.

If you're feeling especially adventurous, you may want to clamber over jagged *a'a* lava flows to investigate some ancient Hawaiian burial caves. They lie inland and around the point from La Perouse Bay, north of Waiakapuhi.

The imposing, black flanks of Haleakala rise up sharply from this starkly beautiful corner of Maui. **Uluapalakua Ranch** and its Tedeschi vineyards are near, but by no means easy to reach. If you're skilled at operating a four-wheel-drive vehicle over primitive terrain, you can journey up a hillside gravel trail from Makena to connect with Highway 31, which leads directly to the property. It is, however, far from a leisurely or comfortable trip. That's why mst travelers prefer to follow Highway 31, the Haleakala-Kula Highway, from Kahului; this connects with Highways 370 and 31 into Ulupalakua.

**HANA HIGHWAY**

The 52-mile (84 km) road from Kahului to the remote village of Hana on Maui's eastern coast may appear deceptively short. It's surely one of the Western Hemisphere's most scenic routes. But if you're driving a rental car, remember to plan a full day for the round trip from the major resort areas.

Take a picnic lunch and depart as early as possible. Otherwise, there are so many tempting stops along the route that you're likely to run out of daylight hours on the return. And it's not advisable to drive the narrow, twisting route at night.

Several tour companies offer automobile or van trips to Hana, if you prefer not to attempt the drive yourself. Inter-island airlines also have flights between Kahului and Hana – but to savor the spectacular scenery en route, try to make the trip by land at least one way, preferably driving in and flying back.

The highway clutches the rugged northern flank of Mount Haleakala much of the way, corniche-like and usually within sight of the sea. The narrow stretch winds up and down steep jungle-clad slopes, crosses innumerable one-lane bridges, and clings to the sides of sometimes precipitous cliffs. It's slow going, yet absolutely enchanting.

All along the route, there are inviting little parks. Side roads to small villages, still resisting the tides of change, have a way of tempting motorists to linger a while ... sometimes longer than planned. Hiking trails lead through tropical jungles and forests of *ohia*, pandanus, *koa*, *kukui* nut and guava trees. Swimmers are enticed by splashing waterfalls, secluded beaches and clear pools. Sooner than you expect, twists and turns become more numerous. Each bend in the road seems to reveal masses of ferns spilling into deep gorges, or stands of bamboo gently swaying in sighing breezes.

At **Kaumahina State Park**, perched on a forested cliff, a viewing point overlooks the sea-girded Keanae Peninsula. You can follow a side road to **Keanae**, a tableland community surrounded by a patchwork of taro fields. This vegetable's tuber roots, when pounded and fermented, produce the paste-like *poi*, a staple of the Hawaiian diet. A carefully maintained coral-stone church more than a century old is still in use in Keanae. Just above the peninsula where the little community sits, the **Keanae Arboretum** preserves a variety of Hawaiian and Pacific plants. You'll be surprised to learn there are more than 30 varieties of taro, producing a *poi* for every taste!

### The Pace of Old Hawaii

From the arboretum, a spur road leads to tiny **Wailua** village, where life still moves mostly at the slower pace of old Hawaii. The miniature lawns of tidy little houses are brilliant with tropical blossoms and the multi-hued leaves of croton plants.

The grounds of serene **St. Gabriel's Church,** garlanded with a trim of painted red hearts are the ideal place for a pleasant stroll. Some of its graveyard markers are embellished with photographs of the deceased. The village's residents are generally reserved, not hostile, and gracefully tolerate the presence of strangers who respect their privacy. Many youngsters frequently gather at the water's edge to bodysurf on homemade boards, just as their ancestors probably did generations ago.

The Hana Highway descends, straightening gradually as it reaches **Puaa Kaa State Park**. Here, in the midst of verdant tropical growth, waterfalls plunge into broad pools to create enjoyable swimming spots. There are dressing facilities and a picnic area in the park.

Eastward, the drive proceeds through the last vestiges of rainforest, then crosses open grazing lands. Just before the final approach to Hana, a sign points down another winding side road to **Nahiku** village, even more preserved in time than Wailua. Isolated houses and a few trees remain from its turn-of-the-century rubber plantation, established before any in North America. Along Nahiku Road are remnants of pipelines built a century ago as part of an impressive trans-Maui irrigation system.

Just beyond Hana Airport is **Waianapanapa State Park,** where shaded picnic tables provide a welcome rest stop. A black-sand beach shimmers in the sun; behind it is the froth-capped, blue-green Pacific Ocean. A short trail leads into a tropical grotto where two watery, rather mysterious-looking caves – actually lava tubes – are connected by an underground stream. A locally popular campsite is situated near the beach.

From the lookout atop **Kauiki Hill**, an ancient cinder cone, the panorama of Hana Bay is spectacular, to say the least. Legend has it that, in ancient times, a demigod stood atop the hill and launched

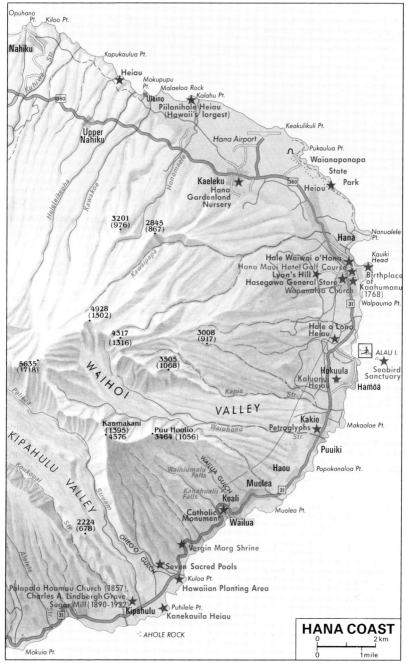

Opuhano Pt.
Kiloo Pt.
**Nahiku**
Kapukaulua Pt.
Mokupupu Pt.
**Heiau**
Malaeloa Rock
**Ulaino**
Kalahu Pt.
**Piilanihale Heiau (Hawaii's largest)**
Keakulikuli Pt.
**Upper Nahiku**
*Hana Airport*
Pukaulua Pt.
**Waianapanapa State Park**
**Kaeleku** Hana Gardenland Nursery
Heiau
Nanualele Pt.
**Hana**
3201 (976)
2845 (867)
Kauiki Head
**Hale Waiwai o'Hana**
Hana Maui Hotel Golf Course
**Lyon's Hill**
**Birthplace of Kaahumanu (1768)**
**Hasegawa General Store**
Wapanalua Church
Walpauma Pt.
4928 (1502)
4317 (1316)
3008 (917)
**Hale o Lono Heiau**
3505 (1068)
5635 (1718)
**WAIHOI**
ALAU I.
**Seabird Sanctuary**
**Hokuula**
Kaluanui Heiau
**Hamoa**
Kapia Str.
**VALLEY**
Waiohonu Str.
**Kaamakani (1395)** 4576
Puu Hoolio 3464 (1056)
**Kakio**
Makaalae Pt.
**Petroglyphs**
**Puuiki**
**KIPAHULU VALLEY**
Koukoual
Waihiumalu Falls
WAILUA GULCH
**Haou**
Popokanaloa Pt.
**Muolea**
Kahahualii Falls
**Koali**
**Catholic Monument**
Muolea Pt.
**Wailua**
Paikea
Aholele Str.
2224 (678)
OHEO'O GULCH
**Vergin Marg Shrine**
**Seven Sacred Pools**
Kuloa Pt.
**Palapala Hoomau Church (1857), Charles A. Lindbergh Grave, Sugar Mill (1890-1922)**
**Hawaiian Planting Area**
Puhilele Pt.
**Kipahulu**
**Kanekauila Heiau**
Mokuia Pt.
AHOLE ROCK

# HANA COAST

0 — 2 km
0 — 1 mile

117

his spear across the sky. It kept invaders at large for many years. Kamehameha the Great ended Maui's independence and isolation.

Kamehameha's favorite wife, the brilliant Kaahumanu, was born in a tree-shrouded cave at Kauiki. A historic marker at the base of the Kauiki Head cliff, near Hana Pier, marks the site.

This is a lovely stretch of road. A lighthouse stands watch on a seaside hill near a crescent beach. The low hills carry peaceful meadows where grazing cattle, clusters of trees, and shadows cast by long, low fences suggest the remote tranquility of Cornwall rather than Hawaii.

### The Mana in Hana

The quaint little town of **Hana** sprawls comfortably across this serene, gently undulating landscape. With a population of

*Above: Harvesting mussels in tidal flats along the Maui coast. Right: A couple finds a bit of paradise at a waterfall.*

118

about 1,000, the community is home to many full or part Hawaiians. Proud yet welcoming, they demonstrate the somewhat indefinable spiritual force the Hawaiians call *mana*. In Hana even the cynical and world-weary may come to believe the *aloha* spirit still exists, transcending easily all those twentieth-century distractions.

Unfortunatly, a long-beloved Hana landmark is no more. The **Hasegawa General Store,** built in 1900, burned down under suspicious circumstances in the summer of 1990. But like the legendary phoenix, it has risen from its ashes to reopen in the guise of the old **Hana Theater**. Memorialized in a popular song, the store was for long the last stop for everything – from gasoline and cold beer to *poi* and potato chips – for motorists continuing north or south on the twisting Hana route.

A welcome recent addition to the town is **Hale Waiwai o'Hana,** the "house of treasures of Hana." Displaying tools, crafts and photographs of local history, it

reflects the architectural style of the nearby, century-old former courthouse. It's operated by the Hana Cultural Center and open daily except Sunday.

Close to the shore stands the historic **Wananalua Church**, built in 1838 by the first missionaries to settle in eastern Maui. Constructed of lava rock (some from an ancient *heiau*, or temple), it still holds Sunday-morning services in both English and Hawaiian.

The renowned **Hotel Hana-Maui**, long a low-key, private retreat for celebrities and international "jet-setters," nestles next door to the church. The luxurious hotel was recently renovated and is now operated by ITT Sheraton. One-story cottage-style buildings overlook private gardens and patios, and are decorated with Hawaiian artwork and artifacts.

The hotel's founder, Paul Fagan, is memorialized by a stone cross on **Lyon's Hill.** This rise, reached by driving through a pasture, affords another splendid view of Hana and its environs. Another 10 miles (16 km) beyond Hana,

a narrow, winding, roughly paved road leads into the **'Oheo'o Gulch** section of **Haleakala National Park.** At least 300 in (7600 mm) of rain fall annually in this rainforest wilderness.

On the approach, as you enter **Wailua Gulch,** you'll spot two pristine waterfalls plunging from the slopes of Haleakala. Just past the falls, a charming "Virgin of the Roadside" image in a tiny shrine is usually draped with fresh flower leis.

As the road winds into 'Oheo'o Gulch, streams flow through a series of scenic pools before plummeting into the sea. These are popularly known as the **Seven Sacred Pools.** You can park and walk down a rather steep bank to delightful (and usually quite crowded) picnicking and swimming spots. Nearby, the U.S. National Park Service has restored a traditional taro farm. Rangers often lead nature walks on more strenuous hikes.

The paved surface of Highway 31 ends under the shadow of the abandoned **Kipahulu Sugar Mill.** Several miles beyond, one can park near a gate on the left

of the road for a short walk to the small, white **Palapala Hoomau Congregational Church**, built in 1850. The famed American aviator-author Charles A. Lindbergh selected his gravesite here before he died on August 26, 1974. Lindbergh spent much of his later life in Hana and helped restore the church. In the late afternoon, the shadow of Haleakala falls across the churchyard, and the last fingers of sunlight touch the epitaph etched on Lindbergh's tombstone: "If I take the wings of the morning and dwell in the innermost parts of the sea."

It's possible to drive further along Maui's rugged southern coast, all the way to **Ulupalakua Ranch**. But it's advisable only during daylight hours, and only if you have a four-wheel-drive vehicle. Hawaii's rental-vehicle companies are very strict about driving on unauthorized roads. It's mandatory that your insurance, or temporary policy, cover such travel.

*Above: The rugged beauty of Haleakala crater, a place to hike or camp.*

## HALEAKALA

Rising 10,023 ft (3,055 m) above sea level, the enormous dormant volcanic crater of **Haleakala** dominates the island of Maui. It's about a 90-minute drive to the rim from Kahului, via Highways 37 and 378. The twisting route leads through tranquil meadows, giving way to rocky terrain as it approaches the **Puu Ulaula Visitor Center** atop Red Hill. Motorcoach sightseeing tours can be booked from all Maui resort areas.

From Kahului, Highway 37 leads southeast, gradually climbing through sugar cane fields, past carnation farms and rolling pasturelands. This is the verdant **Kula District**, an area long popular among Hawaiian families as a site for second homes.

You're at the gateway to upcountry Maui when you reach **Pukalani,** "hole in the heavens." A turnoff here on Highway 400 (Makawao Avenue) leads a short distance into **Makawao.** In this captivating Old West-style town, weathered wood-

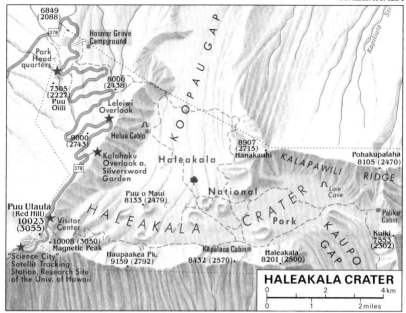

Leleiwi Overlook
Holua Cabin
Kalahaku Overlook a. Silversword Garden
Puu o Maui 8133 (2479)
Puu Ulaula (Red Hill) 10023 (3055)
Visitor Center
· 10008 (3050) Magnetic Peak
"Science City" Satellit Tracking Station, Research Site of the Univ. of Hawaii
Haupaakea Pk. 9159 (2792)
Kapalaoa Cabin 8432 (2570)·
Haleakala 8201 (2500)
Hanakauhi 8907 (2715)
Pohakupalaha 8105 (2470)
KALAPAWILI RIDGE
Laie Cave
Paliku Cabin
Kuiki 7553 (2302)
KAUPO GAP
Haleakala National Crater Park

**HALEAKALA CRATER**
0        2        4 km
0        1        2 miles

fronted shops line Baldwin Avenue, and *paniolos* (Hawaiian cowboys) liven the scene during the popular Fourth of July Rodeo. South of town, the **University of Hawaii College of Tropical Agriculture** has an experimental station where two of Maui's prime crops, macadamia nuts and avocadoes, are grown.

Back on Highway 37, just north of **Waiakoa,** you'll spot the charming octagonal **Church of the Holy Ghost** on a hillside. The 1897 church was built for Portuguese settlers who came to work in the area's agricultural industries. It's still an active parish; its delicate wooden bas-reliefs and handsome Austrian-made altar reflect the settlers' European heritage.

At Kula, signs point off Highway 37 to another **UH agricultural experimental station.** This one specializes in ornamental protea plants, and has magnificent plantings of award-winning roses.

Back in Kula, follow Highway 377 to the **Kula Lodge**, a convenient luncheon stop. A gallery displays the works of artist Curtis Wilson Cost, whose landscapes so aptly capture the Kula District's special ambience.

Ask for directions to the nearby **Upcountry Protea Farm** on Upper Kimo Drive. Here, on a bucolic hillside, many brilliant varieties of decorative protea, a flowering plant native to South Africa and now widely cultivated in upcountry Maui. The proprietors welcome visitors who walk through the gardens and picnic on the grounds. They sell magnificent protea arrangements and will pack and ship the plants, along with orchids, anthuriums and other tropical flora. (Be sure you know the import regulations of your home country.)

A bit further on Highway 377 are the **Kula Botanical Gardens.** Protea, along with some 700 other species of tropical, subtropical and temperate-zone plants, thrive together in this benign climate. Visitors are again welcome to picnic in the grounds.

This is also wine country. **Tedeschi Vineyards and Winery**, on the 18,000-acre (7,285 hectare) **Ulupalakua Ranch**,

121

has a tasting room in a nineteenth-century jailhouse. It's open daily for tasting pineapple wine, Blanc Brut, a sparkling wine, Maui Blush, a white zinfandel and Maui Nouveau, a young table wine. Admittedly, the wines have more novelty than gourmet appeal.

**Thompson Ranch,** en route to the winery, offers morning, sunset and picnic horseback rides.

### "House of the Sun"

Follow Route 37 into 378 for the climb to **Haleakala National Park.** The visitor center overlooks the astonishing crater from an elevation of nearly 10,000 ft (3,000 m). The ascent from sea level to such a rarefied elevation may be physically stressful. It's best not to move around too rapidly once you reach the summit. If you have high blood pressure, a heart condition or other health problems, ask a doctor's advice before making the trip.

Weather conditions near the summit can change dramatically from one day – or even one hour – to the next. It's wise to phone park headquarters (tel. 572-7749) before leaving the lowlands. There's no point in going when the summit is closed in by fog or clouds.

On a clear day, Haleakala – the name means "house of the sun" – offers an incomparable vista. The crater has a valley-of-the-moon appearance: strange, desolate, quite eerie. Streaks of red, yellow, gray and black trace the course of ancient and more recent lava, ash and cinder flows.

Several visitor sites and overlooks within the 28,655-acre (11,597 hectare) national park offer varying views of the remarkable terrain. Just within the park entrance, a side road leads to **Hosmer Grove.** Here in 1910, Dr. Ralph Hosmer,

*Right: The silversword, a bristling set of organic daggers, is a rare sight.*

a naturalist, introduced temperate-zone plants and trees to Hawaii, an experiment in timber production. Today nature trails cut through magnificent stands of spruce, pine and other conifers.

At nearby park headquarters, free maps and brochures describe Haleakala. You can become acquainted with several of Hawaii's state birds, the rare *nene* geese, penned in an outside closure. Park rangers will give advice on hiking into the crater. Permits must be obtained, even for a short walk. Rangers lead walks and hikes during summer months.

**Halemauu Trail** into the crater begins just south of the headquarters. It takes about an hour to reach a fine overlook, enjoyed by visitors who don't want to make the long, strenuous hike down to the crater floor. Further along, the road leads past **Kalahaku Overlook,** where there are more panoramic views of Haleakala's cinder cones.

Near the Kalahaku parking area, you can wander through a garden of rare **silversword** plants. These botanical wonders, which grow naturally throughout the crater and in some sections of the park, are found in only two other places on earth: Mauna Kea and Mauna Loa on the Big Island, and in the Himalayas.

This unique plant is distinguished by its ball of swordlike, gray-green blades. At the age of seven to 20 years, it bursts forth in late spring with the only bloom of its life. Hundreds of yellow and reddish-purple flower heads cluster on a stalk which may reach 9 ft (2.7 m) in height. As seeds develop, the plant slowly dies, leaving a dry, decaying skeleton by late autumn.

### The Rim and the Crater

No roads lead into the crater, but 30 miles (48 km) of well-marked trails traverse the expanse. Guided horseback trips are also available through a privately franchised company.

At **Haleakala Visitor Center**, the views are among the most vivid, weather conditions permitting. It's windy and cool year-round at 10,000 ft (3,000 m), so bring warm clothing and gloves. Within the visitor center, well-designed displays describe Haleakala's unique origin and terrain. Although it has been dormant for at least 200 years, geologists say Haleakala could still erupt again. But there's no indication that volcanic activity will reassert itself on Maui any time soon.

Further along, **Puu Ulaula Visitor Center** offers unobstructed full-circle views of Haleakala and all the major islands of the state of Hawaii, with the exception of distant Kauai.

Nearby, the antennae of the domed **Science City** tower against the sky. Scientists from several universities and institutions study the solar system here and gather data for the U.S. space program. The center isn't open to visitors, but you can enter the grounds to capture more striking views of Maui's south-coast desert.

Active, well-prepared travelers may want to trek into Haleakala crater. There are two main trails. You can divide the hike into half-day, full-day or overnight segments. No matter that it's chilly at the summit; the reverse is true as you descend into the crater.

Three primitive wilderness cabins are found within the crater. Each accommodates 12 persons. Backpackers should bring sleeping bags and food. Cooking stoves and utensils are provided. Reservations must be made at least three months in advance by writing Haleakala National Park, P.O. Box 369, Makawao, Maui, HI 96768, U.S.A.

More sedentary sightseers can book an early-morning tour to Haleakala to view the spectacular sunrise. Departures from the west-coast resort areas are usually around 3am for the drive to the summit. It can be a thrilling experience if weather conditions are clear. But it's also unpredictable, as the sun can't always be counted upon to break through the clouds.

## MAUI
(All area telephone codes are 808)
### Kahului-Wailuku
#### Accommodation
*MODERATE:* **Maui Beach Hotel,** 170 Kaahumanu Ave., Kahului 96732, Tel: 877-0051. **Maui Palms Hotel,** 150 Kaahumanu Ave., Kahului 96732, Tel: 877-0071.
*BUDGET:* **Valley Isle Lodge,** 310 N. Market St., Wailuku 96793, Tel: 244-6880.
#### Attractions
**Alexander & Baldwin Sugar Museum,** Puunene. **Central Maui Park,** Kaahumanu Ave., Wailuku. **Iao Valley State Park,** Iao Valley Rd., 3 mi W of Wailuku. **Kaahumanu Church,** Honoapiilani Hwy. and Iao Road, Wailuku. **Kanaha Bird Sanctuary,** Hwy. 36 and 396, Kahului. **Kepaniwai Heritage Gardens,** Iao Valley Rd., Wailuku, Tel: 244-3085, 9am-5pm daily. **Maui Historical Society Museum, Hale Hoikeke,** Iao Road W of Honoapiilani Hwy., Wailuku, Tel: 244-3326, 10am-4:30pm daily. **Maui Tropical Plantation,** Hwy. 30, Honoapiilani Hwy., Waikapu, Tel: 244-7643, 9am-5pm daily. **Pihana and Halekiiheiaus,** off Waiehu Beach Rd., Wailuku.
#### Restaurants
*AMERICAN:* **Maui Tropical Plantation,** Honoapiilani, Waikapu, Tel: 244-7643.
*CHINESE:* **Moon Hoe,** 752 Lower Main St., Wailuku, Tel: 242-7778. **Red Dragon,** Maui Beach Hotel, 170 Kaahumanu Ave., Kahului, Tel: 877-0051.
*CONTINENTAL:* **Mark Edison's,** Iao Valley Rd., Wailuku, Tel: 242-5555. **Sir Wilfred's,** Maui Mall, Kaahumanu Ave., Kahului, Tel: 877-3711.
*JAPANESE:* **East West Dining Room,** Maui Palms Hotel, 150 Kaahumanu Ave., Kahului, Tel: 877-0071.
*STEAK AND SEAFOOD:* **Aurelio's,** Old Kahului Store, 55 Kaahumanu Ave., Kahului, Tel: 871-7656. **Rainbow Dining Room,** Maui Beach Hotel, 170 Kaahumanu Ave., Kahului, Tel: 877-0051.
*THAI:* **Siam Thai,** 123 N. Market St., Wailuku, Tel: 244-3817.
#### Shopping
**Kaahumanu Center,** Kaahumanu Ave. at Wakea Ave., Kahului, 9am-5:30pm Mon through Wed and Sat, 9am-9pm Thu through Fri, 10am-3pm Sun. **Wailuku Main Street,** Central Ave., Wailuku.
#### Tourist Information
**Hawaii Visitors Bureau,** Suite 112, 111 Hana Hwy., Kahului 96732, Tel: 871-8691.

### West Maui
#### Accommodation
*LUXURY:* **Kaanapali Beach Hotel,** 2525 Kaanapali Pkwy., Kaanapali 96761, Tel: 661-0011. **Kapalua Bay Hotel & Villas,** 1 Bay Dr., Kapalua 96761, Tel: 669-5656. **Napili Kai Beach Club,** 5900 Honoapiilani Rd., Napili 96761, Tel: 669-6271.
*MODERATE:* **Maui Islander,** 660 Wainee St., Lahaina 96761, Tel: 667-9766. **Mauian Hotel,** 5441 Honoapiilani Rd., Napili, Lahaina 96761, Tel: 669-6205. **Plantation Inn,** 174 Lahainaluna Rd., Lahaina 96761, Tel: 667-9225.
*BUDGET:* **Kahili Resort at Kapalua,** 2500 Honoapiilani Rd., Kapalua 96761, Tel: 669-5635. **Napili Shores,** 5315 Honoapiilani Rd., Napili 96761, Tel: 669-8061. **Papakea Beach Resort,** 3543 Honoapiilani Rd., Napili 96761, Tel: 669-4848.
#### Attractions
**Baldwin House Museum and Master's Reading Room,** Front St. at Dickenson St., Lahaina. **Banyan Tree,** Front St., Lahaina. **Carthaginian II Floating Museum,** Lahaina Harbor. **Hale Pa'i,** Lahainaluna Rd. **Historic Lahaina Tours,** Lahaina, Tel: 661- 3042. **Lahaina Jodo Mission,** Lahaina. **Lahaina, Kaanapali & Pacific Railroad,** Lahaina and Kaanapali. **Pioneer Inn,** Front St. opposite harbor, Lahaina. **Richards House,** Front St., Lahaina. **Trilogy Excursions,** 180 Lahainaluna Rd., Slip 99, Maalaea Harbor, Lahaina, Tel: 661-4743. **Waine'e Church and Cemetery,** Front St. at Maluuluolele Park, Lahaina. **Whaling Museum,** Whalers Village, Kaanapali. **Wo Hing Temple,** Front St., Lahaina.
#### Restaurants
*AMERICAN:* **Avalon,** 844 Front St., Lahaina, Tel: 667-5559.
*CHINESE:* **Golden Palace,** Lahaina Shopping Center, Lahaina, Tel: 661-3126.
*CONTINENTAL:* **Kapalua Grill & Bar,** 200 Kapalua Dr., Kapalua, Tel: 669-5653. **Maui Rose,** Embassy Suites Resort, 104 Kaanapali Shores Pl., Kaanapali, Tel: 661-2000.
*FRENCH:* **Chez Paul,** Honoapiilani Hwy., Olowalu. **Gerard's,** Plantation Inn, 174 Lahainaluna Rd., Lahaina, Tel: 661-8939.
*HAWAIIAN:* **Tiki Terrace,** Kaanapali Beach Hotel, 2525 Kaanapali Pkwy., Kaanapali, Tel: 661-0011.
*ITALIAN:* **Bettino's,** 505 Front St., Lahaina, Tel: 661-8810. **Ricco's,** Whalers Village, 2435 Kaanapali Pkwy., Kaanapali, Tel: 661-4433.
*JAPANESE:* **Kobe Steak House,** 136 Dickenson St., Lahaina, Tel: 667-5555. **Seaside Inn,** Front St., Lahaina, Tel: 661-7195.

*MEXICAN:* **Chico's Cantina,** Whalers Village, 2435 Kaanapali Pkwy., Kaanapali, Tel: 667-2777. *SEAFOOD:* **El Crab Catcher,** Whalers Village, 2435 Kaanapali Pkwy., Kaanapali, Tel: 661-4423.

## Shopping

**Lahaina Cannery,** 1221 Honapiilani Hwy., Lahaina, 9:30am-9:30pm daily. **Lahaina Galleries,** 728 Front St., Lahaina, Tel: 667-2152. **Lahaina Shopping Center,** Papalaua St. between Front and Wainee St. **Mariner's Alley,** 844 Front St., Lahaina. **Whalers Village,** 2435 Kaanapali Pkwy., Kaanapali, 9:30am-9pm daily. **The Wharf,** 658 Front St. opposite Banyan Tree, Lahaina, 9am-9:30pm daily.

# Kihei Coast
## Accommodation

*LUXURY:* **Grand Hyatt Wailea Resort & Spa,** 3850 Wailea Alanui Dr., Wailea 96753, Tel: 875-1243. **Maui Prince Makena Resort,** 5400 Makena Alanui Dr., Makena 96753, Tel: 874-1111. **Stouffer Wailea Beach Resort,** 3550 Wailea Alanui Dr., Wailea 96753, Tel: 879-4900. *MODERATE:* **Luana Kai Resort,** 940 S. Kihei Rd., Kihei 96753, Tel: 879-1268. **Maui Banyan,** 2575 S. Kihei Rd., Kihei 96753, Tel: 526-2655. **Maui Lu Resort,** 575 S. Kihei Rd., Kihei 96753, Tel: 879-5881. *BUDGET:* **Kihei Bay Surf,** 679 S. Kihei Rd., Kihei 96753, Tel: 879-8866. **Lihi Kai Cottages,** 2121 Iliili Rd., Kihei 96753, Tel: 879-2335. **Wailana Sands,** 35 Walaka St., (P.O. Box 1471), Kihei 96753, Tel: 879-2026.

## Attractions

**Ahihi-Kinau Natural Area Reserve,** La Perouse Bay, Kanahena. **David Malo's Kilolani Church,** Kihei. **Molokini Isle Diving and Snorkeling,** Tel: 667-7777. **Ocean Activities Center,** Wailea Shopping Village, 3750 Wailea Alanui Dr., Wailea, Tel: 879-4485. **Pacific Whale Foundation,** Slip 52, Maalaea Harbor, Kealia Shopping Plaza, Kihei, Tel: 879-8811.

## Restaurants

*AMERICAN:* **Ocean Terrace,** Mana Kai Maui Hotel, 2960 S. Kihei Rd., Kihei, Tel: 879-2607. *CHINESE:* **Canton Chef,** Kamaole Shopping Center, Kihei, Tel: 879-1988. **Hong Kong,** 61 S. Kihei Rd., Kihei, Tel: 879-2883. *CONTINENTAL:* **Fairway,** 100 Kaukahi St., Wailea, Tel: 879-3861. **Raffles,** Stouffer Wailea Beach Resort, 3550 Wailea Alanui Dr., Wailea, Tel: 879-4900. *JAPANESE:* **Hakone,** Maui Prince Hotel, 5400 Makena Alanui Dr., Makena, Tel: 874-1111. *MEXICAN:* **Senor Gecko's,** Rainbow Mall, S. Kihei Rd., Kihei, Tel: 879-0080.

*STEAKS AND SEAFOOD:* **Kiawe Broiler,** Maui Inter-Continental Resort, 3700 Wailea Alanui Dr., Wailea, Tel: 879-1922. **Sandcastle at Wailea,** Wailea Shopping Village, 3750 Wailea Alanui Dr., Wailea, Tel: 879-0606.

## Shopping

**Azeka Place,** 1280 S. Kihei Rd., Kihei. **Kamaole Shopping Center,** S. Kihei Rd., Kihei. **Kealia Beach Plaza,** 101 N. Kihei Rd., Kihei. **Kukui Mall,** 1819 S. Kihei Rd., Kihei. **Rainbow Mall,** 2439 S. Kihei Rd., Kihei. **Wailea Shopping Village,** 3750 Wailea Alanui Dr., Wailea.

# Hana and Haleakala
## Accommodation

*LUXURY:* **Hotel Hana-Maui,** Hana 96713, Tel: 248-8211. *MODERATE:* **Haikuleana Bed and Breakfast,** 69 Haiku Rd., Haiku 96708, Tel: 575-2890. **Hana Bay Vacation Rentals,** (P.O. Box 318), Hana 96713, Tel: 248-7727. **Hana Plantation Houses,** (P.O. Box 489), Hana 96713, Tel: 248-7248.

## Attractions

**Haleakala National Park,** (P.O. Box 357), Makawao 96768, Tel: 572-9306. **Hana Cultural Center, Hale Waiwai o'Hana,** Hana. **Hasegawa General Store,** Hana. **Helani Gardens,** one mile N of Hana, Tel: 248-8274. **Hookipa Beach Park,** Paia. **Hui Noeau Visual Arts Center,** Makawao. **Keanae Arboretum,** Keanae. **Kula Botanical Garden,** Kula Hwy., Tel: 878-1715. **Maui Downhill Bicycle Touring,** Haleakala, Tel. 871-2155. **Palapala Hoomau Church and Charles A. Lindbergh Grave,** Kipahulu. **Piilanihale Heiau,** Kaeleku, 12 mi N of Hana. **St. Gabriel's Church,** Wailua. **Seven Sacred Pools,** 'Ohe'o Gulch, Kipahulu. **Tedeschi Winery,** Ulupalakua Ranch, Kula Hwy., Tel: 878-6058. **Upcountry Protea Farm,** Upper Kimo Dr., Olinda, Tel: 878-2544. **Waianapanapa State Park,** blowhole and caves, 4 mi N of Hana. **Wananalua Church,** Hana.

## Restaurants

*AMERICAN:* **Picnics,** Baldwin Ave., Paia, Tel: 579-8021. *CONTINENTAL:* **Kula Lodge,** Route 1, Box 475, Kula, Tel: 878-1535. *HAWAIIAN:* **Kitada's,** Hwy. 40, Makawao. *INTERNATIONAL:* **Main Dining Room,** Hotel Hana Maui, Hana, Tel: 248-8211. *MEXICAN:* **Polli's Cantina,** 1202 Makawao Ave., Makawao, Tel: 244-8800. *SEAFOOD:* **Mama's Fish House,** 799 Poho Pl., Kuau, Tel: 579-9672.

## Shopping

**Maui Crafts Guild,** 43 Hana Hwy., Paia.

# MOLOKAI

**WEST MOLOKAI**
**EASTERN MOLOKAI**
**KALAUPAPA PENINSULA**
**LANAI**

The isle of Molokai is one of those places that encourages relaxation and discourages schedules. From one end of the island to the other, Molokai is just 38 miles (61 km) long and 10 miles (16 km) wide. It is small enough so that visitors can take their time and enjoy a 1950s-era Hawaii – a time about which oldtimers reminisce with affection.

Nicknamed "The Friendly Island," Molokai does not offer the standard impersonal tours, crowded beaches, traffic jams, high-rise buildings and general congestion. Instead, its diverse sights and activities are more likely to please outdoor types and nature lovers. They include the world's highest sea cliffs at 3,300 ft (1,000 m), white sandy beaches, mule rides, fishing cruises, ancient Hawaiian fishponds, the scenic drive to lush Halawa Valley, and the haunting beauty of Kalaupapa.

A large portion of Molokai's allure is the overall feeling of space. The 6,500 people who call the island home share an open and easygoing lifestyle, and seem to know each other well.

*Preceding pages: Molokai's north coast is a magnificent wilderness of tall sea cliffs and deep, verdant valleys. Left: There are many native Hawaiians living on Molokai.*

Molokai is far more complex than meets the eye. Its early history is filled with harmony, spirituality and mystery. But contact with outside influences in the nineteenth century sparked one of the most tragic chapters in Hawaiian history – the separation of victims of Hansen's disease (leprosy) from their families, the exile of these patients to Kalaupapa, and the subsequent suffering that afflicted this tiny, isolated peninsula.

### Island History

A plain connects Molokai's two major land masses, each a volcanic mountain that rose from the sea floor an estimated 1.5 million years ago. (A later eruption produced the Kalaupapa Peninsula.) In time, streams carved large canyons in east Molokai and marine erosion shaped the sheer cliffs on the windward coast.

One of the earliest recorded human settlements in Molokai, indeed in the entire Hawaiian chain, can be traced to the paradisical setting of Halawa Valley, probably about A.D. 650. The area is believed to have been settled by Polynesians who migrated across the open ocean from the Marquesas and Tahiti.

The settlers respected and lived closely with nature's bounty. Inland, these early Hawaiians raised such staples as taro and

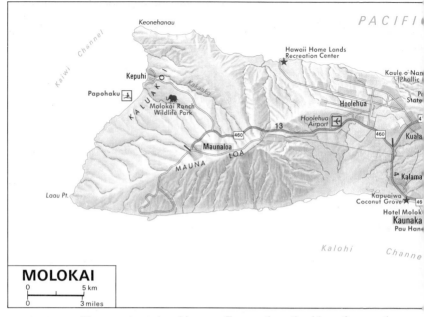

**MOLOKAI**

0  5 km

0  3 miles

sweet potatoes. They constructed sophisticated fishponds along the southern shoreline, probably in the 1400s. More than 60 fishponds line Molokai's coast today. This form of aquaculture was developed long before the practice became a popular one, demonstrating the ancient people's intelligence and sensitivity to their natural world.

Hawaiian spirituality appears to have been especially powerful on Molokai, for it served as a retreat and is home to some of the most impressive shrines found in the islands. A renowned Hawaiian prophet, Lanikaula, lived here during the late 1600s; pilgrims from other islands traveled to Molokai to solicit his advice. In the eighteenth century, Molokai was known throughout Hawaii for the effectiveness of its prayers and rituals.

Interaction with foreigners was limited until the early 1800s, when Western missionaries introduced a different value system. For one example, the Great Mahele of 1848 changed a cooperative land division to one of individual ownership.

For another, the idea of separation, alien to Hawaiian thinking, was imposed on natives suffering from leprosy in the mid 1800s. Hawaiians could not understand isolation, since it ran contrary to their society of extended families.

But fear of this little-known disease prevailed. Patients were torn from their families, herded onto boats at Honolulu, and abandoned near Kalaupapa, cut off from the rest of the world by ocean and sheer cliffs. Forsaken in a harsh, windy environment, many died from despair and neglect until the arrival of such compassionate people as Mother Marianne Cope and Father Damien Joseph de Veuster in the late nineteenth century.

During his lifetime at Kalaupapa, Father Damien molded the leper colony into a community. He, too, succumbed to leprosy in 1899.

Other aspects of Molokai changed by the late 1800s as well. The island's greener east side was dotted with individual family holdings, while the dry west and central areas became the vast,

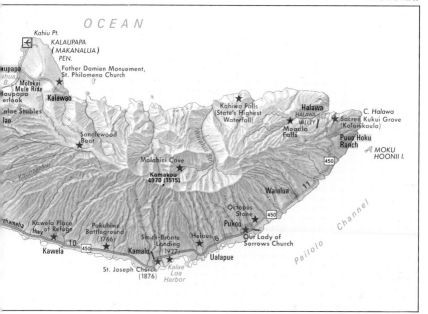

rolling pastures of the Molokai Ranch, controlled by King Kamehameha V.

Through the years, various American business interests owned Molokai Ranch. In the early 1900s, a descendant of a missionary, Charles M. Cooke, bought out his partners, generated the second largest cattle ranch in Hawaii, and later leased parts of it to big-time pineapple growers.

Due mainly to high production costs, however, Molokai's pineapple industry had virtually disappeared by 1990. Today the island's people, faced with change, are looking toward other economic mainstays, including tourism and diversified agriculture – bell peppers, onions and watermelons, to name a few crops.

## WEST MOLOKAI

Sightseeing is a relatively easy activity on this slender island. The main town of Kaunakakai sits in central Molokai, on its southern coast. North and almost directly across the island is **Kalaupapa Overlook**, which offers a sweeping view of Kalaupapa below. The major resort development of Kaluakoi is on the island's sunny and dry west side. **Halawa Valley** on the east end remains tropical and luxuriant, thanks to the generous amount of rainfall the area experiences.

The 8-mile (13 km) drive from **Hoolehua Airport** offers a colorful introduction to the somewhat sleepy community of **Kaunakakai.** The land may appear barren first, but the scenery closer to town brightens up considerably, especially with the sparkling blue-green waters on the shore. Across the way lie **Kalohi Channel** and the island of Lanai.

Near town, look for **Kapuaiwa Coconut Grove,** once the home of thousands of coconut trees planted by Kamehameha V in the 1860s. Since the trees that remain are largely untrimmed, beware of falling coconuts!

Kaunakakai itself resembles an Old-West town, a throwback to turn-of-the-century Hawaii when cowboys and horses teemed here. Today, families gather at wooden false-front buildings to

131

"talk story" and indulge in local foods such as the fresh-baked bread and cookies of the **Kanemitsu Bakery**, tasty Chinese dishes of the **Hop Inn**, grilled fresh fish at the **Mid-Nite Inn.**

For a genuine island experience, head for either the **Pau Hana Inn** or the **Hotel Molokai**, two oceanside cottage-style hotels that offer Hawaiian music, lovely dinners and dancing.

A different kind of experience is the **Molokai Mule Ride**. It can be enjoyed (or endured) beginning at the **Kalae Stables**, located just north of Kaunakakai, right in the middle of the island. This is where sure-footed mules and their riders begin the 1,600-ft (500 m) descent to the **Kalaupapa Peninsula** by means of 26 switchbacks down a narrow, winding trail. For the visitor who is not afraid of heights or riding, this adventure combines splendid views and lots of history.

*Above: Mule riders descend from "topside" Molokai. Right: The Phallic Rock was used by those seeking the blessings of fertility.*

Only a few hundred yards past the mule barn is **Paalau Park**, where residents and visitors enjoy picnicking on the grassy lookout above Kalaupapa and the Makanalua Peninsula. **Phallic Rock**, a curious 6-ft (1,8 m) rock formation within the park, was once the site of fertility pilgrimages by Hawaiian women.

The 6,800-acre (2,752 hectare) resort and residential community of **Kaluakoi** is about 12 miles (7.5 km) west of Hoolehua Airport. So far, Kaluakoi is Molokai's only major visitor complex, the site of the luxury 288-room Kaluakoi Hotel and an 18-hole championship golf course. Near the hotel at **Papohaku** lies a lovely stretch of white-sand beach, ideal for jogging or beachcombing but sometimes dangerous for surfing or swimming, as the waters are often choppy.

One of the most popular spots at Kaluakoi is the **Molokai Ranch Wildlife Park**, home to such animals as giraffes, ostriches, antelope and deer. Weather permitting, visitors may arrange for a "camera safari" by contacting the Ka-

luakoi Hotel's reservations desk. Tours are usually canceled on rainy days.

For shopping or snacking in the area, residents and visitors frequently head for **Maunaloa**, a former plantation town that is home to a handful of quaint shops and eateries. Maunaloa and Kaluakoi are surrounded by acres and acres of pastures belonging to the **Molokai Ranch**, the island's major private landowner.

## EASTERN MOLOKAI

Kamehameha V Highway provides the 30-mile (48 km) southern coastline route from Kaunakakai to Halawa Valley. Pack some food and refreshments, and allow at least half a day for a leisurely round-trip drive. The journey is filled with some of Hawaii's best scenery.

The east side is noted for its spiritual qualities; for the *heiau* (temples or sacred sites) that lie in the mysterious mountains (and are best left undisturbed); and the numerous ancient fishponds that grace the coastline.

Typically, the fishponds were enclosures built up of stones and coral blocks rising 6 feet (1.8 m) above the water. Small fish from the sea entered through wooden gratings and eventually grew too large to escape. A few ponds have survived the centuries, but a great number has been ruined by time and people.

During this drive, a multitude of diverse images greet the eyes. Little pockets of white sandy beach pop up from time to time. Inland, horses and cows graze. Chickens and ducks roam the roadsides. Humble wooden houses with tin roofs stand across the road from rambling estates.

Visitors often stop by **St. Joseph's Church** at **Kamalo**, one of three surviving churches built by Father Damien on Molokai. Nearby is the **Smith and Bronte Landing** where, in 1927, Ernest Smith and Emory Bronte crashed unceremoniously ending the first civilian trans-Pacific flight from California.

The church faces the waterfalls and dense forests of **Mount Kamakou**,

Molokai's highest elevation at 4,970 ft (1,515 m).

Father Damien, a carpenter-priest, also built the next little church on the way: **Our Lady of Sorrows.** Soon after it the road narrows, then twists and climbs through Puu o Hoku ("Hill of Stars") Ranch. The view is truly phenomenal: blue skies, blue ocean and Maui, in the distance across the Pailolo Channel.

The path down to **Halawa Valley** is a bumpy one, but the reward for a slow and shaky drive is indeed worthwhile. Halawa Valley, home to only a few people, is a particularly magnificent spot. Fronting the valley are twin bays that resemble a picture postcard. It's no wonder that people stop for long moments and simply stare at the beauty of it all.

Some adventurous souls wander inland through a rainforest, and stop at **Moaula Falls** for a swim in the cool, clear water.

*Above: A typical Molokai homestead. Right: Various species of antelope are the primary attraction in the Molokai Wildlife Park.*

Before embarking on the journey, it's wise to load up on mosquito repellent and get specific directions. Hike on a clear day only: Heavy rains and mud can sometimes erase well-traveled trails and spoil an otherwise wonderful hike.

Beyond Halawa is Molokai's North Shore, where some of the most exquisite terrain and sea cliffs are hidden from the world. However, the beauty of this rugged and inaccessible nature can be best appreciated from the vantage point of a helicopter or an offshore boat tour. Because rough seas are also a hazard, boat trips are usually undertaken only in the calmer summer months.

### KALAUPAPA PENINSULA

One place, accessible year-round, gives a hint of life on Molokai's forbidding North Shore. It takes some doing to get there – by foot, air, or mule – but the majesty of **Kalaupapa** makes any effort extremely worthwhile for those who dare to come.

Visitors who arrive by foot or mule, for instance, are greeted at the bottom of the cliff by a mini-bus. The tour goes through Kalaupapa, a village consisting of a few small houses, churches, a general store, social hall and a nearby meadow filled with gravestones.

Kalaupapa is surrounded by rainforest and green valleys. East, across the peninsula, is the abandoned site of **Kalawao**, where the first leprosy patients, mostly native Hawaiians, were purposely stranded in 1866. Five years after Father Damien's arrival in 1873, the settlement moved from rocky and windy Kalawao to the drier leeward side of the peninsula.

Today, reminders of the past hover over the haunting landscape of Kalawao. There are thousands of unmarked graves in the area. **St. Philomena's Church,** finished by Father Damien in 1873, stands in full view of that section of ocean into which the sick arriving to the island were sometimes thrown. Some made it to shore. Others did not. A monument to the selfless priest graces the

church's adjacent cemetery, but Father Damien's grave itself is empty. His remains were returned to his native Belgium in 1936.

In time, life in Kalaupapa did improve thanks to education and, above all, the discovery of sulfone drugs that started being used in the late 1940s to arrest leprosy. They were administered by the Department of Health of first the territory, and finally the State of Hawaii. One side-effect of Washington's concern was that Kalaupapans, faced with the frustrations of a faraway bureaucracy, became a close-knit community.

A controlled visitor program was begun by the patients themselves in 1957. Through land tours prearranged with a resident Kalaupapa guide, thousands now make pilgrimages each year to this spot.

The Kalaupapa Peninsula and three adjoining valleys were declared a national park in 1980, with the aim of preserving their natural beauty for posterity. Within the next decade, St. Philomena's Church, rotted from years of neglect, was restored by Hawaii's people. It stands as a symbol of an important aspect of island history.

Today, fewer than 100 lepers live at Kalaupapa. They are free to come and go as they please. Most choose to stay in the pristine setting enyoying a quiet lifestyle and their memories.

## LANAI

If there is any one island that epitomizes the charm of an earlier Hawaii, it is **Lanai**, long known as "The Pineapple Island." For decades, Lanai has been the get-away-from-it-all hideaway enjoyed by veteran visitors seeking rugged trails and natural wonders.

This third smallest of the eight major Hawaiian Islands is rocky and pear-shaped – just 17 miles (27 km) long and 13 miles (21 km) wide – , and it rises to a height of 3,370 ft (1,027 m) at the rainforest of Mount Lanaihale, Lanai's highest elevation. When viewed from nearby Maui or Molokai, Lanai resembles a gently arching mound, usually crowned by white puffs of clouds. Hence its name: Lanai, "the hump."

Lanai's peaceful face can be deceiving. The island offers breathtaking contrasts. For one, its almost eerie tranquility is starkly different from Honolulu's hustle-and-bustle and Waikiki's bright lights. By day, residents and visitors alike don sturdy footwear and trek Lanai's few paved roads, or conquer the wilderness in their Jeeps, the easier way to get around. They discover desert-dry landscapes, lovely beaches, pine forests, red-dust trails and stunning views of Molokai and Maui from Lanaihale's summit. Some carry their snorkeling gear and head for the clear waters of Hulopo'e Bay.

Lanai's people live amidst an estimated 14,000 acres (5,665 hectares) of pine apples. These spiny green-and-gold fruits line the red-dirt roads of Lanai's fertile (and sometimes foggy and ghostly) **Palawai Basin**, located on the floor of an extinct volcanic crater. The pineapple groves date from 1922 when Jim Dole purchased most of the island from a missionary family for $1.1 million.

Dole's pineapples and a plantation-style economy gave rise to the island's only town, tiny **Lanai City.** In turn, the town was populated by immigrant laborers of various races, from Filipino and Japanese to Portuguese and Chinese. Stately pine trees dot the landscape, originally planted around 1910 by naturalist George Munro, after whom Lanai's Munro Trail is named.

Now, as then, the immigrants' lives away from the fields revolve around Lanai City's single post office, small mom-and-pop eateries and modest wooden homes with tin roofs and vegetable gardens. Lanai's oldtimers know each other well and share their worries, food and supplies. For many, the best of old-fashioned hospitality comes at twilight when friends and neighbors gather to "talk story" on the front porch of the ten-room **Hotel Lanai**. From 1923 to 1990, this plantation-style home served as the heart and soul of Lanai – the island's only hotel and its main social center.

For most of Lanai's 2,500 permanent residents, Hotel Lanai may serve as a historic landmark by which to gauge future changes. The island itself, however, is a symbol of a rich past, some of which is preserved in traditional chants.

### Island History

Historically Lanai has been perceived in different ways. Early Hawaiians, for instance, avoided Lanai for a long time, fearing it was inhabited by ghosts. Ancient chants spoke of a "Red Lanai," referring to the windswept dust that colored everything it touched a rusty hue.

When Hawaiians no longer feared Lanai's ghosts, they gradually migrated from the neighboring islands, probably around A.D. 1400. The people derived

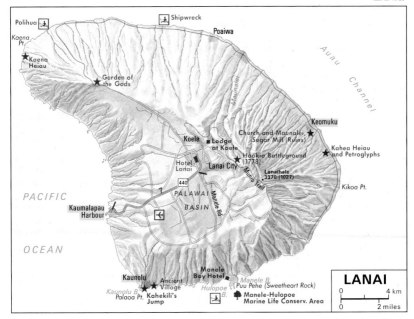

sustenance from the sea, but eventually found the fertile interior lands ideal for raising taro and yams. Until their contact with outsiders, Lanai's people lived in harmony with their environment.

From the late 1700s, Westerners started to take notice of Lanai, albeit in different ways. Captain George Vancouver circled the island in 1792 but did not land. Vancouver's ship's surgeon noted Lanai's "naked appearance ... thinly covered with shriveled grass in a scorched state."

But King Kamehameha liked what he saw. Not long after the warrior-king consolidated his control over most of the Hawaiian Islands in 1795, he kept a summer home at the southwestern coastal village of Kaunolu Bay. The event marked Lanai's transition into modern history.

By the mid 1800s, business people, missionaries and others pursued their own dreams for Lanai. Chinese entrepreneur Wu Tsin arrived in 1802, noticed wild sugar cane along the coast, and produced Hawaii's first commercial sugar crop. But he soon learned that Lanai was too dry for any substantial sugar yield.

The two Maui-based missionaries Dwight Baldwin and William Richards arrived in 1836 to preach, but encountered a people who preferred their traditional belief. The missionaries departed. Mormons reached Lanai's shore in 1854, established a City of Joseph in Lanai's fertile central plains, but left after such natural disasters as drought and insects destroyed their crops and dreams.

By the beginning of the twentieth century, Lanai's people were mostly fishermen or workers on goat-and-sheep ranches, belonging to Maui's Baldwins. The arrival of Dole's pineapples changed the face of the island.

The rise of the pineapple industry altered the island, though for six decades life continued moving at a slow pace. Today, Lanai's cooperative lifestyle is facing different stresses as the economic base shifts from pineapples to tourism. The changing cost of foreign labor has deeply affected its pineapple industry.

With the dawning of the 1990s, the once-solitary Hotel Lanai was joined by two larger luxury resorts: the 102-room **Lodge at Koele** and the 248-room **Manele Bay Hotel.** Both are owned by Castle & Cooke, a Los Angeles-based real-estate development company that became Lanai's major landowner when it acquired Dole's assets in 1961.

In contrast to the Hotel Lanai's home-style simplicity, the new resorts are opulent. The Lodge at Koele, for instance, is patterned after a sprawling English country estate, complete with elegant verandas, stone fireplaces, gardens, tea salon, floors of dark rich woods and butler service.

The oceanside Manele Bay Hotel, surrounded by lavish gardens and waterfalls, perched high above the soft white-sand beach of beautiful Hulopo'e Bay possesses what one might describe as genuine island atmosphere.

### Exploring Lanai

New resorts notwithstanding, it is the Hotel Lanai that serves as a convenient guidepost for newcomers. The center of Lanai City is just a short walk downhill from the hotel.

Three paved primary roads – about 30 miles (48 km) in all – spread like rays from Lanai City. Southwest is the working port of **Kaumalapau Harbor**; south is lovely Hulopo'e Beach

The 7-mile (11 km) drive between Lanai City and Kaumalapau Harbor provides a nice introduction to the island. It is the same route workers have taken for years as they hauled millions of crated pineapples to the barges for shipment to Honolulu canneries about 60 miles (95 km) away.

Off the highway, a rough trail leads to **Kaunolu Bay** and Kaunolu Village, where one finds the ruins of Kame-

*Above: The Garden of the Gods in Lanai.*
*Right: Camping on Lanai. Following page: A ripening pineapple awaits harvest.*

hameha's summer home. Visitors are advised to approach such cultural sights with the appropriate degree of respect.

At **Kahekili's Jump** warriors once tested their bravery by running along a narrow path and jumping into the sea – but not before clearing a ledge that juts 15 ft (4,5 m) from the cliff wall.

The more hardy may want to hike east to **Hulopo'e Bay**, but a drive on Manele Road from Lanai City is quicker. Near Hulopo'e Bay and its beach is **Manele Bay**, where recreational sailboats share the waters with the family fishing boats of Lanai's anglers.

Windward Lanai provides another mood for hikers and beachcombers. At the end of the paved road, near the shoreline, a left turn onto a smaller trail leads to **Shipwreck Beach**. This is aptly named, since powerful trade winds between Maui and Molokai occasionally swept ships toward its destructive reefs. The setting is eerie: a deserted beach, shards of driftwood, and the remains of a World War II liberty ship in plain view.

Certainly one of Lanai's strangest sights is a geological curiosity located 7 miles (11 km) north of Lanai City. The **Garden of the Gods** is actually a windswept canyon with an aura of otherworldliness to it: Large boulders of many colors look as if they were dropped from the sky by a playful god. Close by, a rough road leads down to **Polihua Beach**, a deserted 2-mile (3.2 km) strand.

A nice way to cap a Lanai vacation is to hike to the summit of **Lanaihale** by means of the **Munro Trail**. It begins about a mile above the Lodge at Koele. The trail winds through dense forests and Norfolk pines, another gift from naturalist George Munro: They have proved to be beneficial, collecting moisture from the air and supplementing the island's precious supply of ground water.

Like the rest of Lanai, the summit of Lanaihale surrounds the visitor with a calmness of nature that remains unencumbered by machines, artificial noises and buildings, a natural elegance that is the source of Lanai's appeal.

## MOLOKAI
(All local area telephone codes are 808)

### Accommodation

*LUXURY:* **Colony's Kaluakoi Hotel & Golf Club**, (P.O. Box 1977), Maunaloa 96770, Tel: 552-2555, 800-367- 6046.
**Kenani Kai**, Kalua koi Route, Manualoa, Molokai HI 96770, Tel: 552-7261.
*MODERATE:* **Hotel Molokai**, (P.O. Box 546), Kaunakalai, Molokai, HI 967 48, Tel: 553-5347, HNL 531-4004.
**Wavecrest Resort**, Star Route, Molokai, HI 96743, Tel: 558-8238, 800-367-2980.
**Paniolo Hale**, (P.O. Box 146), Maunaloa 96770, Tel: 552-2731, 800-367-2984.
*BUDGET:* **Pau Hana Inn,** (P.O. Box 860), Kaunakakai 96748, Tel: 553-5342, 800-367-5072.

### Attractions

**Damien Molokai Tours**, Kalaupapa.
**Father Damien Monument**, Kalawao.
**Halawa Valley**, Halawa.
**Ka Ule o Nanahoa, Phallic Rock,** Kalae Hwy., Kalae.
**Kahiwa Falls**, Molokai Forest Reserve, Pali Coast, northeast shore.
**Kakahaia Wildlife Refuge**, Kawela. **Kalae Stables**, Great Molokai Mule Train Ride, Kalae Hwy., Kalae.
**Kalanikaula Sacred Kukui Grove,** Puu-o-Hoku Ranch.
**Kalaupapa National Historical Park**, Kalaupapa and Kalawao.
**Kaluaaha Church**, Kamehameha V Hwy., Kaluaaha.
**Kapuaiwa Coconut Grove**, Maunaloa Hwy., Kaunakakai.
**Kawela Place of Refuge**, Kawela. **Moaula Falls**, Halawa Valley.
**Molokai Ranch Wildlife Park**, Maunaloa.
**Octopus Stone**, Kamehameha V Hwy., Puko'o.
**Our Lady of Sorrows Church**, Kamehameha V Hwy., Kaluaaha.
**Palaau State Park**, Kalae Hwy., Kalae.
**Papohaku Beach**, Kaluakoi.
**Puu-o-Hoku Ranch and Lodge,** Kamehameha V Hwy., near Halawa.
**St. Joseph's Church**, Kamehameha V Hwy., Kamalo.
**St. Philomena's Catholic Church,** Kalawao.
**Siloama, Church of the Healing Spring**, Kalawao.
**Smith and Bronte Landing Site**, off Kamehameha V Hwy., Kamalo.

### Restaurants

*AMERICAN:* **Mid-Nite Inn,** Kaunakakai.
*CHINESE:* **Hop Inn,** Kaunakakai.
*CONTINENTAL:* **Paniolo Broiler,** Kaluakoi Hotel, Maunaloa, Tel: 552-2555.
*STEAK AND SEAFOOD:* **Ohio Lodge,** Kaluakoi Hotel, Maunaloa, Tel: 552-2555.

### Tourist Information

**Hawaii Visitors Bureau**, Suite 112, 111 Hana Hwy., Kahului, Maui 96732, Tel: 871-8691.

## LANAI
(All local area telephone codes are 808)

### Accommodation

*LUXURY:* **The Lodge at Koele**, (P.O. Box 774), Lanai City 96763, Tel: 565-7300, 800-321-4666.
**Manele Bay Hotel**, (P.O. Box 774), Lanai City 96763, Tel: 565-7700, 800-321-4666.
*BUDGET:* **Hotel Lanai,** (P.O. Box A-119), Lanai City 96763, Tel: 565-7211, 800-624-8849.

### Attractions

**Garden of the Gods**, 7 mi NW of Lanai City.
**Halulu Heiau**, Kaunolu Bay.
**Hookio Gulch battle site,** Munro Trail E of Lanai City.
**Kahea Heiau**, Halepalaoa Landing.
**Kahekili's Jump**, Kaunolu Bay.
**Kanepu'u Preserve**, Koele.
**Keomoku townsite ruins**, east shore.
**King Kamehameha Summer Home Archeological Site**, Kaunolu Bay.
**Lanai City Service**, Manele Bay, Tel: 565-7227.
**Manele-Hulopo'e Marine Life Conservation Area,** Manele and Hulopo'e bays.
**Munro Trail**, Lanaihale.
**pineapple fields**, Palawai Basin.
**pineapple shipping port,** Kaumalapau Harbor.
**Polihua Beach,** west shore.
**Shipwreck Beach**, north shore.

### Restaurants

*AMERICAN:* **Hotel Lanai Restaurant,** Hotel Lanai, Lanai City, Tel: 565-7211.
**Main Dining Room,** The Lodge at Koele, Lanai City, Tel: 565-7300.
*CONTINENTAL:* **Malele Bay Restaurant,** Manele Bay Hotel, Hulopo'e Bay, Tel: 565-7700.

### Tourist Information

**Hawaii Visitors Bureau**, Suite 112, 111 Hana Hwy., Kahului, Maui 96732, Tel: 871-8691. Normal business hours.

# BIG ISLAND

**HILO**
**PUNA**
**VOLCANOES NATIONAL PARK**
**KONA COAST**
**KOHALA COAST**
**HAMAKUA**

The island of Hawaii is the oldest of the Hawaiian islands – and the youngest. This was the cradle of Hawaiian history and culture, the site of the first landing of peoples from elsewhere in Polynesia, the birthplace of King Kamehameha and the place from which the other islands were conquered and unified.

Geologically speaking, Hawaii is only teen-aged. It's still experiencing growing pains, as repeated volcanic activity attests. Lava flows slowly continue to stretch the isle's size to the south and southeast.

The island of Hawaii is better known as "The Big Island," and not just to differentiate it from the state as a whole. It's by far the largest of the state's islands – 4,050 square miles (10,900 sq km), greater than all the other Hawaiian islands put together.

Not surprisingly, it also has the widest variety of landscapes, climates and scenic attractions. The Big Island boasts bleak lava deserts and lush tropical rainforests, quiet beaches and snow-capped moun-

*Preceding pages: Lava glows in Hale-maumau crater atop Kilauea volcano in a 1974 eruption. The most recent eruption series, which started in 1983 and continues, sees lava flowing into the sea. Left: One of the waterfalls along the Hamakua Coast.*

tains, vast cattle ranches and tiny gardens of orchids and anthuriums, 1,000-year-old Polynesian artifacts and futuristic observatories seeking out the secrets of outer space.

But the Big Island isn't all pristine wilderness. Hilo, with 42,000 people, is the state's second city. The Kona and Kohala coasts have some of the state's most extravagant resort hotels. And Hawaii Volcanoes National Park displays one of the rarest and most awesome spectacles in the United States.

The first Polynesians are believed to have settled here in the middle of the eighth century, but they were unknown to the Western world for yet another 1,000 years, until Captain James Cook landed in 1778. On his second visit to the Big Island in 1779, Cook was killed in an unfortunate dispute with native Hawaiians at Kealakekua Bay, midway along the west coast of the Big Island.

Just reaching full adulthood at the time of Cook's visits was a young *ali'i* (chief) named Kamehameha. Born near modern Mo'okini Heiau, perhaps the most ancient of Hawaiian temples at the northernmost tip of the Big Island, Kamehameha became known as the greatest of Hawaiian rulers. When his king, Kalaniopuu, died in 1782, he was elevated to full ruler of the northern and western

145

districts of Kohala and Kona. Over the following decade, he gained control of the entire Big Island through a series of wars with other isle chieftains.

But Kamehameha's ambition was not yet fulfilled. In 1795, he launched an invasion of Maui, and from there moved on to Oahu and Kauai. By 1810, he had become the first king to reign over all the Hawaiian islands.

Kamehameha III transferred Hawaii's capital from Kailua-Kona to Honolulu, and the Big Island became of lesser political and economic importance in the islands. But it experienced the same outside influences and changes. Missionaries, sugar, Asian immigration, revolution, U.S. territorial status and statehood all radically affected its development.

In the years following World War II, nature and tourism have been the leading factors shaping the Big Island. Hilo was devastated by tidal waves in 1946 and 1960. The second time the town was rebuilt on higher ground. The well-known volcanoes add acres to the island but also devour homes and other property.

In the meantime, the Kona and Kohala coasts have become one of Hawaii's three primary tourist magnets, along with Oahu's Waikiki Beach and Maui's Kaanapali Coast. Some of the state's most famous developments line this coastline, sharing the natural setting with ancient fishponds, petroglyphs, *heiaus*, and other reminders of Hawaii's long and rich history.

## HILO

As the Big Island's largest city, **Hilo** is a romantic introduction to the sights and experiences that await the visitor.

Curling around a deceptively peaceful crescent bay midway down the island's east coast, Hilo (pronounced "heel-oh") sits on the divide between Mauna Kea and Mauna Loa. And in much the same way that the serene, often snow-capped

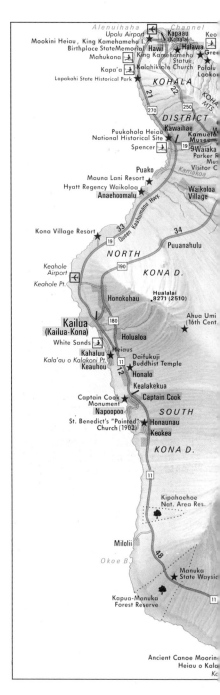

Kakuihaele
Waipio
Macadamia
Nut Factory
HAMAKUA
19 16
Honokaa
Paauilo
Kukaiau 19
Milo Village
hio
ltage
elu
ry
Kalopa State
Rec. Area
*Laupahoehoe Pt.*
Laupahoehoe
COAST
NORTH HILO
Kahinahina Trail
David Douglas
Historical Monument
19
37
Honomu
HAMAKUA D.
ii
Mauna Kea
13796 (4205)
Mauna Kea
Observatory
Complex
200 26
Mauna Kea
St. Rec. Area
DISTRICT
Akaka Falls
Pepeekeo
Onomea
Papaikou
Paukaa
Hawaii Tropical
Botanical Garden
*Pepe'ekeo Scenic Drive*
PACIFIC
Saddle
Road
29
Wailuku R.
Naha Stone
Rainbow Falls
Wailuku River
St. Pk.
SOUTH
200
Dirt Road
*Hilo B.*
Hilo Trop. Gardens
Hilo
Nani Mau Gardens
Macadamia Nut Factory
and Orchards
*Paki B.*
na Loa
rvatory
a Loa
(4169)
Hawaii
Volcanoes
Nat. Pk.
HILO D.
Kulani Honor
Camp
Panaewa Zoo
Equestrian Center
Kurtistown
Stainback Hwy.
Mountain View
21
Haena
Keaau
HAWAIIAN
PARADISE
PARK
130
Old Hawaiian
Canoe Shed
Glenwood
11
Hawaiian Flower
Exports(Anthurium
Gardens)
Pahoa
Kapoho
446 (136)
*C. Kumukahi*
Kumukahi Lighthouse
*Kapoho Pt.*
PUNA
Volcano
Thurston
Lava Tube
4078 (1247)
Kilauea Caldera
CHAIN OF CRATERS
DISTRICT
Lava Tree
State
Monument
137
130
Kalani Honua
Kaimu
Star of the Sea
Church
Ancient Footprints
in Lava Ash
KAU
DISTRICT
11
35
KAU DESERT
Hilina Pali
Lookout
Puu Loa
Petroglyphs
Kalapana
Cave of Refuge
Park Visitor Center,
Wahaula Heiau
Kaimu Black Sand
Naula Sea Arches
OCEAN
Turtle Cave
Pahala
Henry
Opukahaia
Church
Twain's
eypod
aiohinuu
Naalehu
(1942)
Punaluu
Seamountain Ninole Golf Course
Punaluu,
Black Sand
Honuapo
Wittington

# HAWAII – BIG ISLAND

| 0 | 10 | 20 | 30 km |
|---|----|----|-------|
| 0 | 5 | 10 | 15 miles |

older mountain shares the island with the dynamic and volatile younger peak, Hilo is a charming blend of old and new.

The contemporary state and county buildings that house the island's seat of government stand in the middle of Hilo. Close by is the octagonal **Wailoa Center**, with visitor information services and art and cultural exhibits. Behind these buildings is one of several modern indoor shopping complexes.

But "modernity" is only a small part of the story in downtown Hilo. One- and two-story tin-roofed wooden buildings house all manner of local shopkeepers, from vendors of Chinese preserved fruit and Japanese mochi to soda fountains with spinning stools. "Talk story" with the local merchants in cluttered, wooden-walled stores as they total up your purchases with paper and pencil, abacuses, or old-fashioned cash registers that literally "ring" up the prices.

Many downtown structures have been refurbished through the national Main Street program. These revitalized businesses and buildings are preserving Hilo's special charm and creating jobs in new restaurants and shops.

Begin a walking tour of downtown Hilo by stopping at the Main Street project office on Kamehameha Avenue and picking up the self-guided tour brochure published by the American Association of University Women (AAUW). As you stroll, don't miss the **East Hawaii Cultural Center** on Kalauaka Street. There is a good chance you will see an exhibit by local artisans and perhaps a play or hear a poetry reading.

The home of Hilo's earliest missionaries, the Lymans, has been preserved in museum fashion. The **Lyman House Memorial Museum** on Haili Street was built in 1839, and today offers the visitor a glimpse of Hawaii's missionary era. The adjacent **Island Heritage Gallery** preserves ancient Hawaiian artifacts, and ethnic memorabilia of the different cul-

tural and ethnic groups that have immigrated to Hawaii. There are also geological exhibits.

Just down Haili Street is **Haili Congregational Church.** It was built in 1859 by the Waiakea Mission Station, established by New England missionaries. The Rev. Titus Coan and David Lyman conducted services in the new church as the congregation sat on mats on a dirt floor. Services today are conducted in the recently renovated sanctuary, rededicated after a fire in the bell tower in 1979.

**Banyans and Blossoms**

Elsewhere in and around the town of Hilo are numerous scenic attractions. **Banyan Drive,** which fronts the city's leading tourist hotels, is lined with a row of imposing banyan trees planted in the 1930s by visiting celebrities and dignitaries such as baseball star Babe Ruth.

The Banyan Drive also leads to the elaborate **Liliuokalani Gardens.** This 30-acre (12 hectare) park, designed and maintained in authentic Japanese style, is one of the largest formal oriental gardens outside Japan. Wedding parties often use the gardens as a setting for a portrait.

Although all of lush Hilo is like a garden, two gardens in particular feature orchids, anthuriums and other tropical flowers blooming profusely. **Hilo Tropical Gardens**, on Kalanianaole Avenue, has an elegant orchid collection. **Nani Mau Gardens,** off the highway to Volcano, claims to have every flowering plant found in the state on its 22 acres (8.7 hectares).

If you're up with the sun, stop at **Suisan Dock**, at the end of Banyan Drive, for the fish auction. Each morning at dawn, the fleet chugs in with its catch. The excitement begins about 8am with a lively auction conducted in two or three languages, including Pidgin English, Hawaii's own special linguistic blend. The early riser might also take a drive to

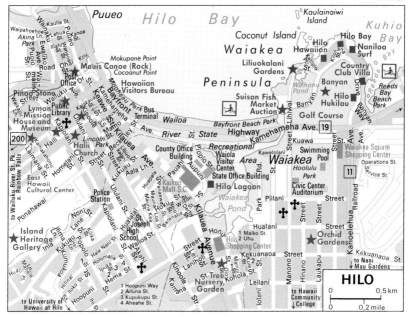

**Wailuku River State Park**, the site of **Rainbow Falls**. The best viewing time is early in the morning, when the sun tops the mango trees and forms a rainbow in the mist created by the falls crashing into the huge pond below.

Natural materials have been cleverly interwoven with the lush vegetation at **Panaewa Rainforest Zoo.** Animals roam in an environment much like their natural habitats; many of the animals and birds at the zoo are native to Hawaii. Additional natural and exotic plantings create a botanical garden within the zoo. Located 5 mi (8 km) south of Hilo on Stainback Highway. It's open from 9am to 5pm daily.

The **University of Hawaii-Hilo** is the second largest of Hawaii's nine-campus statewide system of higher education. UH-Hilo includes the two-year **Hawaii Community College** with a traditional four-year College of Arts and Sciences, a four-year College of Agriculture, and a Center for Continuing Education and Community Service.

History lovers find Hilo to be a treasure trove of Hawaiian stories and legends. Hawaiians told their cultural history through legend, and it seems that everything in Hilo has a story behind it.

For example, two enormous stones stand in front of the **Hawaii Public Library** on Waianuenue Avenue. One, the **Pinao Stone**, was once the entrance pillar to an ancient *heiau*. The **Naha Stone** stood in front of the temple. In true Arthurian fashion (just like the "sword in the stone"), it was used by the royal Naha clan to test royal legitimacy by challenging young nobles to budge the gigantic boulder. Any warrior strong enough to turn it over would have the strength to conquer and unify all the islands of Hawaii. It is said that King Kamehameha the Great overturned the 2.5 ton stone as a young boy, fulfilling the prophecy in manhood when he unified the islands under his rule.

Many of Hawaii's legends are put into chant and song and choreographed for Hilo's annual summertime **Merrie**

**Monarch Festival**. Hula *halau* (schools) from Hawaii and the mainland gather to tell history in dance and music.

## PUNA

South of Hilo, the **Puna District** forms the easternmost tip of the Big Island. A short drive in this direction on Highway 11, followed by a 3-mile (5 km) turnoff through macadamia nut orchards, leads to the **Mauna Loa Macadamia Nut Visitor Center**, orchard and factory. You may see workers harvesting the nuts from the ground. At the visitor center, samples of the nuts are available; in fact, the snack shop serves only products made from macadamia nuts. From special viewing stations on a second-story walkway, you can look into the factory where signs explain the cracking, weighing, sorting, cooking, salting, candy-making and

*Above: High chiefs and warriors in full costume rededicating the Puukohola heiau (temple). Right: Rainforest on Big Island.*

packaging processes that all take place at the plant. Next door, workers cover macadamia nuts with chocolate.

As you drive deeper into Puna, fields of papayas, anthuriums and orchids dot the countryside. Watch for "Visitors Welcome" signs outside the nurseries. Puna is Hawaii's major producer of papayas and anthuriums. About 2,5 miles (4 km) east of Pahoa, 18 miles (29 km) from Hilo, is the **Lava Tree State Park**. Found in a lush tropical forest on Highway 132, it preserves an area where an eighteenth century lava flow engulfed a grove of large *ohia* trees and left behind an eerie forest of lava tree molds. At the end of Highway 132 is the lighthouse at **Cape Kumakahi**, the easternmost point in Hawaii. In 1960, the lighthouse was in the path of a lava flow, but miraculously was left standing when the molten river split and passed on either side of it, leaving it quite untouched.

Less fortunate in the same eruption was the village of **Kapoho**. A 420-ft-high (128 m) cinder cone along Highway 132

marks the site of this buried town.

**Kalani Honua**, along coastal Highway 137 between Kapoho and Kaimu, is a rural retreat for those engaging in Hawaiian cultural studies, or enjoying performing and visual arts and recreation. The center offers comfortable cedar lodges for individuals or groups who have come to participate in the activities or taking part in seminars and camps.

One of the long-standing attractions on Puna's southern coast has been obliterated by recent volcanic action. The **Kaimu Black Sand Beach** and Kalapana, near the junction of Highways 13 and 137, is no longer. But just as Kaimu Beach was formed by the meeting of fire and water thousands of years ago, new pockets of black sand are now being created. The jet-black sands are formed when hot lava flows into the cold Pacific and is broken into tiny bits by steam explosions, then ground and polished to minute, glistening grains by the friction of constant wave action.

Two diametrically opposed reminders of Hawaii's spiritual past and present are situated fewer than 5 miles (8 km) apart on Highway 13.

The **Waha'ula Heiau**, adjacent to a Hawaii Volcanoes National Park visitors center, has been threatened by recent lava flows. Built more than 700 years ago by the Tahitian priest Paao, it was a major temple for the sacrifice of humans to the Hawaiian gods.

The **Star of the Sea Church** has brilliant pictures and murals covering its interior; these were the work of Father Evarist Gielen, a Catholic priest from Belgium who finished his artistic labors in 1929. On the shore by the church, a canoe ramp dating back to the Stone Age is still used as a launching site.

### North of Hilo

Lush mountain slopes and vast fields of sugar cane border coastal Highway 19 north of Hilo. 6 miles (10 km) from the city, a side road turns off toward the coast. This is the 4-mile (6.5 km) **Pepe'ekeo Scenic Drive**. Passing tropical forests, charming old churches, and a derelict gas station that opens for business only when its local patrons call the owners to request a sale, you'll come to a bluff overlooking the beautiful **Onomea Bay**. A natural sea arch collapsed several years ago, leaving behind an unusual notched formation.

The **Hawaii Tropical Botanical Garden** at Onomea Bay offers visitors the opportunity to walk along the salty shoreline, beside a cool mountain stream and through the dense jungle vegetation. A small yellow church has been converted to a visitor center. Sign up here for the garden walks, then climb aboard vans for the short ride to the garden.

At **Honomu**, turn inland 3,5 miles (5.5 km) to **Akaka Falls State Park**, a 66-acre (27 hectare) slice of the Garden of Eden, fragrant with wild ginger, tropical trees, plants and flowers. Pathways

weave through the dense foliage, bringing you to Akaka Falls, which plunges 420 ft (128 m) into a mountain pool, and Kahuna Falls, which drops from a height of 100 ft (30 m).

## VOLCANOES NATIONAL PARK

**Hawaii Volcanoes National Park** is the most popular visitor attraction on the Big Island – and rightfully so. Containing the world's most active volcano, **Kilauea**, on the southeastern flank of **Mauna Loa**, the park is a draw for adventurous travelers from all over the world. Since 1983, the ever-temperamental Madame Pele has embarked on a series of eruptions that have poured flows of lava down the slopes of Kilauea into the Puna district. These flows have made their way to the sea, consuming forests,

*Above: Molten lava flowing into the sea, causing giant clouds of steam. Right: The steep walls of Halemaumau, Kilauea volcano's summit caldera.*

homes and sections of the Chain of Craters Road, making the loop between national park headquarters and the village of Kalapana impassable. Acres of new land have been added to the island.

Many visitors, especially those who can afford a helicopter or small-plane excursion, have been able to view the explosion of steam where the molten lava pours into the ocean. But seeing an explosive lava eruption remains, purely and simply, a matter of luck.

Since 1980, Kilauea has erupted some 60 times; Mauna Loa, just once. Rarely do the eruptions offer the perfect drive-in convenience of staging themselves in **Halemaumau Crater**, directly in front of the **Hawaiian Volcano Observatory**. More frequently, they occur along the more distant **East Rift**.

But even for those visitors not fortunate enough to see an eruption, Kilauea is a dramatic experience. The National Park Service has done a wonderful job of protecting this natural treasure and enhancing its accessibility for all visitors.

Hawaii Volcanoes National Park is located just 28 miles (45 km) from downtown Hilo, via a broad, uncrowded highway that climbs past tree ferns and through a few small communities.

Established in 1916, the 229,000-acre (92,675 hectare) park sprawls down the southern and eastern flanks of Kilauea and up the slopes of Mauna Loa to its 13,679 ft (4,169 m) summit. Also part of the national park are nearly 30 miles (48 km) of rugged coastline, including the ancient and historic Hawaiian temple, **Waha'ula Heiau.**

At park headquarters is the **Kilauea Visitor Center**, a comprehensive orientation stop where new arrivals collect area maps and view films of recent eruptions in a 220-seat theater.

Next door, housed in the carefully restored 1877 **Volcano House** hotel, is the rustic **Volcano Art Center**, an active gallery that displays a full range of works by area artists and craftspeople. In recent years, **Volcano Village** – just outside the park – has evolved into a small but vital artists' colony. Besides browsing or buying, visitors can sign up for seminars and special events held by the Volcano Art Center throughout the year.

The contemporary Volcano House has been perched rimside, just across Crater Rim Road since 1941. It has 37 pleasant but old-fashioned rooms, a dining room and lounge with remarkable views across Kilauea Crater, and a living-room-like lobby with deep-cushioned seating around a blazing fireplace. It gets cold here, 4,000 ft (1,220 m) above sea level.

About 3 miles (5 km) away, on the west rim of Kilauea Crater, are the **Hawaiian Volcano Observatory** and the new (1987) **Thomas A. Jaggar Museum.** Both have an almost bird's-eye view of Halemaumau, the steaming firepit near the center of Kilauea Crater. The Jaggar Museum, which details the park's volcanology through exhibits, murals and videos, is considered by many

to be the finest museum in the National Park system.

Also within the park's boundaries are support facilities for scientific research, several campgrounds and visitor cabins, picnic grounds and a golf course. There are, as well, a variety of scenic drives and 150 miles (240 km) of hiking trails.

### Signs of Pele

And everywhere are the signs of the area's ever-changing geology. Fumaroles hiss at the roadside. Firepits smolder. Sulfur banks emit their pungent, sinus-piercing odor. The once-molten lava has hardened into a coal-black lunar landscape of bizarre, otherworldly patterns.

The Hawaiian people say the volcanoes are the home of Pele, the goddess of fire. Her moods, they say, determine the area's level of activity – a tantrum here, a peaceful lull there. Pele is regularly appeased by gifts of gin, *ti* leaves, and *ohelo* berries tossed ceremoniously into Halemaumau Crater. Many swear

they've seen her in the form of a mysterious, white-robed old lady.

It's a severe exception, though, for any of the 2 million annual visitors to the park to lay eyes on the ancient goddess. The few thousand who venture out of their buses or rental vehicles and onto the backcountry trails probably stand a better chance of seeing her.

In spite of the roads, however, the vast majority of the national park's acreage can be reached only on foot. Yet only a handful of hikers and campers test the rambling wilderness of the backcountry – making the volcanoes' park a backpacker's uncrowded delight.

Several trails lead across and around Kilauea Crater to Halemaumau. Others lead across smaller craters, down **Devastation Trail**, to the mazelike **Thurston Lava Tube** or to remote campgrounds. But the park's hardiest hike is the one to the summit of Mauna Loa, a three- or

*Above: Stylized petroglyphs, a pastime of the ancient Hawaiians.*

four-day excursion over 18 miles (29 km) of difficult and treacherous trail.

To the pleasure of the majority of visitors, however, many of the park's points of interest can be reached by car. From Crater Rim Drive, motorists can venture down **Chain of Craters Road** past its many smaller volcanic craters. The 11-mile (17.5 km) route from park headquarters also passes lush rainforests and great areas of devastation. Pumice is piled high from recent eruptions, and lava flows, cover much of the landscape. The dramatic drive is, in fact, a close-up look at the lava flows' march to the sea.

The Chain of Craters Road was covered by lava flows from Mauna Ulu from 1965 to 1979. Reopened in June 1979, it has been frequently closed by lava flows from additional eruptions on Kilauea's east rift since 1986. When it is open, visitors enjoy direct access from the Kilauea area to the park's coastal section.

Coastal attractions include the powerful surf eating into lava sea cliffs, and **Puu Loa**, one of the great concentrations

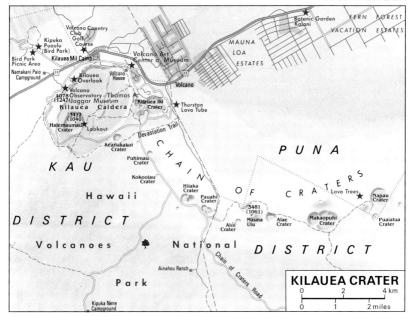

**KILAUEA CRATER**

| 0 | 2 | 4 km |

| 0 | 1 | 2 miles |

of petroglyphs in Hawaii. The **Waha'ula Visitor Center** adjoins the ancient *heiau* of the same name. One of the most significant religious sites in ancient Hawaii, this temple is believed to be the one where the practice of human sacrifices was begun. Before lava flows cut off the road just past Waha'ula, motorists could continue out of the park via sleepy Kalapana village for a complete circle tour back to Hilo. A turnoff from the Chain of Craters Road leads to **Hilina Pali**, a steep cliff that affords a spectacular view of the Big Island's southeast seacoast.

Further information on Hawaii Volcanoes National Park can be obtained by writing to park headquarters in Volcano, HI 96718. An automatic answering service provides updates on ongoing volcanic eruptions or potential activity: phone (808) 967-7977, 24 hours a day.

### The Ka'u Desert

As Highway 11 proceeds southwest out of Hawaii Volcanoes National Park, it passes through the district of **Ka'u**, the southernmost part of the Big Island – and of the United States. Historically, the Ka'u Coast is recognized as a very special, sacred place by Hawaiians. Many believe it to be the landing site of the first Polynesians to arrive in Hawaii.

Not truly a desert, Ka'u is drier in climate than other areas of the island, but is rich in macadamia nuts as well as sugar cane and cattle-feeding grasses. Flowers such as the yellow *mamani* and white *alahe'e* speckle the land in the most unusual places, particularly during spring and winter rains. Sugar cane grows at higher levels here than anywhere in the country, at altitudes of 3,300 ft (1006 m).

Ka'u is a quiet, friendly land of old plantation communities. Highway 11 winds past the sugar-mill town of **Pahala** and continues to **Naalehu,** the southernmost town in the United States. The community is a gathering place for local residents, with the shopping center always a hub of activity. Here, women do their grocery shopping, students congre-

155

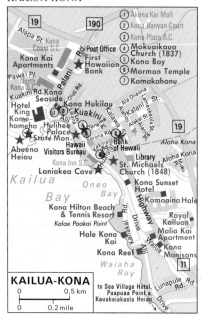

KAILUA-KONA

① Akona Kai Mall
② Kona Banyan Court
③ Kona Plaza S.C.
④ Mokuaikaua Church (1837)
⑤ Kona Bay
⑥ Mormon Temple
⑦ Kamakahonu

0        0,5 km
0        0,2 mile

gate at the snack bar, and retirees get together to talk about the old days.

There are two very different places to spend a night in Ka'u. The **Shirakawa Hotel** in **Waiohinu,** just past Naalehu, resembles a large house set in park-like grounds. Close to the hotel is Mark Twain's monkeypod tree. The original, planted by Twain in 1866, was felled by a storm in 1957, but a new one sprouted from its roots. Also in Waiohinu is **Kauahaao Church**, a pretty, colonial-style frame church built more than 100 years ago.

**Sea Mountain**, at **Punalu'u**, between Pahala and Naalehu, is a recreational-residential complex built with elegant simplicity on the lower slopes of Mauna Loa, with views of the Pacific. It has attractive and functional condominiums for rent, a golf course, tennis courts, a restaurant and a branch of the Aspen Institute for Humanistic Studies.

*Right: Thurston Lava Tube is one of the attractions in Hawaii Volcanoes National Park.*

Perched high on a hill above the Punalu'u settlement is a tiny church commemorating Henry Opukahaia, a young man from this village who left for New York in 1809. While there he converted to Christianity and influenced missionaries to come to Hawaii and spread the teachings of the Church. Punalu'u is also known for its black-sand beach, one of two that are accessible on the island.

Picnickers have a choice of parks. They can stay at **Punalu'u Beach Park**, visit **Whittington Beach Park**, or take a 15-mile (24 km) drive west on Highway 11 to **Manuka State Park**. There are excellent picnic and camping facilities at Punalu'u. Manuka, a botanical garden of native and imported plants, has beautifully landscaped areas and hiking trails.

Reserve some time for visiting **Ka Lae**, or South Point. The most southerly point in the United States, Ka Lae also boasts the Big Island's only green-sand beach, made of minute volcanic olivine particles. However, it is accessible only by foot or in four-wheel-drive vehicles. There are archeological findings here that date back to A.D. 750: ancient canoe moorings set in solid rock, petroglyphs and the ruins of the Kalalea Heiau.

## KONA COAST

The Kona Coast is the Big Island's playground, a mecca for sun-worshipping, ocean-loving vacationers, golfers and game fishermen. The western flanks of Mauna Loa and her younger sister, Hualalai, fall gradually into the Pacific along the Kona Coast, their lava-rich soils providing perfect conditions for the world-famous Kona coffee beans that grow here. This is a dry region, bordering even on desertic conditions. Prevailing winds push heavy rainclouds over the higher locations and over the eastern shores, saving little for this sheltered coastline. Few holidaymakers complain about the overabundance of sunshine.

Kailua-Kona (as different from the Honolulu suburb of Kailua, Oahu) is the main resort center. It has a wide choice of first-class hotels and fine restaurants, and a wide range of exquisite shops and night clubs.

To many, Kailua is a 1,5-mile (2,4 km) stretch of busy street called Ali'i Drive. At its north end is the **Hotel King Kamehameha**; on the south is the **Kona Hilton Beach & Tennis Resort.** Between are many other hotels and visitor attractions. The built-up area, however, stretches south 7 miles (11 km) to the **Kona Surf Resort,** on the south side of Keauhou Bay, and inland to Highway 11 (the Hawaii Belt Road) through a mixture of residential and rural backdrops to the town of **Keauhou**.

Kailua and the Kona Coast are much more than hotels, however. The community and region are inseparable from the history of the Hawaiian people. Along the South Kona coast are the **Pu'uhonua o Honaunau National Historical Park**, a "place of refuge" of ancient Hawaiians;

and **Kealakekua Bay**, where Captain James Cook anchored and where he died. In Kailua itself are **Kamakahonu**, from where King Kamehameha reigned in his final years; **Hulihe'e Palace**, King Kalakaua's summer home, now a museum; and **Mokuaikaua Church**, the first Christian church in the islands.

### Kailua-Kona

Most visitors to the Kona Coast fly into the **Keahole Airport,** a small but modern facility 9 miles (15 km) north of Kailua-Kona, in the midst of an ancient lava desert. A new highway delivers you from the airport to Kailua in about 15 minutes.

It is useful to indoctrinate yourself with Kailua's history before indulging completely in the late twentieth century. A good place to start is **Kamakahonu**, a national historic landmark on the grounds of the Hotel King Kamehameha. The great king made this thatched-roof complex the center of the islands' governmental activities from 1813 until his

death in 1819. **Ahu'ena Heiau**, a traditional temple facing Kailua Bay, was the focal point. It has been restored by Amfac Resorts and the **Bishop Museum**. After Kamehameha's death, his son and queen regent toppled the ancient *kapu* system, setting the stage for the gradual decline of traditional Hawaiian ways.

Nearby, in the center of Kailua-Kona on Ali'i Drive, is **Hulihe'e Palace,** a gracious, two-story coral-and-lava home built in 1837-8 by Kuakini, brother-in-law of Kamehameha and governor of the island. The building served later as a vacation residence for royalty and as the summer palace of Kalakaua. It has been completely restored, furnished in the Victorian style of the last century. As a museum operated by the Daughters of Hawaii, it contains many mementoes of royalty and exhibits a strong missionary influence.

*Above: Some participants literally personify the Ironman Triathlon.*

Directly across Ali'i Drive is **Mokuaikaua Church**, the first Christian church in the islands. The lava rock and coral building was first dedicated in 1823 and completed 14 years later by Hawaii's first missionaries. Visitors are welcome; services are still held on a regular schedule.

The first Catholic mission on the **Neighbor Islands** was established nearby in 1848 at **St. Michael's Church,** at the south end of Kailua town, on Ali'i Drive facing **One'o Bay**. Further south, on Kahalu'u Bay near Keauhou, the tiny blue-and-white **St. Peter's Catholic Church** stands beside an ancient Hawaiian temple, **Ku'emanu Heiau.**

Other Hawaiian temple ruins in the area include **Kaukaiakaola Heiau**, on Puapua'a Point beside Kona by the Sea Hotel; **Kealakowa'a Heiau,** in Kilohana near the junction of Highway 11 and the Kuakini Highway; and a trio of *heiaus* – **Kapuanoni, Hapai Ali'i** and **Ke'eku** – on Kala'au o Kalakoni Point, adjacent to the Keauhou Beach and Kona Lagoon hotels.

**Keauhou Bay**, the birthplace of Kamehameha III (there is a marker), and once the center of Kona fishing activity, now is dominated by a resort atmosphere, especially from the expansive Kona Surf Resort. But reminders of the past abound, including **Keauhou Holua Slide**, a hand-built rock slide down which kings and chiefs of old rode on wooden sleds. Situated on the east side of Ali'i Drive, it has been designated a national historical landmark.

### Beaches and Billfish

There are numerous fine beaches along the Kailua-Keauhou strand. Among the best are **Kahalu'u Beach Park**, on the south shore of Kahalu'u Bay, popular among picnickers; **Keauhou Bay,** with its calm waters; and **White Sands (Disappearing Sands) Beach Park,** which can be treacherous for weak swimmers but fine for experienced body surfers. (The sands actually do disappear from time to time, exposing lava below.) You'll find other coves and inlets along the rocky, irregular coastline.

Kailua is well known for its various fishing competitions, which include the renowned **Hawaiian International Billfish Tournament** every August. Daily charter boats are available for some of the world's best sport fishing, as well as glass-bottomed boats, yachts and catamarans. There are boats for whale watching and scuba diving, for dinner and sunset cruises.

Among the many reliable charter services is **Discovery Charters,** a 45-ft (13,5 m) custom-built sailboat offered for half-day, full-day and overnight cruises. Owners Bob and Carol Hogan came to Kailua to compete in the **Ironman Triathlon** in 1982 and 1983 (each won trophies in their age group) and wound up staying.

That Ironman Triathlon World Championship is a great event for the spectator as well as the participant. Competitors in this grueling event, held on a Saturday in October, swim 2.4 miles (3.9 km), bicycle 117 miles (188 km), and conclude with a 26-mile (42 km) marathon run. Events begin and end in the heart of Kailua.

There's golf at the beautiful but challenging **Kona Country Club** and tennis at any number of spots.

North of Kailua-Kona, on **Keahole Point** near Keahole Airport, is an indication that this island is indeed as much a part of the future as of the past. The **Natural Energy Laboratory of Hawaii** was established in 1974 to study and develop ocean thermal energy conversion technologies. The process uses the temperature difference between the ocean's warm surface water and its cold deep water to produce energy.

NELH also applies the cold seawater, piped from a depth of about 2,000 ft (650 m), to aquaculture. The lab has met with great success in cultivating edible seaweeds, abalone and sea urchins, salmon and oysters.

The cold water is even used to stimulate the growth of tropical strawberries! Public tours are offered at 10am Tuesdays and 2pm Thursdays.

Twelve miles (19 km) north of Kailua-Kona, off Highway 19 (the Queen Kaahumanu Highway), is the **Kona Village Resort**, where visitors can live like Hawaiian royalty in splendid isolation. No one who is unknown or not expected gets past the gatehouse. Ancient Polynesia comes to life when guests check into their private thatched-roof bungalows (*hales*) tucked along lagoons, nestling in lush tropical gardens or facing a sandy, palm-shaded cove. Traces of Kona's royal past can be found on the resort's 15-acre (6 hectares) petroglyph field. People come here to get away – there is no telephone, no television, no radio, no cars. There is, however, a 2-to-1 staff-to-room ratio.

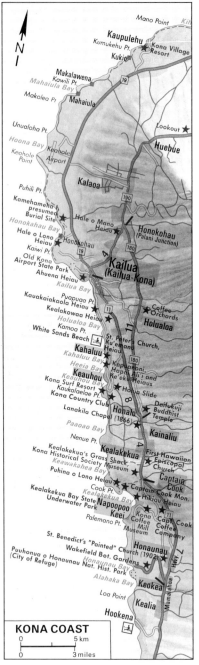

KONA COAST

0        5 km

0        3 miles

Some 1,300 ft (400 m) above Kailua-Kona, 5 miles (8 km) southeast on the slopes of Hualalai, the quaint art colony of **Holualoa** occupies what was once a ramshackle coffee plantation. Some of the best contemporary art in Hawaii is created in the series of galleries here. Some of the galleries are as creative as the work itself, such as one inspired by Zen Buddhism, complete with a stream-stone floor. There's bed-and-breakfast for those who choose to tarry.

### South Kona

For better or worse, the name **Kealakekua** is synonymous in history with that of Captain James Cook. The famed British navigator and explorer made his first landfall here in 1778 and was hailed as the god Lono.

A year later, however, when Cook visited again, animosities broke out between the Hawaiians and the British. A battle on the beach ensued, and Cook was killed in the early morning on February 14, 1779. The **Captain Cook Monument** on the north shore of **Kealakekua Bay** commemorates the event.

The bay is about 15 miles (24 km) south down the Kona coastline from Kailua-Kona. Travelers heading south from their hotels in rental vehicles will take Highway 11 (the Hawaii Belt Road). At the village of **Honalo** are a series of interesting and appetizing sights, including **Teshima's Inn,** a long-established and popular Japanese restaurant, and the **Daijukuji Mission,** an attractive Buddhist temple. A short distance further is **Kainaliu,** which serves as a shopping center for area residents. Just beyond is the community of Kealakekua.

A popular Hawaiian song lilts, "I want to go back to my little grass shack in

*Right: Macadamia nuts are one of a new generation of export crops.*

Kealakekua, Hawaii." There really is a grass shack in Kealakekua, albeit not the one of the popular song. **The Grass Shack of Kealakekua** is a gift shop offering local arts and crafts, and boasting a small botanical garden. Elsewhere in the town, which blends the bustle of a modern business center with the rustic serenity of an old, rural community, are the **Kona Historical Society Museum** in an 1875 building and the **First Hawaiian Episcopal Church**, built in 1867. Lovers of marine life should make a point of seeing James Watt's whale photographs, published by **Ocean Editions** in Kealakekua (tel. 322-9528).

Another mile down Highway 11 (the Mamalahoa Highway) is the turnoff to Kealakekua Bay. The narrow, winding road descends 4 miles (6.5 km) through coffee country – the only place in the United States where coffee is commercially grown. Toward the end of the downhill trip is the **Kona Coffee Mill Museum,** where visitors are invited to browse and sip Kona coffee.

At the end of the road are the few houses that make up the settlement of **Napo'opo'o**, just a short distance from the curve of Kealakekua Bay. A **memorial** to Henry Opukahaia honors this son of Napo'opo'o for encouraging the first Christian missionaries who came to Hawaii.

The memorial, ironically, is situated close to the **Hikiau Heiau,** the ancient Hawaiian temple where Cook was celebrated as a Hawaiian deity after he arrived in 1778. As mentioned, a year later his "divine" origins were not honored, and he was unceremoniously killed.

Besides its historical significance, Kealakekua Bay is a valuable marine preserve. There's excellent swimming and snorkeling in the sheltered cove. Cruise boats, catamarans and Zodiac boats from Kailua-Kona visit frequently.

On the hillside above Kealakekua Bay, back on Highway 11, is the town of **Captain Cook.** Among the attractions here is the **Captain Cook Coffee Company,** whose headquarters are on the west side

of the Mamalahoa Highway, south of town. Established in 1984, the company produces more than 20% of all Kona coffee, which holds a solid reputation for tastiness. Fields, mill and warehouse are higher on the west slopes of Mauna Loa; at this facility, from July to March, the coffee fruit is pulped, bagged, and prepared for shipment.

Visitors can view the coffee-making process virtually from the picking of the bean on. The bright red fruits, called "cherries" in the business (each of which contains two beans), have their coats removed and are soaked overnight in plain water. In the morning, they are dried on beds or in tumblers until the pairs of beans are separated. Then the hulls (or "parchment") are removed and the beans are roasted before shipment.

*Above: God figures standing guard outside the Temple of Keawe in Pu'uhonua o Honaunau, the City of Refuge. Right: Thatched houses used to display local crafts in Pu'uhonua o Honaunau.*

## The City of Refuge

About 6,5 miles (10,5 km) south of Captain Cook, at Keokea, Highway 160 turns west toward the coast. **St. Benedict's "Painted" Church,** a tiny Gothic structure perched on a hillside overlooking the South Kona coastline, is a delightful sight indeed: Biblical scenes cover the walls, ceilings and columns. They were painted about 1902 by Father John Berchmans Velghe, a Belgian priest who used his art to pictorially convey Christianity to many Hawaiians who were still illiterate. The church frequently hosts televised Christmas specials.

Further down the road are the **Wakefield Botanical Gardens,** which offer a spectacular array of tropical plants.

At the bottom of the road is one of the Kona Coast's most significant attractions, **Pu'uhonua o Honaunau National Historical Park,** once known as the City of Refuge. This is the best preserved and restored of all *pu'uhonua* (places of refuge) in Hawaii.

In ancient Hawaii, the death penalty could be exacted upon those who broke the sacred laws of *kapu*. There was one salvation for the *kapu* breaker: If he could reach a *pu'uhonua*, he could be spared. At a *pu'uhonua*, made sacred because it was associated with the burial site of royalty, a *kapu*-breaker could be absolved by a *kahuna* (priest) and thus might return shortly to normal life. A *pu'uhonua* was also a sanctuary during war for those who could not fight, and for those defeated in battle. They could stay in safety until the battle passed or peace came.

Honaunau was also the residence of the ruling chief of South Kona, whose palace grounds adjoined the refuge. Between the palace grounds and the sacred place is the **Great Wall**, a massive hand-built mortarless barrier of lava rock 1,000 ft (305 m) long, 10 ft (3 m) high, and 17 ft (5 m) wide. The wall was constructed in about 1550 in honor of the chief of that time, Keawe-kuike-kaai.

The area received its sanctity from the *heiau* that housed the sacred bones of royalty. It was believed that the spiritual power of chiefs, their *manu*, remained in their bones after death.

Within the 181-acre (73 hectare) Pu'uhonua o Honaunau are two *heiau* dating from before 1550. A third, Hale-o-Keawe, was built in 1650 at one end of the Great Wall. It served as a temple mausoleum until 1818, housing the bones of no less than 23 chiefs, giving additional sacredness to the *pu'uhonua*. The complex also includes house and temple foundations, many restored with thatched roofs, burial caves, petroglyphs and recreational slides for chiefs, all nestling along a palm-fringed shoreline.

There were two ways for those wishing sanctuary to reach the *pu'uhonua* – by foot from the south or by water from the north. Those from the north had to swim or canoe in, since the high chief resided on that side and commoners were forbidden to set foot on royal grounds.

After Kamehameha II abolished the *kapu* system in 1819, there was no more reason for *pu'uhonua* to exist. For-

tunately, a few have been preserved to serve as a reflection of Hawaii's heritage and a link to its past.

Many of the arts and skills of old Hawaii are revived and practiced in the royal setting at Pu'uhonua o Honaunau. Visitors can watch as the *tapa* (bark cloth) is pounded, the *lauhala* (pandanus leaf) is woven into baskets or mats, or as capes, leis and helmets are made from feathers.

The park's annual three-day cultural festival is held on the weekend closest to July 1, the park's establishment date. Visitors can try their hand at *lauhala* weaving, lei making, *poi* pounding, making fish nets, or even helping to pull in the big fish net during a *hukilau* (fishing festival). The royal court, dressed in feather cloaks and helmets made during the year at the park, preside over the festivities.

On the first Friday in February and November, Hawaiian sports are the focus

*Above: Hawaiian face in Kohala. Right: One of many Big Island world-class golf courses.*

of Pu'uhonua o Honaunau's day-long **La Pa'ani celebration** (coming together for sports and games). Visitors can watch Kona school children compete in such Hawaiian sports as dart sliding, arm wrestling and spear throwing.

The **Mamalahoa Highway** south from Honaunau crosses several twentieth-century lava flows, including flows from 1919, 1936 and 1950. The **Kipahoehoe National Area Reserve** about 16 miles (26 km) from Honaunau protects the returning vegetation and wildlife of one such flow. Just inside the boundary of the Ka'u district is the **Manuka State Wayside,** with a botanical garden and picnic area.

## KOHALA COAST

**Kohala** is best known to tourists as the location of the Big Island's most extravagant resorts – the Mauna Kea Beach Hotel, the Hyatt Regency Waikoloa, the Mauna Lani Resort.

But there is more, much more. This is the cradle of modern Hawaiian history – the birthplace of King Kamehameha the Great, and the place from which he set off on his conquest of the entire chain. And, remarkably, it's the location of America's second largest cattle ranch!

Driving northward along the Queen Kaahumanu Highway from Kailua, travelers enter the Kohala district at **Anaeho'omalu**, a popular state park with a white-sand beach that curves between a turquoise bay and an ancient fish pond.

The Waikoloa Beach resort community is along this strand, including the spectacular **Hyatt Regency Waikoloa** hotel, **The Royal Waikoloan** hotel and the **Aston Shores at Waikoloa** condominium resort.

The Hyatt is a veritable Disneyland of the Pacific. It should be: it's the most expensive resort ever built, with a price tag of $360,000,000. Upon 62 oceanfront acres (25 hectares) of what was once a

vaste bleak, black lava desert, Hyatt constructed a matchless self-contained fantasy world.

The resort's 1,241 guest rooms (in three towers) surround a tropical garden interlaced with lagoons and waterways. Guests not in the mood to walk from their rooms to any of the seven restaurants or the huge health spa can take a monorail or a Venetian-like gondola (on an underwater track). Those who do walk will find the mile of hallways adorned with museum-quality artwork from Asia and the Pacific.

There are three 18-hole golf courses designed by Robert Trent Jones Jr.; and a free-form swimming pool, nearly an acre in size, with waterfalls, twisting water slides and a hidden grotto bar. And, of course, there are all the things you'd find at any major oceanside resort – snorkeling and swimming, tennis and horseback riding, a huge health club and expansive conference facilities, for instance.

But the Hyatt has one more feature that no other hotel can boast – not dancing with wolves, but swimming with dolphins – a truly magical experience.

Eight Atlantic bottle-nosed dolphins, under the care of two marine-mammal specialists, cavort in their private lagoon. Hotel guests draw lots for the opportunity to spend a half-hour in the water with the creatures. Special times are set up just for children.

The adjacent hotel, the Royal Waikoloan, a former Sheraton property with 543 rooms, is built on a beautiful beach around historic royal fishponds and amidst petroglyph fields. A historic walking tour is offered from the hotel, but the rich heritage of the region is even more obvious from the next hotel complex to the north, **Mauna Lani Resort.**

Hawaii's largest fields of petroglyphs – simple images carved in stone that tell how the ancients lived, fished, played and communicated – are found in the South Kohala and North Kona districts. Most often, they are clustered in protected settings near caves. Mauna Lani's historic park, which centers around the

165

Kalahuipua'a fishponds, contains a remarkable cave complex where ancient Hawaiians lived, worshipped, and buried their dead between the thirteenth and seventeenth centuries. Ancient burial sites have been sealed and camouflaged to discourage vandalism, but a walking trail passes large shelter caves with skylights, cross-ventilation openings, tool-manufacturing areas, even a one-of-a-kind petroglyph of a helmeted Hawaiian warrior. Mullet, milkfish and native red shrimp are raised in 15 acres (6 hectares) of ponds, today's finest examples of working Hawaiian fishponds.

The Mauna Lani Resort, though a far cry from the Hyatt's fantasy land, is no slouch in the resort business. It boasts a 354-room hotel and another 466 condominium units, along with six restaurants and outstanding golf, tennis and beach facilities. The new **Ritz-Carlton Mauna Lani** adds another 542 guest rooms.

*Above: Guests get a chance to swim with the dolphins at the Hyatt Regency Waikoloa.*

Oldest and, to many, most esteemed of the Kohala Coast resort hotels is the **Mauna Kea Beach Hotel,** built by Laurance Rockefeller in 1964. Still consistently ranked as the No. 1 resort in Hawaii, it continues to set a standard by which other island resorts are judged. The hotel has a marvelous beach, golf and tennis facilities considered among the best in the world, five outstanding restaurants, and an original Rockefeller collection of Asian and Pacific art.

### Historic North Kohala

The 8 miles (13 km) from Waikoloa to the Mauna Kea Beach Hotel offer modern oases amidst a black-lava desert. When leaving the Mauna Kea, you also leave the twentieth century. The Queen Kaahumanu Highway offers access to a rocky brushland that conceals Hawaii's best preserved and most valuable archaeological sites.

Among them is **Pu'ukohola Heiau National Historical Site** at Kawaihae, near the origin of the Akoni Pule Highway (Highway 270). This hilltop temple was built in 1791 to honor Kuka'ilimoku, the family war god of Kamehameha I. The great ruler worshipped and offered human sacrifices at the altar here before setting out on his voyage of conquest. This old complex once included carved wooden images and thatched houses, but all that remains today is the massive stone platform on the hill, Kawaihae's most imposing presence.

Twelve miles (19 km) north of Kawaihae is the ancient seaside village of **Lapakahi**, Hawaii's only state historical park. Guides (or self-guided trails) lead visitors through the 600-year-old fishing village. Stone implements, game boards, canoe sheds, house sites and shrines tell the story of a hardy, resourceful people who sought shelter among the barren coves and gleaming coral beaches of Lapakahi. Also a part of Lapakahi State Historical Park, but further up the road, are **King Kamehameha's birthplace** and **Mo'okini Heiau.** A bumpy dirt road past Upolu Airfield leads to both. The *heiau*, believed to have been constructed some time about A.D. 480 , was a temple where royalty fasted, prayed and offered human sacrifices to their gods – principally the war god, Ku. It stands on an isolated hillside enveloped in silence and solemnity. The temple is built of waterworn basalt rocks, and is said to have been constructed in a single night by a human chain which passed the rocks from the Pololu Valley, 14 miles (22 km) distant. Kamehameha was born 1,000 ft (300 m) from the *heiau*, the first Hawaiian site on the National Registry of Historic Sites.

**Hawi** and other small towns of North Kohala are surrounded by thick green fields and sugar mills that have seen better days. They recall the era of King Cane, when five sugar plantations supported life in Kohala. Today, only an occasional field of waving cane breaks the

pastureland, but small sugar communities such as Hawi carry on, their clapboard houses fronted by tidy lawns, their "dry goods" and "general merchandise" stores open for business.

East of Hawi lies **Kapa'au**. In front of the North Kohala Civic Center stands the original **King Kamehameha Statue**, cast in Florence, Italy in 1880 and given to the island by its American sculptor. Lost at sea, the statue was salvaged and restored only after a replica – the much-photographed tourist favorite in front of the Judiciary Building in downtown Honolulu – had been commissioned and elaborately unveiled. Today the original appropriately reigns near Kamehameha's birthplace.

One of North Kohala's important spiritual landmarks is the **Kalahikiola Congregational Church,** built at Kapa'au in 1855 by the Rev. Elias Bond, a New England missionary. After gales destroyed the first thatched houses of worship raised by Bond in 1841, his Hawaiian congregation carried sand in tattered

bags, coral in canoes, and stones on their shoulders to rebuild the church. Kalahikiola has since weathered earthquakes and storms, and it stands as a monument to Bond and the faith of his congregation. Restored in 1973, the church is set at the end of a graceful carriage road with a canopy of royal palms and Norfolk pine. Its gleaming white exterior is matched by a spotless interior, brightened by window views of Kapa'au and the Kohala hills.

Continuing eastward now, it becomes obvious that rainfall is more and more plentiful. Pasturelands turn into woods and the quiet stretch of road encourages you to slow down and enjoy the intrigue of a native Hawaiian forest.

**Greenbank,** the 1850 estate of Scottish doctor-botanist James Wight, is located near the community of Halawa, near the end of the road. Wight, who was shipwrecked here, wound up bringing Hawaii its first orchids and ironwood

*Above: The landscape around Hawi includes this type of pastoral, agrarian scene.*

trees. The private estate today has more than 22 acres (9 hectares) of botanical gardens, an arboretum and lowland tropical rainforest encompassing ancient taro fields.

Kohala calls every inviting cove or sandy beach a park, and such scenic spots are quite numerous. **Hapuna State Beach Park** is famed for swimming, bodysurfing and picnicking. **Spencer Beach Park** is ideal for family outings with its camping and cooking facilities. **Mahukona Beach Park,** once a sugar-shipping port, and **Kapa'a Beach Park** are excellent for fishing and snorkeling. One of the loveliest, **Keokea Beach Park**, is set on a grassy flat overlooking a small bay near the end of Highway 270.

The view from the car window is only an introduction to the majestic **Pololu Valley** and its famous "hanging cliffs." A trail leads from the parking area and lookout to the black sand beach below, about a 30-minute walk. Plan for a picnic here. More difficult trails penetrate further valleys and offer lovely views.

The best way to see this spectacular **Hamakua Coast** is to take a 50-minute helicopter flight from Keahole Airport or Waikoloa. Among the most experienced operators is **Kenai Helicopters.** Tours cross the Kohala Mountains from Parker Ranch and trace the coastline from Pololu to Waipi'o.

## Cattle Country

Backtracking to Hawi, take the Kohala Mountain Road (Highway 25) south about 20 miles (32 km) through the Kohala Mountains to **Kamuela**, the center of Hawaii's cattle industry.

Ironwoods line the two-lane highway and windbreaks of Norfolk pine and eucalyptus shelter the highland livestock. Stone fences stretch across fields, recalling the days when labor was more plentiful than barbed wire. At this 2,000-ft (650 m) elevation, a panorama unfolds from sometimes snow-capped Mauna Kea to the crashing surf and to Mount Haleakala on Maui.

**Kamuela**, also known as Waimea, owes its bustling life to 250,000-acre (100,000 hectare) **Parker Ranch**, one of the largest in America under individual ownership. John Palmer Parker, a Massachusetts sailor who arrived in Hawaii in 1809, established his ranch around 1815 from stock descended from wild cattle landed by the English Captain George Vancouver.

Mexican, Portuguese and Indian cowboys, known as *paniolos* (the Hawaiian pronunciation of "Espanol"), arrived in the 1830s. They taught the trade of cowpunching and shared stories, serenades and a lifestyle. They made a lasting impression as Hawaiian folk heroes.

The Parker Ranch Visitor Center provides a narrated slide show of the ranch and the Hawaiian cowboy's life, along with a museum of Hawaiiana and Parker Ranch memorabilia. Check here also for information on visiting the **Puuopelu**

**Gallery,** which offers the fine art collection of ranch owner Richard Smart, a descendant of John Parker. Adjacent is the original Parker house, which Smart has moved from the old Mana homestead.

Kamuela is a regional shopping center. Houses have frostings of gingerbread woodwork and yards are filled with flowers. This was home to Protestant missionary Lorenzo Lyons. Lyons' **Imiola Church**, built in 1857 and restored several times since, has a typical New England spire that seems oddly at home in the green hills of Kohala.

## HAMAKUA DISTRICT

The Hamakua District is small but remarkable. It certainly offers Hawaii's greatest elevation difference – from the 13,796-foot (4,205m) summit of Mauna Kea to the palm-fringed Hamakua Coast line in just 18 miles (29 km). Its historical perspective is equally dramatic, ranging from the centuries-old taro-farming colonies of the Waipi'o and Waimanu valleys to the state-of-the-art astronomical observatories atop Mauna Kea.

Most of the coastal strip retains the ambience of old sugar plantation towns. Wood-frame churches, vintage movie theaters, houses with iron roofs and a dog in every yard are part of the village atmosphere of another time.

Traveling north from Hilo on Highway 19, **Laupahoehoe Point** marks your arrival in Hamakua. This finger of lava that juts into the Pacific is beauty and poignancy in one. The well-tended picnic grounds and the peaceful whisper of the waves belie the violence that wrecked the area nearly half a century ago. Memories of the devastating 1946 tidal wave that rolled over a nearby school, killing 20 young children and four teachers, are still fresh in the minds of the local people. Today, a monument stands at the ocean's edge, a commemoration of the lives that were lost in nature's wrath.

**Kalopa State Recreation Area** contains 600 acres (240 hectares) of majestic *ohia*, eucalypatus and *koa* forests on the lower slopes of Mauna Kea. Picnic areas, drinking water and restrooms are on the grounds, as well as camping facilities for those willing to rough it, and cabins for those not so adventurous.

**Honokaa,** a quiet plantation town, is generally hailed as the macadamia nut capital of the world. The first macadamia nut trees in Hawaii were planted in Honokaa over a century ago in 1881, but the macadamia nut title comes more from the **Hawaiian Holiday Macadamia Nut Company** that is based in Honokaa. The company's factory retail store (open 9am to 6pm daily) offers free samples as well as a view of candy-making and nut-processing in the factory next door. The way to the factory is marked by a series of "nutty" signs from downtown Honokaa.

*Above: Observatories dot the summit of Mauna Kea. Right: A snow-capped cinder cone atop Mauna Kea.*

It is only fitting that **Waipi'o Valley**, once a favorite spot of Hawaiian royalty, is often called the Valley of Kings. From a black sand bay at its mouth, Waipi'o runs back 6 miles (10 km) between the vertical 2,000-ft (600 m) cliffs of the Kohala Mountains. At its head, twin 1,200-ft (360 m) waterfalls tumble into the valley.

Historians estimate that as many as 40,000 Hawaiians lived in Waipi'o in the centuries preceding Captain Cook's arrival in 1778. Nowadays, the pastoral valley is only sparsely populated by a few dozen taro farmers and other families reluctant to give up the simplicity and beauty of Waipi'o and the Hawaii of yesteryear. These residents live in virtual seclusion amid an abundance of wild fruit and colorful birds, enduring tsunami, storms and floods.

Helicopter tours allow a bird's-eye view of the Waipi'o and neighboring valleys. You can also view this magnificent piece of nature from a lookout point, or proceed by the **Waipio Valley Shuttle** into the valley itself for a guided tour.

## "White Mountain"

It's possible to access **Mauna Kea** from Honokaa via a series of dirt roads, but these – like the Keanakolu Road and the Kahinahina Trail – are best left to those equipped with four-wheel drive vehicles. Most visitors to Polynesia's highest point approach it from Highway 200, the somewhat less strenuous Saddle Road between Hilo and Kohala.

Ancient Hawaiians dubbed the state's highest elevation *mauna kea*, "white mountain," for the snow that blankets its peak in winter. Hardy skiers, most of them transplanted mainlanders longing for a little taste of winter, or members of the armed services stationed on Oahu, often test their skills here between January and March – renting four-wheel-drives in Hilo, as there are no lifts on the mountain. But these outdoor types must be cautious, and not just of the usual injuries: The direct sunlight at this height, reflected off the snowy surface, can severely burn unprotected eyes and lips,

so it is advisible to wear glacier glasses protected at the side as well. What's more, ascending too quickly from sea level can bring on elevation sickness. It's wise to pause overnight at the state-owned Pohakuloa cabins at **Mauna Kea State Recreation Area,** on the Saddle Road at 6,500-ft (1,980 m).

All the astronomers who work atop Mauna Kea live in the **Ellison S. Onizuka Astronomy Complex** at 9,200 ft (2,800 m), named for the U.S. astronaut – and Big Island native – killed in the explosion of the *Challenger* space shuttle in 1986.

Eight major observatories, flying the flags of the United States, Canada, the Netherlands, France and Great Britain, sit atop Mauna Kea. Japan plans to join the summit meeting in 1994. The $85 million W.M. Keck telescope, built in 1991 by the California Institute of Technology, is the largest in the world.

Measured from the adjacent ocean floor, Mauna Kea measures 32,000 ft (9,750 m), higher than Mount Everest.

## BIG ISLAND
(All local area telephone codes are 808)

### Hilo-Puna
#### Accommodation
*MODERATE:* **Hawaii Naniloa Hotel,** 93 Banyan Dr., Hilo 96720, Tel: 969-3333. **Hilo Hawaiian Hotel,** 71 Banyan Dr., Hilo 96720, Tel: 935-9361. **Uncle Billy's Hilo Bay Hotel,** 87 Banyan Dr., Hilo 96720, Tel: 935-0861. *BUDGET:* **Country Club Hotel,** 121 Banyan Dr., Hilo 96720, Tel: 935-7171. **Hilo Bay Youth Hostel,** 311 Kalanianole Ave., Hilo 96720, Tel: 935-1383. **Lanikai Hotel,** 100 Puueo St., Hilo 96720, Tel: 935-5556.

#### Attractions
**Akaka Falls State Park,** Honomu, 15 miles N of Hilo. **East Hawaii Cultural Center,** 141 Kalakaua St., Hilo, Tel: 961-5711. **Hawaii Tropical Botanical Garden,** Onomea Bay, 7 miles N of Hilo, Tel: 964-5233. **Hilo Tropical Gardens,** 1477 Kalanianaole Ave., Hilo. **Kaumana Caves,** Waianuenue Ave., 5 miles W of Hilo. **Kumukahi Lighthouse,** Cape Kumukahi, 10 miles E of Pahoa. **Liliuokalani Park and Coconut Island,** Banyan Dr., Hilo. **Lyman Mission House & Museum,** 276 Haili St., Hilo, Tel: 935-5021. **Mauna Loa Macadamia Nut Mill,** Macadamia Road, Kea'au, Tel: 966-8612. **Nani Mau Gardens,** 421 Makalika St., Pana'ewa, Hilo, Tel: 959-9442. **Pana'ewa Rainforest Zoo & Equestrian Center,** Stainback Hwy. S of Hilo. **Rainbow Falls,** Waianuenue Ave. W of Hilo. **Wailoa Culture and Visitor Center,** Hilo Lagoon, Hilo, Tel: 961-7360.

#### Restaurants
*AMERICAN:* **Fiascos,** Kanoelehua Ave. near Waiakea Square, Hilo, Tel: 935-7666. **Ken's House of Pancakes,** 1730 Kamehameha Ave., Hilo, Tel: 935-8711. *CAJUN:* **Roussels,** Bishop Trust Building, 60 Keawe St., Hilo, Tel: 935-5111. *CHINESE:* **Sun Sun Lau,** 1055 Kinoole St., Hilo, Tel: 935-2808. **Ting Hao Mandarin,** Puainako Town Center, Hilo, Tel: 959-6288. *CONTINENTAL:* **Capers,** 235 Keawe St., Hilo, Tel: 935-8801. **Harrington's,** 135 Kalanianole Ave. at Banyan Dr., Hilo, Tel: 961-4966. *JAPANESE:* **Nihon Restaurant & Cultural Center,** 123 Lihiwai St., Hilo, Tel: 969-1133. *STEAK AND SEAFOOD:* **Reflections,** Hilo Lagoon Center, 101 Aupuni St., Hilo, Tel: 935-8501.

#### Tourist Information
**Hawaii Visitors Bureau,** Suite 105, Hilo Plaza, 180 Kinoole St., Hilo 96720, Tel: 961-5797.

### Volcano-Ka'u
#### Accommodation
*LUXURY:* **Colony One at Seamountain,** (P.O. Box 460), Pahala 96777, Tel: 928-6200. **Seamountain at Punalu'u,** (P.O. Box 70), Pahala 96777, Tel: 928-8301, 800-367-8047 ext. 145. *MODERATE:* **Kilauea Lodge,** (P.O. Box 116), Volcano 96785, Tel: 967-7366. **Volcano House,** (P.O. Box 53), Hawaii Volcanoes National Park, Volcano 96718, Tel: 967-7321. *BUDGET:* **Shirakawa Motel,** (P.O. Box 467), Naalehu 96772, Tel: 929-7462. **Volcano Bed & Breakfast,** 19-3950 Keonelehua St., (P.O. Box 22), Volcano 96785, Tel: 967-7779, 800- 733-7713.

#### Attractions
**Akatsuka Orchid Gardens,** Volcano Hwy., Glenwood, Tel: 967-7660. **Hawaii Volcanoes National Park,** Volcano, Tel: 967-7643. **Thomas A. Jaggar Museum,** Crater Rim Drive, Tel: 967-7643. **Ka Lae, South Point,** 11 miles, S of Mamalahoa Hwy. **Ka'u Center of History and Culture,** Punalu'u. **Punalu'u Black Sand Beach Park,** Punalu'u. **Mark Twain Monkeypod Tree,** Naalehu. **Volcano Art Center,** Volcano, Tel: 967-7511. **Waha'ula Heiau,** S end Chain of Craters Rd., Hawaii Volcanoes NP.

#### Restaurants
*AMERICAN:* **Seamountain Broiler,** Seamountain at Punalu'u, Hwy. 11, Pahala, Tel: 928-6222. *CONTINENTAL:* **Ka Ohelo Dining Room,** Volcano House, Hawaii Volcanoes National Park, Tel: 967-7321.

### Kona
#### Accommodation
*LUXURY:* **Kona Hilton Beach & Tennis Resort,** 75-5852 Ali'i Dr., (P.O. Box 1179), Kailua-Kona 96740, Tel: 329- 3111. **Kona Surf Resort & Country Club,** 78-128 Ehukai St., Kailua-Kona 96740, Tel: 322-3411. **Kona Village Resort,** Ka'upulehu, (P.O. Box 1299), Kailua-Kona 96740, Tel: 325-5555. *MODERATE:* **Holualoa Inn,** bed and breakfast, Mamalahoa Hwy., (P.O. Box 222), Holualoa 96725, Tel: 324-1121. **Hotel King Kamehameha,** 75-5660 Palani Rd., Kailua-Kona 96740, Tel: 329-2911. **Keauhou Beach Hotel,** 78-6740 Ali'i Dr., Kailua- Kona 96740, Tel: 322-3441. *BUDGET:* **Adrienne's Bed & Breakfast,** 85-4577 Mamalahoa Hwy., Route 1, Box 8E, Captain Cook 96704, Tel: 328- 9726, 800-328-9726. **Kona Lodge & Hostel,** (P.O. Box 645), Kealakekua 96750, Tel: 322-9056. **Manago Hotel,** (P.O. Box 145), Captain Cook 96704, Tel: 323-2642.

## Attractions

**Ahu'ena Heiau,** Hotel King Kamehameha, Kailua-Kona, Tel: 329-2911. **Captain Cook Coffee Co.,** Captain Cook, Tel. 328-9795. **Hawaiian Mountain Gold Coffee Plantation,** Holualoa, Tel: 322-6713. **Hikiau Heiau and Captain Cook Memorial,** Kealakekua Bay. **Hulihe'e Palace,** 75-5718 Ali'i Dr., Kailua-Kona, Tel: 329-1877. **Kona Art Center,** Holualoa. **Kona Historical Society Museum,** Kealakekua, Tel: 323-3222. **Mac Farms of Hawaii,** Captain Cook, Tel: 328-2435. **Mokuaikaua Church,** Ali'i Drive, Kailua-Kona. **Natural Energy Laboratory of Hawaii,** Keahole Point, Tel: 329-0648. **Pu'uhonua o Honaunau National Historical Park,** Honaunau, Tel: 328-2326. **St. Benedict's Painted Church,** Honaunau. **Wakefield Botanical Gardens,** Honaunau, Tel: 328-9930.

## Restaurants

*AMERICAN:* **Kona Ranch House,** 75-5653 Ololi St., Kailua-Kona, Tel: 329-7061.
*CHINESE:* **Royal Jade Garden,** Lanihau Center, Palani Rd., Kailua-Kona, Tel: 326-7288.
*FRENCH:* **La Bourgogne,** Kuakini Plaza South, 77-6400 Nalani St., Kailua-Kona, Tel: 329-6711.
*HAWAIIAN:* **Manago Hotel,** Mamalahoa Hwy., Captain Cook, Tel: 323-2642.
*INDONESIAN:* **Cafe Sibu,** Kona Banyan Court, Ali'i Dr., Tel: 329-1112.
*INTERNATIONAL:* **The Beach Club at Kona by the Sea,** Kailua-Kona, Tel: 329-3743.
*JAPANESE:* **Kanazawa Tei,** 75-5845 Alii Dr. Kailua-Kona, Tel: 326-1881. **Teshima Inn,** Kealakekua, Tel: 322-9140.
*MEXICAN:* **Kona Amigos,** 75-5669 Alii Dr., Kailua-Kona, Tel: 326-2840.
*STEAKS AND SEAFOOD:* **Jameson's by the Sea,** 77-6452 Ali'i Dr., Kailua-Kona, Tel: 329-3195. **The Pottery,** Kuakini Hwy. at Walua Rd., S of Kailua-Kona, Tel: 329-2277.
*THAI:* **Poo Ping,** 75-5744 Ali'i Dr., Kailua-Kona

## Tourist Information

**Hawaii Visitors Bureau,** 75-5719 W. Alii Dr., Kailua-Kona 96740, Tel: 329-7787.

## Kohala
### Accommodation

*LUXURY:* **Hyatt Regency Waikoloa,** 1 Waikoloa Beach Dr., Kohala Coast 96743, Tel: 885-1234. **Mauna Kea Beach Hotel,** 1 Mauna Kea Beach Dr., Kohala Coast 96743, Tel: 882-7222. *MODERATE:* **The Royal Waikoloan,** HCR 2, Box 500, Kohala Coast 96743, Tel: 885-6789. **Waikoloa Villas,** Lua Kula Dr., (P.O. Box 3498), Waikoloa Village Station, Kamuela

96743, Tel: 883-9144. *BUDGET:* **Kamuela Inn,** (P.O. Box 1994), Kamuela 96743, Tel: 885-4243. **Parker Ranch Lodge,** (P.O. Box 458), Kamuela 96743, Tel: 885-4100.

## Attractions

**Greenbank Estate,** Halawa, Tel: 883-9254. **Hapuna Beach State Park,** Kawaihae. **Kamuela Museum,** Wai'aka, Tel: 885-4724. **Kamehameha's Birthplace,** Upolu Point. **Kalahikiola Congregational Church,** Kapa'au. **King Kamehameha Statue,** Kapa'au. **Koai'e Cove State Underwater Park,** Lapakahi. **Lapakahi State Historical Park,** Kapa'au, Tel: 889-5566. **Mauna Lani petroglyph fields,** Mauna Lani Resort, Tel: 885-6677. **Mo'okini Heiau,** Upolu Point. **Parker Ranch Visitor Center,** Kamuela, Tel: 885-7655. **Pololu Valley Lookout,** Halawa. **Pu'ukhola Heiau National Historical Site,** Kawaihae, Tel: 882-7218. **Puuopelu and Mana Home,** Parker Ranch, Tel: 885-7655, 10am-3pm Fri-Sat and Mon.

## Restaurants

*AMERICAN:* **Don's Family Deli,** Kapa'au, Tel: 889-5822. *CONTINENTAL:* **Bree Garden,** Kinohou St., Kamuela, Tel: 885-5888. *GERMAN:* **Edelweiss,** Kamuela, Tel: 885-6800. *HAWAIIAN:* **Merriman's,** Opelo Plaza, Kamuela, Tel: 885-6822. *ITALIAN:* **Cafe Pesto,** Kawaihae, Tel: 882-1071. *STEAKS AND SEAFOOD:* **Waimea Corral,** Parker Ranch Shopping Center, Kamuela, Tel: 885-7366.

## Hamakua
### Accommodation

*LUXURY:* **The Treehouse,** Waipio Valley, (P.O. Box 5086), Honokaa 96727. Tel: 775-9518. *BUDGET:* **Hotel Honokaa Club,** (P.O. Box 185), Honokaa 96727, Tel: 775-0678 or 775-0533. **Waipio Wayside Bed & Breakfast Inn,** Waipio Overlook, (P.O. Box 840), Honokaa 96727. Tel: 775-0275.

## Attractions

**Hawaiian Holiday Macadamia Nut Co.,** Honokaa, Tel: 775-7255. **Kalopa State Recreation Area,** near Honokaa. **Kipuka 'Ainahou State Nene Sanctuary,** Saddle Road, Mauna Kea. **Laupahoehoe Beach Park,** Laupahoehoe. **Mauna Kea Observatory,** summit of Mauna Kea, Tel: 935-7606 or 935-3371. **Mauna Kea State Recreation Area,** Saddle Road, Mauna Kea. **Waipio Valley Lookout and Shuttle,** Kukuihaele, Tel: 775-7121.

## Restaurants

*AMERICAN:* **Herb's Place,** Main St., Honokaa, Tel: 775-0668. *ITALIAN:* **Honokaa Pizza & Subs,** Main St., Honokaa, Tel: 775-9966.

# KAUAI

**LIHUE**

**POIPU**

**WEST KAUAI**

**WAIMEA CANYON**

**HANALEI**

**NIIHAU**

The two-lane coastal highway that meanders around perhaps 80% of Kauai traditionally has been "the road less traveled" by visitors to the Hawaiian Islands. Yet the Garden Isle is considered the most beautiful and lush in the chain.

Dubbed "the separate kingdom" by historian Ed Joesting, Kauai was the only island not conquered during Kamehameha the Great's unifying drive in 1790. Though Kauai was Captain James Cook's first landfall in 1778, it is only recently that many visitors have added this unique destination to their itinerary rather than visit Oahu, Maui or the Big Island for a second, third or fourth time.

The beauty of Kauai is legendary. Its velvety mountains look as if some giant's fingers had creased green ridges down sheer sides and, at their bases, sprinkled glistening half-moons of sand around the edges of translucent turquoise bays. Waterfalls cascade off the cliffs of 5,243-ft (1,598 m) Mount Waialeale, touted as the wettest place on earth with a rainfall often measured not in inches, but in feet: 40 ft (12 m) per year is average.

*Preceding pages: The rugged Na Pali Coast wilderness. 16-kilometers accessible only on foot or by boat on Kauai's north coast. Left: Visitors receive a Hawaiian serenade at the Fern Grotto.*

One main highway, numbered 50 to the west and 56 to the east, follows the circular contour of the island. On its northwestern leg, it branches into Highway 550. Roughly horseshoe-shaped on a map, the road ends in the northwest at Kokee State Park, where backpackers begin the trek inland into Waimea Canyon, sometimes called the "Grand Canyon of the Pacific." Over the same ridge, on the north rim of the island, is the lush, green Kalalau Valley.

The eastern spur of the horseshoe highway runs through the little towns of Kapaa, Kilauea and Hanalei, and ends at Ke'e Beach, trailhead for the Kalalau Valley. It's a considerable 11-mile (18 km) backpack between Ke'e Beach and the back of Kalalau to complete a visual circle.

Slightly to the east of the horseshoe's base is Lihue, the hub of Kauai's government and business. The majority of the island's 45,000 residents make their home here.

## Kauai History

Archaeological evidence suggests that Kauai was probably among the first of the islands of the Hawaiian chain to be populated, around A.D. 750, by Polynesians navigating their boats by the stars.

But legend has it that a race of small but industrious people lived on Kauai as many as 300 or 400 years before the Polynesians arrived. These were the shy *menehune*, the exceptional stonemasons who accomplished incredible feats of building during the night, retiring to the cool recesses of the forest by day. It is said that if the rays of the morning sun touched these leprechaun-like people, their 2-ft-tall (61 cm) bodies would immediately turn to stone.

Today, the existence of structures like the **Menehune (Alakoko) Fishpond** is attributed to this mysterious little people. Inland from Nawiliwili Harbor in the Huleia River, a 900-ft-long (275 m) rock wall, 4 ft (1,2 m) high and 5 ft (1,5 m) wide, cuts off a bend of the stream. The wall is said to have been built by the *menehune* to hold fish for a prince and princess, on the condition that no one would watch them as they worked. But the royal couple couldn't resist; they spied on thousands of *menehune* working in the dark of the night. As punishment, they were turned to pillars of stone that can still be seen on the mountainside above the dam. As in early times, mullet are raised in this impressive pond system.

When the Polynesians arrived in the eighth century, they established their villages on the banks of the Wailua River. It was at the birthstones of Wailua that the last ruling king of Kauai, Kaumualii, was born to the chiefess Kamakahelei, fathered by Kaeo, high chief of Maui and king of Kauai. Kaumualii, who became ruler at the age of 16, refused to surrender his kingdom when King Kamehameha I attempted to conquer all the islands in the 1790s. In 1796, intent on victory, Kamehameha sailed from Oahu with an armada of 1,500 war canoes and 10,000 warriors – but he was forced to give up his plans halfway across the Kaieie Waho Channel, when the canoes overturned in waters churned to fury by an unexpected and ferocious storm.

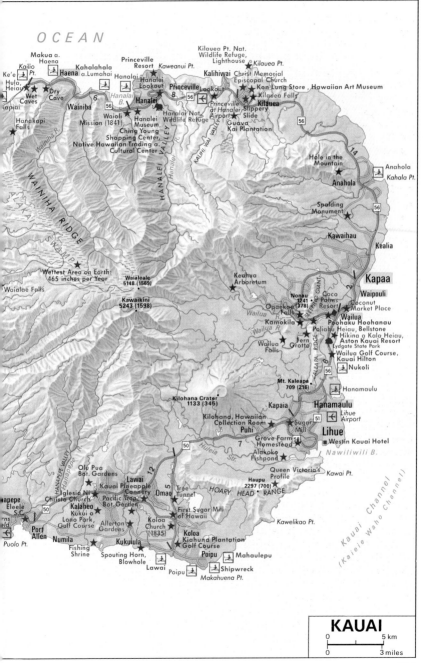

OCEAN

Makua a. Haena
Kahalahala a.Lumahai
Kailio Pt.
Ke'e
Hula, Heiau
Princeville Resort
Kaweanui Pt.
Kilauea Pt. Nat. Wildlife Refuge, Lighthouse
Kilauea Pt.
Haena
Wet Caves
Dry Cave
Wainiha
Hanalai Lookout
Hanalei
56
Hanalei B.
Princeville
8
56
Lookout
Kalihiwai
Christ Memorial Episcopal Church
Kon Lung Store , Hawaiian Art Museum
Kilauea Falls
Kilauea
Kapaia
Hanakapi Falls
Waioli Mission (1841)
Hanalei Museum, Ching Young Shopping Center, Native Hawaiian Trading a. Cultural Center
Hanalei Nat. Wildlife Refuge
Princeville at Hanalei Airport
Guava Kai Plantation
Slippery Slide
56
WAINIHA RIDGE
SWAMP
Hole in the Mountain
Anahola
Kahala Pt.
Anahola
Spalding Monument
56
Waialeale 5148 (1569)
Wettest Area on Earth: 465 inches per Year
Waialae Falls
Kawaihau
Kealia
Kawaikini 5243 (1598)
Keahua Arboretum
Nonau 1241 (378)
Coco Palms Resort
Kapaa
Waipouli
Coconut Market Place
Opaeka'a Falls
Wailua
Poohaku Hoohanau
Paliahu Heiau, Bellstone
Hikina a Kala Heiau, Aston Kauai Resort
Lydgate State Park
Wailua Golf Course, Kauai Hilton
Nukoli
Kamokila
Fern Grotto
Wailua Falls
56
Mt. Kaleapa 709 (216)
Hanamaulu
Kilohana Crater 1133 (345)
Kapaia
Kilohana, Hawaiian Collection Room
Puhi
Grove Farm Homestead
Alakoko Fishpond
Hanamaulu
Sugar Mill
51
Lihue Airport
58
Lihue
Westin Kauai Hotel
50
7
Hueia Str.
Nawiliwili B.
Olu Pua Bot. Gardens
Lawai
Kauai Pineapple Cannery
Pacific Trop. Bot. Garden
Omao
5
Tree Tunnel
Queen Victoria's Profile
Haupu 2297 (700)
HOARY HEAD RANGE
Kawai Pt.
Iglesia Ni Christo Church
Eleele S.C.
Kalaheo
Kukui o Lono Park, Golf Course
Allerton Gardens
First Sugar Mill of Hawaii
Kawelikao Pt.
50
Port Allen
Numila
Koloa Church (1835)
Koloa
Kiahuna Plantation Golf Course
Poipu
Mahaulepu
Kukuiula
Fishing Shrine
Spouting Horn, Blowhole
Lawai
Poipu
Shipwreck
Makahuena Pt.
Puolo Pt.
Kauai Channel (Kaieie Waho Channel)

HANAKAPI VALLEY
HANALEI VALLEY
KALIHI WAI VALLEY
KILAUEA RIDGE
SLEEPING GIANT
KALEPA RIDGE
Wailua R.
Wailua R.
Hanapepe R.
6

**KAUAI**
0 — 5 km
0 — 3 miles

It was eight years before Kamehameha attempted once again to conquer Kauai. In the meantime, Captain Cook had made his first landfall at Waimea, Kauai, on January 18, 1798, in the *HMS Resolution* and *HMS Discovery*. Cook found Kauai "a fair island of good water and friendly people" who traded pigs and fresh produce for the iron nails brought by his men. The ship's artist, John Webber, sketched the huts along the seashore and the nearby *heiau* (stone temple), and five days later Cook moved on to Niihau and eventually to the island of Hawaii.

By the time Kamehameha made his second attempt at quelling the rebellious Kauai populace in 1804, both sides had acquired Western weaponry. Kamehameha had muskets, cannon, swivel guns, several armed schooners and 50 Europeans to aid him and his men. But again, fate intervened. His forces were

literally struck down with fever and hundreds of warriors died.

It wasn't until 1821, after Kamehameha's death, that his successor, Liholiho, actually kidnapped Kaumualii on Kauai and brought him to Oahu, where he was married off to Kaahumanu, Kamehameha's widow. That action established Kauai as part of the united kingdom. Kaumualii died on Oahu three years later.

The subsequent years brought great change to the island. Sandalwood forests were quickly depleted as chiefs traded shiploads of the fragrant wood for Western goods. The missionaries arrived in 1820; the old *kapu* system was discarded and Christianity was embraced; and sugar cane became the mainstay of the economy. The first sugar plantation on Kauai was built at Koloa in 1835. Soon the great swaths of swaying cane required the importation of low-cost indentured labor, establishing the racial mix of Chinese, Japanese, Portuguese and Filipino that exists on Kauai – and on many other islands – today.

*Above: Fast food, oldfashioned style. Right: Mother and child, Hawaiian-style.*

## LIHUE

Kauai's capital retains much of the simplicity of its plantation background. Streets stained with the rich red volcanic earth of the surrounding cane fields are lined with mom-and-pop businesses. Painted wooden storefronts alternate with modern fast-food outlets, banks and other business buildings. Skyscrapers don't exist on Kauai, as early building laws decreed that the height limit could be no taller than the tallest coconut tree.

A good place to start an investigation of the charms of Kauai is at the lava-rock **Kauai Museum**, 4420 Rice St. in the center of the **Lihue** business district. A compact and interesting introduction to island history and culture is offered here. Dioramas, a continuous film presentation, and displays of early artifacts depict the eruption of the single shield volcano that formed the twin peaks of **Waialeale** and **Kawaikini** 60 million years ago. The exhibits trace Kauai's history through the fascinating folklore of the *menehune*, years of fierce warfare, the arrival of the white man, the establishment of sugar plantations and finally statehood.

Much of the history of sugar cane on Kauai can be painlessly absorbed at a pair of graceful plantation estates on the outskirts of Lihue. Both belonged to the Wilcox family, and the restored homes reflect their former grandeur.

**Grove Farm Homestead**'s original plantation house dated to before 1864. The house, its 1915 annex, the plantation office, worker and guest cottages, and 80 acres (32 hectares) of gardens and orchards are open to the public as a working museum. Small groups are guided through the house, located beside Nawiliwili Road, to view the Wilcox family's portraits, furniture and a fine collection of Hawaiian quilts and calabashes. Also displayed are such artifacts as *poi* pounders, adzes and rare *makaloa* mats from Nii-

hau. The tour culminates in the kitchen – located in a detached building, as was common on plantations – where refreshments are served by an elderly woman who was a family servant for more than 40 years. It is wise to write for advance reservations, as tours are given only on Monday, Wednesday and Thursday at 10am and 1pm. Write to P.O. Box 1631, Lihue, HI 96766 (tel. 235-3202). Admission is $3 for adults, $1 for children aged five to twelve.

### Plantation Parties

Drive *mauka* (toward the mountains) on Nawiliwili Road, turning left at Kukui Grove Shopping Center, and watch on your right for another Wilcox family home, **Kilohana**, at 3-2087 Kaumualii Highway. Built in 1835 as the home of Gaylord and Ethel Wilcox, the 35-acre (14-hectare) estate was restored and opened as a shopping, restaurant and theme-party complex in 1987. A visit to Kilohana is pure nostalgia, from the Cly-

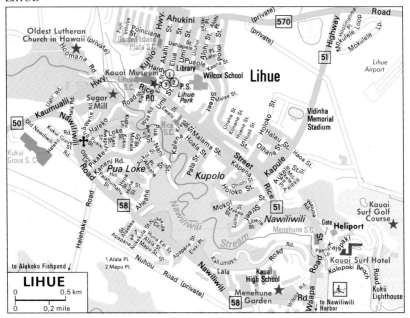

desdale-and-carriage rides offered at its entrance, to the beveled mirrors and original turn-of-the-century furnishings inside. *Al fresco* dining is featured at **Gaylord's,** where the veranda tables all overlook a pleasantly shaded courtyard. A stroll on the pathway that wanders through the grounds takes you past tiny old plantation cottages turned photo studio or stationery shop. A thriving garden is guarded by an old-fashioned scarecrow. Coffee, mango, macadamia nut, papaya and avocado trees flourish.

Groups can choose from eight theme parties including "Murder Mystery," "South Pacific," "Paniolo" (Hawaiian cowboy), and "Polo Party." Even F. Scott Fitzgerald might think the Great Gatsby had returned when players from the Kauai Polo Club gallop across Kilohana's lawn during the 45-minute exhibition game for the Polo Party, while guests savor champagne and hors d'oeuvres.

Inside, the shops carry a wide range of interesting items. **Island Memories** has one-of-a-kind creations from Thailand, Sumatra and Bali. The **Hawaiian Collection Room** features Niihau shell necklaces, rare Hawaiian coins and stamps and more. Each quaint bedroom or sitting room showcases something special: lacquerware, woodblock prints, and *tansu* chests.

Shoppers seeking conventional resort wear, souvenirs, groceries and sundries might prefer to check out the 50 shops and restaurants at nearby **Kukui Grove Center**, 3-2600 Kaumualii Highway. This mall is equipped with all the phenomena of modern travel, including a gas station, a Burger King and a Taco Bell, to speed you on your way. Or if you're more in the mood for local flavor, drop in on the **Hamura Saimin Stand** or the **Tip Top Motel**, which doubles as a restaurant and bakery. (If you do, don't miss out on Tip Top's legendary macadamia-nut cookies.)

Heading east, Kaumualii Highway 50 curves around **Lihue Mill**. The thick aroma of molasses emanates from these rusty tanks and dilapidated buildings, which, in spite of their outside appearance, process much of the cane that covers the island's fields. Here, the highway becomes Kuhio Highway 56.

At the curve, a Hawaiian warrior sign marks Hoomana Road; about 500 ft (150 m) up the hill is the **Lihue Lutheran Church.** In the 1860s, this area was called German Hill because so many Germans – who had been brought in as *lunas* (foremen) for the sugar plantations – settled here. The neat gray-and-white church, built in 1883, has lovely stained-glass windows and a pretty choir loft.

The Nawiliwili Road passes the aforementioned **Alakoko Fishpond** before leading to Kauai's principal commercial harbor, **Nawiliwili Harbor.** The *USS Constitution* and *USS Independence*, two luxury cruise ships of the American Hawaii line, dock here weekly during their journey through the islands. Buses, limousines and taxis transport the ship's passengers to nearby visitors' attractions, shops, hotels and restaurants.

### A Resort Par Excellence

Not far from the harbor is the spectacular **Westin Kauai Resort Hotel**, an 846-room total destination resort. When it opened in 1987, it caused a major furor. Not only did it receive a height variance that allowed its towers to soar to 11 stories; *kamaainas* (long-time residents) lamented the demise of their favorite gathering place, the Kauai Surf Hotel.

Today, however, the Westin Kauai adds a splash of glamour to this comfortable town. The resort has the only escalator on the island, descending with a tunnel-like, Alice-in-Wonderland ambience to emerge beside a huge reflecting pool with water fountains surrounding an enormous sculpture of seven marble horses rearing into the air. Beyond the reception area, overlooking **Kalapaki Beach**, is the most massive continuous swimming pool in the islands. Around its

rim, waterfalls splash next to five smaller, more private alcoves, each of which shelters a Jacuzzi in pillared splendor.

This playground of tropical diversions was the ultimate indulgence of developer Chris Hemmeter, whose spree of whimsy (the Westin Maui, the Grand Hyatt on the Big Island and the newly completed Hyatt Regency Kauai) changed the complexion of island resorts in the late 1980s and early 1990s. Hemmeter constructed a private road from Lihue Airport, five minutes away from the Westin Kauai, so that guests would not add to nor be inconvenienced by the painstakingly plodding traffic through downtown Lihue during morning and afternoon rush hours – a good time to avoid city thoroughfares, by the way.

Two of the island's finest golf courses are located at Westin Kauai Lagoons: the **Kiele Course** and the **Lagoon Course**. Both are renowned for their spectacular settings overlooking both the ocean and miles of specially dredged lagoons.

### POIPU

From Lihue, follow Highway 50 southwest to the popular Poipu resort area. En route, you'll pass the tiny old plantation town of **Puhi** in the shadow of **Queen Victoria's Profile**. Search the Hoary Head Mountains for Haupu Ridge, and with a little stretch of the imagination, you might be able to identify Victoria's head adorned with a crown; a nearby small peak is said to be her finger pointing skyward. Older legends have it that this was the profile of Hina, the goddess mother of Molokai. Hawaiians considered the finger-like peak a phallic stone and believed Hina and the stone were always together because they symbolized male and female. In these mountains grows the *mokihana* berry. Found only on Kauai, these berries intertwined with the *maile* vine comprise the traditional lei of the island.

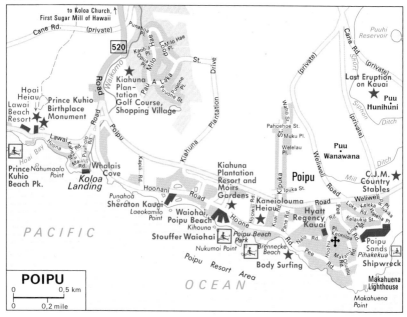

Turn left on Highway 520 to reach **Poipu Beach**. You'll travel through Kauai's famed **Tree Tunnel**, a stretch of road planted on both sides with towering eucalyptus trees. On the aptly named **Maluhia** or Serenity Road, the leafy green canopy of branches overhead creates a cool, peaceful twilight zone on the way to the little plantation town of **Koloa**.

Koloa means "long cane." It was founded by three New Englanders who leased land from Kamehameha III to plant sugar. As Hawaii's first plantation town, it became the mercantile center for Kauai's south side. Both Kauai's first public school and its first doctor's office were established at Koloa. Stroll along the boardwalk fronting the old buildings and you'll find hand-painted resort wear floating in the breeze; a cook-your-own-steak restaurant called the **Koloa Broiler**; **Fez's Pizza**; and toward the end of Main

Street, the **Koloa Ice House and Deli**. This homey establishment offers a shave-ice or ice-cream cone, munch a deli sandwich at an outdoor table, or request picnic fare packed to go.

Before you continue south on Poipu Road, wander back across the street to the ruins of Kauai's **first sugar mill**, built in 1841. Nearby, protected within a curved cement wall, is a vivid monument to plantation laborers sculpted by Oahu artist Jan Fisher. As you continue toward Poipu, on the right you'll see **Koloa Church**, built in 1835.

Koloa was once a lively community serving Koloa Landing, then Kauai's largest seaport. At night, when the trees and buildings glitter with miniature lights and music drifts from **Mango's Tropical Restaurant and Bar**, it's easy to imagine the appeal the soft tropical air and unrestricted lifestyle must have had for early New England immigrants.

It is 3 miles (5 km) from Koloa to the resort area of **Poipu**. You'll see **Kiahuna Golf Course** on the left.

*Right: Princeville offers some of the most spectacular golf anywhere.*

### Hotels and Beaches

Take the left fork in the road, saving the right-hand route until later. Beautifully landscaped areas interspersed with driveways indicate resort entrances; patches of *kiawe* brush spring up before the civilized façade of another hotel presents itself. But don't let the country fool you. Beautiful white-sand beaches, only partially hidden by luxurious but discreetly low-rise hotels, stretch all along this area.

A pleasant stop is the **Kiahuna Plantation Resort and Gardens** (tel. 742-6411), next door to the Sheraton Kauai Hotel. Admission is free to the gardens, the former estate of Hector Moir and his wife. Their house, with its spacious stone-walled lanai, is now the attractive **Plantation Gardens restaurant**. Gardens, landscaped with lava-rock pools, are planted with 4,000 varieties of plants, including orchids and aloes. A free tour is conducted daily at 10am.

On the other side of Poipu Road, golfers will find the **Kiahuna Golf Course** and the casual **Kiahuna Shopping Village**. The Kiahuna Golf Village Restaurant is a low-cost alternative to Sunday-morning brunch at any of the hotels ... though if you want to be thoroughly indulgent, it's fun to dine at the **Stouffer Waiohai Beach Resort** (tel. 742-9511). This buffet feast with champagne deserves many leisurely hours of a diner's attention.

Further along Poipu Road, turn down Honowili to Ho'one Road to find the public beach parks. Across from **Poipu Beach Park**, a pleasant grassy seaside expanse with swings and other playground equipment for children, is **Brennecke's Beach Broiler** (tel. 742-5788). Dining takes place upstairs in this open-sided restaurant with a wonderful ocean view. In addition to the all-American hamburger, fresh fish broiled over *kiawe* wood and exceptional homemade des-

serts are served. You'll want to sample the mango and guava sherbets.

Poipu Beach Park is known for its petroglyphs on the sandstone ledges. Adjacent is **Brennecke's Beach**, a spot you can't miss because every bodysurfer on Kauai eventually has a go at the offshore surf. The beach area is small and attracts more local people than visitors.

If you continue your drive on Poipu Road, you'll come to the new **Hyatt Regency Kauai**. This mind-boggling complex, beautifully conceived by developer Hemmeter, will have a major impact on Kauai's economy. You can't miss the resort's white-stucco buildings with green-tile roofs. Nearby, another elaborate golf course is being developed at the end of what used to be a little-traveled cane road – leading to **C.J.M. Country Stables** (tel. 742-6096). When nearby **Shipwreck Beach** and **Mahaulepu Beach** will become accessible as Poipu Beach Park, all dreams of romantic walks or horseback rides along deserted beaches will disappear.

Shipwreck Beach got its name from the ribs and keel of a wooden ship that lay half-covered with sand until Hurricane Iwa swept the debris into the ocean in November 1982. The hurricane, a rare occurrence in Hawaii, devastated the Poipu area, actually destroying one hotel. Today, there is little evidence of the vicious winds that downed houses and palm trees just a few years ago.

### The Road to Spouting Horn

Retrace your route along Poipu Road and take the right-hand fork from Koloa. You're now on Hoonani Road. Cross over the bridge and stop for a view of **Koloa Landing**. There's not much to see here now, as this rocky little bay was last used as a port in 1928. Until the decline of whaling, it was the third busiest port in the islands.

*Above: The Spouting Horn, Poipu. Right: A fisherman throws his net in traditional Hawaiian style.*

Past **Prince Kuhio Beach Park** and **Lawai Beach** is the most famous visitor attraction at Poipu, **Spouting Horn.** With all the sidewalk vendors next to the parking lot, you can't miss it. Many of these vendors sell intricately woven and very dear Niihau shell necklaces. Otherwise, their wares consist mostly of inexpensive wood and shell jewelry. If you do decide to purchase a Niihau necklace here , ask for an address for repairs, in the event that you should ever crush one of the tiny, rare shells.

Spouting Horn is a rather fascinating geyser that sprays into the air with an eerie moaning sound as the water escapes through an ancient lava tube connected to the ocean. Keep your camera ready, and hope for a day when the waves are big to snap the most dramatic pictures.

If you continue past the maintained road, you'll be at the back entrance to the **Allerton Estate** at Lawai Kai. But little of this beautiful valley can be seen from here. John Greg Allerton was the son of a Chicago millionaire who bought the val-

ley in 1937. Much of the upper valley was McBride sugar-cane land when the Allertons began turning it into gardens to show off the waterfall and ponds that once were part of an early Hawaiian village complete with a *heiau* site and terraces planted in taro. Robert Allerton also was instrumental in establishing the 400-acre (162 hectare) **National Tropical Botanical Garden**. Tours of both gardens can be arranged Monday through Friday. The visitor center is off Koloa Road at the end of Hailima Road.

## WEST KAUAI

To proceed from Poipu to the western part of the island, first of a return to Koloa and prepare for a little back-road exploring. Turn left on Highway 530, which will eventually rejoin the main Highway 50 at Lawai.

Before the roads join, you'll find the defunct **Kauai Pineapple Cannery** on the right. It now houses dozens of souvenir vendors under the auspices of the Hawaiian Trading Post. Juice is free at the entrance or you can get a hot dog from Mustard's Last Stand. Children play a round of miniature golf while Mom and Dad shop.

You might miss **Kalaheo**, the next village on Highway 50, if you blink. So be alert for this partially Portuguese community for the pretty white **Iglesia di Cristo** church. Then, if you've got a picnic lunch, turn left on Papalina Road and climb to **Kukuiolono Park** and golf course.

Kukuiolono, which means "light of the god Lono," was once part of the McBride sugar estate. Now its serene Japanese gardens and rich display of Hawaiian artifacts are overgrown. Still, the view is wonderful and with greens fees at $5, the nine-hole golf course is one of the cheapest to play on Kauai.

Back on Highway 50, you'll find another garden, **Olu Pua Botanical Garden**, marked by a Hawaiian Warrior sign just outside Kalaheo. Olu Pua means "floral serenity." This former pineapple

187

plantation estate has opened 12.5 acres (5 hectares) to public viewing for an admission fee. A guide answers questions as you browse through the Front Lawn, the Jungle and the Kau Kau, Hibiscus, and Palm Gardens. Call (tel. 808/332-8182) to make reservations for tours.

A well-marked look-out at the 14-mile marker on Highway 50 is worth a stop to savor the view of **Hanapepe Valley and Canyon**. The outlines of old *taro* terraces can still be spotted in the brush of this historic valley. Here the last great battle between opposing Hawaiian chiefs took place in 1824. Kaumualii's son, Humehume, revolted against Kamehameha's rule, but was defeated by an army of Liholiho's men from Oahu.

Proceeding west, you'll come upon a turnoff for **Port Allen,** a major port until the 1930s when a breakwater was constructed at Nawiliwili so Kauai's shipping terminal could be closer to Lihue.

*Above: Hanapepe Valley is one of numerous scenic lookouts on a circuit of Kauai.*

**Hanapepe**

Angle to the right on Awawa Road to visit the original main street of the picturesque little town of **Hanapepe**. Once a thriving market town and gathering place because it was an "open" town not owned by the sugar plantations, Hanapepe's glory has faded to dilapidated wooden buildings with peeling paint. But in recent years, *kamaainas* and newcomers are banding together in an effort ,at historic preservation. Neatly painted and restored art galleries (like **James Hoyle's**, pictured in the television mini-series *The Thorn Birds)* stand side-by-side with faded, clapboard structures.

Walk the length of the town for the full dichotomy of old vs. new. Stop by **Longie's Crack Seed Shop** to sample the salty, succulent preserved nuts so popular among island residents, or quench your thirst with a shave-ice (snow-cone). The Hanapepe River runs *mauka* (mountainside) of the main street, and if you slip through an alleyway, you can cross the stream on an impressive suspension bridge once used by Chinese rice farmers in the valley to shorten their walk to town.

Back in your car, continue down the main street, cross over another bridge into the oldest part of town, and turn right up **Hanapepe Valley** for a drive into yesteryear. Pig, taro and truck farmers inhabit this fertile valley, tilling the earth much as the Hawaiians once did.

When Highway 50 was built in 1939, it bypassed Hanapepe town. A spate of businesses were located on the new main street. If you return to the highway the way you came and continue northwest, you'll find three enterprises that are mainstays of the town. At **Kauai Kookies**, Mabel and Norman Hashisaka produce nine varieties of cookies – from Kona coffee to guava macadamia – that visitors from neighboring islands buy to take home to family and friends. **Lappert's Ice Cream** is a relative newcomer, established in 1984 by Walter Lappert, who moved over from the mainland but decided he couldn't bear retirement. Finally, the **Green Garden Restaurant**, a family endeavor since 1948, is a locally favored dining spot known for its *lilikoi* (passion fruit) chiffon pie.

Hanapepe has two other claims to fame. In 1929, the first air travel between the islands was inaugurated by Inter-Island Airways (today's Hawaiian Air) at **Burns Field**. Nowadays the little airport is used mainly by gliders and helicopters. **Niihau Helicopter Tours** (see following chapter) use this field as a base, and **Tradewinds Glider Flights** (tel. 335-5086) offer a quiet, inspiring flight over beaches and mountains – wind permitting.

Helicopter tours, by the way, are a popular way to see the hidden beauty of Kauai. Helicopters depart from Lihue, Princeville and Burns Field. Three reputable owner-operated companies are **Jack Harter Helicopters** (tel. 245-

3774), **Preston Myers Safari Helicopter Tours** (tel. 246-1036), and **Will Squyres Helicopter Service** (tel. 245-7541).

## The Salt Ponds

In summer, the red mud flats next to the Burns Field airstrip become a maze of shallow square wells, or salt pans, carefully dug in the same location year after year after year, dating all the way back to before Captain Cook's landing. Salt water seeps into these wells and, as it evaporates, a coarse salt, milder than iodized rock salt, piles up. Board of Health rules do not allow the sale of this salt, but anyone may go and talk to resident gatherers, who certainly won't object if you want a taste. **Salt Pond Beach Park** preserves this stretch of shoreline.

Captain Cook actually replenished his ship's stores with Hanapepe salt when he anchored at Waimea Bay – by today's **Lucy Wright Beach Park**, just offshore of **Waimea**, the next town along Highway 50. As you pass through town, you'll see a statue of the illustrious British sea captain in a small grassy park to the right of the highway. In town, **Kashuba Fine Arts and Gifts International** (tel. 338-1750) supports a mini-museum with exhibits and a video detailing the life of Captain Cook.

Before the park, stand the ruins of the **Russian Fort,** or Fort Elisabeth, to the left of the road. The fort was built in 1815 by Dr. Georg Anton Shaeffer, who hoped to convince Kaumualii to turn over Kauai to Russia in return for protection against Kamehameha's invading forces. As it turned out, Russia decided against the deal. The walls, still 12 ft (3,5 m) high in some places, can be scaled for a vantage point view of the circular enclosure. Entry to the fort is free, as is the use of the well-maintained on-site toilets.

A walking-tour map of Waimea town can be obtained at the Waimea Branch Library (on the ocean side of the highway).

189

It details such points of interest as the **Waimea Foreign Church**, built in 1845 of sandstone blocks, and the coral-block **Gulick-Rowell House**, an example of early missionary architecture.

Drive inland on Menehune Road a couple of miles, and stop at the suspension bridge. Across the road is a portion of **Kiki a Ola**, the "Menehune Ditch." Archaeologists say this stone was cut and fitted together in a way unknown to Hawaiians, and in fact, its construction probably predates the Polynesians' arrival. In 1793, Captain George Vancouver described the wall as being 24 ft (7,3 m) above the level of the river and 20 ft (6 m) thick at its base. The construction of the road destroyed this view of the ditch, but the water still courses along the stone waterway whose construction, for want of a better explanation, is ascribed to the industrious *menehune*.

*Above: The beautiful depths of Waimea Canyon. Right: Kalalau Valley from the lookout in Kokee State Park.*

An interior route, Highway 550, leads to Waimea Canyon from here. But it is easier to follow Highway 50 to **Kekaha** and turn inland there on Kokee Road, saving the less-traveled and rougher Waimea Canyon Road for the return.

Highway 50 goes beyond Kekaha, past **Barking Sands Beach**, the Pacific Missile Range facility, to a dead-end at **Polihale State Park**. Framed by sheer cliffs, this unspoiled white-sand beach is never crowded. Swimming can be dangerous because of strong southern currents and pounding surf, so take to the water with extreme care.

## WAIMEA CANYON

It is about 19 miles (31 km) from Kekaha to the last lookout over Kalalau Valley. Along the way, there are numerous viewpoints into **Waimea Canyon**. Kokee Road traverses the 1,800-acre (728 hectare) **Waimea Canyon State Park** and 4,345-acre (1,758 hectare) **Kokee State Park**. This road ultimately reaches the 4,120-ft (1,255 m) elevation of Kalalau Lookout. Temperatures can be nippy, especially when the mists roll in, obscuring the warming rays of the sun and the wind picks up, so a sweater or jacket are advisable.

There are 45 miles (72 km) of trails in Kokee State Park, but if you're just in the area for the day, the easiest might be the **Iliau Nature Lookout Trail**, halfway between the 8-mile and 9-mile road markers. Plants endemic to Hawaii are labeled along this level, 0.3-mile (0.5 km) trail, which leads to a kaleidoscope view of the canyon, broken by Waialae Falls on the opposite cliff wall. Three later lookouts – **Waimea Canyon**, **Puu Ka Pele** and **Puu Hinahina** – all furnish similarly accessible, spectacular views of the canyon, which is approximately 3,600 ft (1,100 m) deep, 2 miles (3.2 km) wide and 10 miles (16 km) long.

At Puu Ka Pele, Hawaiians once felled the best *koa* trees for canoe construction. Traces of the route by which the trees were dragged to the coast can still be detected, as can the ruins of a *heiau* on the ocean side of the hill. At Hinahina Lookout, a large *koa* tree, with light-green leaves shaped like a sliver of the moon, is to the left of the pathway.

Turn off to **Kokee Lodge** and the **Kokee Natural History Museum.** The museum, which survives partly on donations, contains displays of birds and other wildlife, and if you pause for lunch at one of the picnic tables in the peaceful green glade outside, you might even hear the songs of some of the birds on display within. Throughout the peaceful park you'll see blossoms of hydrangea, ginger, red lehua and a riot of orange, lavender, gold and pink lantana.

The rustic Kokee Lodge (tel. 335-6061), with its cheery fireplace, is open for breakfast and lunch daily. Dinner is served only from 6 to 9pm, Friday and Saturday. If you have a desire to explore this idyllic area in depth, phone the lodge

for information regarding campsites or the rental of a furnished cabin.

To squeeze in the last two views, continue on the main road to the 18-mile marker. Take the left fork to peer over the **Kalalau Lookout** to an incomparable panorama of the ocean far beyond and below. Or follow the right fork for a view of the canyon from **Puu o Kila Lookout**, 4,120 ft (1256 m) above sea level. From here, a hike along Pihea Trail leads to the **Alakai Swamp**, the wet depression atop Mount Waialeale that is the habitat of rare and endangered flora and fauna, including many birds. With an average annual rainfall of 450 in (about 1,200 cm), the Alakai Swamp overflows down Mount Waialeale to supply water to Kauai's seven major rivers.

Too tired to travel all the way back to your hotel? Or perhaps you've become caught up in the fascinating history of Kauai, and want to relive a small portion of a bygone era. Then watch for the **Waimea Plantation Cottages** to the right of the road as you retrace your route

to Waimea. Mike Faye, son of an early plantation owner, has enlisted the aid of general manager Ray Blouin to restore 28 original plantation cottages set amid a coconut grove beside a nearly deserted 1,5-mile (2,4 km) stretch of black-sand beach. The bungalows have 1950s-style rattan furnishings, wide, pleasant verandas and old-fashioned claw-footed tubs, and are thoroughly equipped with dishes, flatware, cooking utensils and colorful linens. A spacious oceanside pool is built in a classic style reminiscent of the 1920s. Weekly rates begin at $300. For reservations and other information, write to 9600 Kaumualii Highway, Box 367, Waimea, HI 96796.

## HANALEI

The east and north shores of Kauai are so beautiful that the area has been sought out time after time by filmmakers. Years

*Above: Hikers enjoy the tropical beauty of the Na Pali Coast.*

ago, the Hanalei area starred in *South Pacific*, *Pagan Love Song*, *Birds of Paradise* and *Miss Sadie Thompson*, while more recently, *Raiders of the Lost Ark*, *10*, *China Beach* and the remake of *King Kong* have brought Kauai's northeastern beaches and jungles to the big screen.

**Ke'e Beach** at the end of the road is an easy 58-mile (93 km) excursion from Lihue. But the number of hours it takes to get there will depend upon your own curiosity.

Starting at the Lihue Mill, proceed north on Highway 56. The few vintage buildings of old **Kapaia** town will slip by almost unnoticed. Just beyond the town, at the bottom of the hill, turn left onto Highway 583 to make the 4-mile (6,4 km) drive through cane fields to **Wailua Falls**. If these falls seem vaguely familiar, it's because they were pictured during the opening scenes of the old *Fantasy Island* television series. Footpaths from the parking area lead to the base and the top of the 80-ft (24 m) waterfall, but when these paths are muddy, the going is treacherous. People have been injured, and some even killed, when they slipped into the stream and were carried over the falls.

Back on the main highway, you'll pass through another blink-of-the-eye town, Hanamaulu. **Hanamaulu Beach Park** is off to the right, while **Mount Kalepa** is on the left. The slopes of this range were once forested with thick stands of sandalwood.

There's a family dining opportunity here at the **Hanamaulu Restaurant and Tea House** (tel. 245-2511). Ask for a tea room by the gardens and carp ponds. Won ton soup, crispy fried chicken and shrimp, teriyaki beef skewers, *sashimi* and tempuras are delicious and reasonably priced, in this restaurant that is now in its seventh decade of business!

The first hotel along the main highway is the **Kauai Hilton**, beside Nukolii Beach. More canefields follow, broken only by Wailua Golf Course. **Lydgate State Park** appears next, near the mouth of the Wailua River and beside another hotel, the **Aston Kauai Resort.**

### Fern Grotto

Just before the **Wailua River**, turn inland at the marina to book a trip to Kauai's famed **Fern Grotto.** Two tour outfits, both of which charge the same rates, run the riverboats. Smith's Motor Boat Service has been around much longer than Waialeale Boats, but the latter tends to be less crowded. Both, however, are embarrassingly hokey, with audience participation expected in shouting "Aloha!" and doing a hula wiggle – so you must simply set your mind to enjoying the silly fun. The upriver trip and the grotto are so beautiful, everyone must go at least once. Hundreds of weddings take place among the ferns each year, and you'll hear the clear acoustics demonstrated in a live performance of *The Hawaiian Wedding Song.*

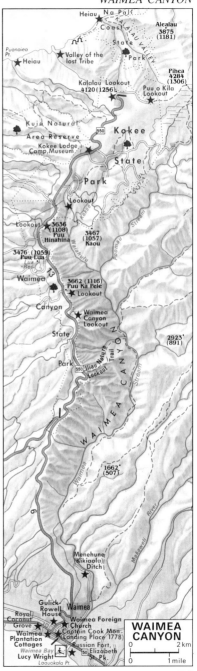

A little further up the Fern Grotto road is **Smith's Tropical Paradise** (tel. 822-4111). Filipino, Japanese and Polynesian villages sprout among the foliage that covers 30 acres (12 hectares). In the evening, a Hollywood-style Polynesian spectacular takes place under the stars. If you wish to make an evening of it, you can purchase the whole dinner package, including garden entry, buffet dinner (with some *luau* items) and show. Otherwise, walking tours are available at reasonable entry fees.

Return to the highway, cross the river and turn inland (left) again on Highway 580. Called the **King's Highway** because ancient royalty were carried along the road so that their feet wouldn't touch the ground, this route skirts a number of historic sites. Seven *heiau* were built along the Wailua River by Hawaiians who first settled in this area. **Hikina a Ka La Heiau**, on the site where the rays of the rising sun first touch Wailua, is below the highway near the mouth of the river.

Upstream, along the King's Highway, **Poohaku Hoohanau** is a birthstone that stood beside the grass hut where royal births took place. About a mile up the highway, a bumpy dirt lane leads to a path that descends to a **bellstone** beside the river. Announcements of royal births were made by striking the bellstone with another stone, so that a ringing sound pealed out across the valley.

The overlook for **Opaekaa Falls**, named for the "rolling shrimp" that once churned at its base, is a few hundred yards further up the highway, just beyond another looping road that takes in **Poliahu Heiau**. Across the road from the falls, look down on **Kamokila**, a restored Hawaiian village. It is struggling to survive, and guides provide a very personalized look at early Hawaiian artifacts, foods, customs and dwelling places.

*Right: The serene waterfalls are part and parcel of any tropical paradise.*

For visitors interested in tropical plants, a stop at the **Alexander Nursery**, about a mile beyond Opaekaa Falls, is worthwhile and doesn't cost a cent. The museum's 10 acres (4 hectares) are described as "an oasis of life" by owners Dorothy and Herbert Alexander, who are pleased to share their knowledge of plants and their menagerie of animals with you.

### Coco Palms and Coconuts

By the mouth of the Wailua River, off Highway 56, is the **Coco Palms Resort**, located on land once owned by the queen of Kauai. Coconut palms are planted all around the lagoons and buildings on this 45-acre (18 hectare) resort (tel. 822-4921). A small free museum, tennis courts and swimming pool create a Polynesian fantasy, parts of which were seen in the old Elvis Presley movie *Blue Hawaii*. A torchlighting ceremony, featuring barechested and barefooted young men in *malos* running along the pathways with flaming torches, takes place every day at sunset.

The little towns of **Waipouli** and **Kapaa** run together in a confusing way, but a new restaurant – just beyond Waipouli Town Center at Kauai Village – makes it worth figuring out where these communities lie. Chef Jean-Marie Josselin began preparing imaginative Pacific Rim cuisine at his **Pacific Café** (tel. 822-0013) in 1990. His menu changes daily, but entrées like grilled *ono* with ginger vinaigrette sauce, and scallops with red pepper sauce, are welcome additions to the Kauai dining scene.

However, the north shore beckons. When you see the Hawaiian Warrior sign, glance toward the mountains to pick out the **Sleeping Giant**, Puni, on **Nounou** ("throwing") **Mountain**. Puni is said to have died when he accidentally swallowed some rocks thrown to wake him from an afternoon nap.

In Kapaa, the **Ono Family Restaurant** (tel. 822-1710) is a favorite casual stop for breakfast or lunch. Buffalo burgers (the shaggy beasts are raised in Hanalei) are lower in cholesterol than beef, and are about as fancy as this restaurant gets.

You'll pass a number of side roads that lead all down to small beaches over the next stretch of highway. Not so far beyond the 13-mile marker, you can take Anahola Road to **Anahola Beach**, whose white-sand bay is framed with lacy ironwood trees.

Further out on Highway 56, a sign points to **Kilauea** beyond the 23-mile marker. Kilauea was in danger of becoming a ghost town when its sugar plantation closed in the 1970s, but community spirit kept it alive. Two industries – aquaculture and guava orchards – have been introduced, and the town has become a tourist stop of sorts.

Pause first at **Christ Memorial Episcopal Church**, built in 1941 of lava, with stained-glass windows imported from England. The wooden altar was carved by Mrs. William Hyde Rice, born into one of the prominent missionary families of Kauai.

Proceeding down Lighthouse Road, keep an eye out for **Kong Lung Store** at Keneke Street. This old plantation store was originally opened in 1896 by the Lung family. It carries a wonderful selection of gifts and collectibles.

Today, the store is the anchor of the Kong Lung Center. It includes a popular restaurant, **Casa di Amici**, serving Italian country cuisine. Also in the complex is **The Bread Also Rises**, a bakery in competition with Kilauea's other bakery – **Jacques Atlan's French Bakery**, in a hut one block *mauka* on Oka Street. The croissants and onion bread are recommendable.

### Kilauea Point

Save the picnic until after you visit **Kilauea Point National Wildlife Refuge and Lighthouse** at the end of the road. A $2 fee allows all family members

to take a self-guided tour of the light-house, which was erected in 1913 but has not been operated since 1976. Visitors can also view the sea birds that are protected on this northernmost point of the main Hawaiian islands. Hours are 10am to 4pm Monday through Friday.

On the return trip to Kilauea, you might want to detour to the left on Kolo Road, where you'll find the **Hawaiian Art Museum and Book Store.** It is operated by a cooperative of artisans to market local arts and crafts, Hawaiian books and music.

Further along Kolo Road, Kilauea Stream flows under a bridge. The stream is broken by Kilauea Falls and the **Kilauea Slippery Slide**, a cement tube with water rushing through it. It was constructed for the movie *South Pacific*, but is no longer open for public use.

Upon returning to Highway 56, proceed *mauka* up Kuawa Road to

*Above: Village meeting in Hanalei valley.*
*Right: Bringing in a load of tuna.*

Guava Kai Plantation, operated by C. Brewer Co., to see its modern visitor center, opened in 1989. Here you can sample free guava juice and take a self-guided tour to pick your own guava along the **Nature Walk**. The loading area of the processing plant is also open for viewing. Naturally, a gift shop has plenty of jams, jellies, kitchen accessories and so forth.

Scenery is spectacular all the way to Hanalei, but the **Kalihiwai Valley and Waterfall Lookout** at the 25-mile marker is particularly idyllic. Kalihiwai means "the edge of a stream," and if you turn right on Kalihiwai Road off the highway, you'll see parts of the stream. Keep bearing left onto Anini Road and descend to **Anini Beach Park**. Windsurfing lessons are generally available from a local vendor who carries his boards atop a truck. Across from the beach is a polo field, where actor Sylvester Stallone sometimes drops by on weekends for a game (called a "chucker") or two.

A short distance further, you'll see Princeville Airport on the left side of the

road. To the right is the **Princeville Resort**, begun on 11,000 acres (4,450 hectares) in 1969. Best known for its beautiful 36-hole golf course designed by Robert Trent Jones Jr., and populated by condominium-dwelling residents and visitors, Princeville has a shopping center and three small beaches with rough surf. The **Beamreach Restaurant** in the Pali Ke Kua complex at Princeville has a reputation for tasty and reasonably priced dining. The former Sheraton Mirage Princeville Hotel was closed in 1991 for remodeling.

Highway 56 becomes 560 as you come upon the **Hanalei Valley Lookout.** From here, it is 10 miles (16 km) to the end of the road. This lookout offers probably the most photographed view on Kauai. You'll want to stop to breathe in the beauty of this green panorama. The one-way truss bridge at the valley entrance was built in 1912, and over the years Hanalei residents have opposed widening it, not wanting to encourage increasing amounts of traffic along the road.

Near the bridge, a buffalo-shaped sign marks the only commercial bison farm in Hawaii. Chinese and Japanese farmers grew rice in the Hanalei Valley until it finally became cheaper to import California rice in the early 1900s; now the valley is planted in square patches of wetland *taro*. Karol Haraguchi, a descendant of one of the original rice growers has renovated the **Haraguchi Rice Mill** with remarkable efforts. She arranges special tours for schoolchildren and senior-citizen groups, but the rice mill is not yet open to the public.

The lower 917 acres (371 hectares) of the valley constitute the wonderful **Hanalei National Wildlife Refuge**. This area has been set aside for endangered water birds, so you may look but not enter.

Near the 2-mile marker is the old **Hanalei Museum**, no longer in operation. The museum occupied the former home of Ho Pak Yet, who built the house in 1860 with money he earned from the sandalwood trade of those days.

197

### Hanalei Town

Hanalei proper is simply a short block of shops on the side of the highway, plus the **Ching Young Shopping Center**. This center has a grocery store for last-minute provisioning by Na Pali Coast hikers. It also includes the **Native Hawaiian Trading and Cultural Center**, which occasionally showcases craft demonstrations or entertainment. The upstairs mini-museum is run by a Kauai artisans guild.

**Waioli Mission House** across the street is one Hanalei visitor attraction that should not be missed. Missionary teachers Abner and Lucy Wilcox – ancestors of the Wilcoxes of Lihue – built the house of coral limestone blocks in 1837. Their granddaughters restored the tidy house, with its clean and spare *koa* furniture, in 1921. Today it is open for half-hour guided tours Tuesdays, Thursdays and Sat-

urdays. Call 245-3202 for information. Next door, the **Waioli Mission Hall** and its bell tower date from 1841. Originally the hall had a stone floor and a thatched roof. Services, in Hawaiian and English, are still held next door in the white **Waioli Huiia Church**. The parish itself was founded in 1834, although this building actually dates from 1912.

In sharp contrast to the prim and proper missionary mentality are the lively goings-on at **Tahiti Nui**, a bar considered an institution in Hanalei. Family-style luaus are sometimes staged at the Tahiti Nui. It's a colorful place to stop for a beer and "talk story" with the locals.

The life of Hanalei revolves around the ocean. To get there, turn right on Aku road and right again on Weke Street. (Even the streets are named for ocean fish.) Here you'll find picturesque **Hanalei Pier**. Narrow-gauge tracks, on which old railcars once carried rice to ships, still run out along the pier. **Hanalei Beach Park** is beside the mouth of the Hanalei River. With ironwood trees for

*Above: The charming town of Hanalei. Right: A wahine (woman) from Kauai.*

shade, tables and restrooms, this is a popular gathering place, although the swimming is not always safe.

Two tour operators are headquartered in Hanalei: **Na Pali Adventures** (tel. 826-6804) and **Captain Zodiac** (tel. 826-9371), both of whom offer inflatable raft trips along the north shore, weather permitting. The beauty of the natural arches and the serenity of the rugged shoreline make an excursion worthwhile. If you want an exciting, wild, wind-in-your-hair ride, sit in the front of the craft. If you prefer a more sedate pace, sit as far back as possible.

The scenery beyond Hanalei consists of wave-washed beaches, stretches of emerald jungle and pasture, and weathered houses with chickens running about and dogs snoozing in the yards. **Kahalahala Beach** abuts a black-rock peninsula and continues on the other side for a half-mile as **Lumahai Beach**. You'll recognize the trailhead on the steep embankment by the number of cars parked alongside the road. Lumahai became famous as the beach in the movie *South Pacific*, but a funny thing happened on the way to the silver screen: the beach pictured was actually Kahalahala!

The Zodiac raft expeditions take off for the Na Pali Coast from **Makua Beach**, located at the end of a narrow dirt road off Highway 56, about 9 miles (14 km) from Hanalei town. Snorkelers might want to don their masks and flippers to swim inside the reef here. The beach has been dubbed "Tunnels" by surfers because of the tube-shaped waves that predominate on days when the surf is up.

### The End of the Road

Next along the highway is **Haena Beach Park**, a county park with campsites as well as showers and restrooms. A lunch wagon often sets up business by the park. Across the road is **Maniniholo Dry Cave**, worth a look for the ruins of

stone terraces inside, to the left of the entrance. Legend says this cave was built by a *menehune* who was searching for an evil spirit. It once extended about 300 ft (90 m) through the mountain, but sand has since shortened it.

You might find the wet caves to the left of the highway more intriguing than the dry one. **Waikanaloa** is beside the road, but take a short uphill walk to **Waikapalae** ("water of the lace fern"). Both caves are said to have been tunneled out by Pele, the volcano goddess. A swim in Waikapalae is a chilly, slightly spooky adventure, but scuba divers have braved the cold to explore about 100 yd (90 m) into the cave.

The road ends at **Ke'e Beach Park**. White sand, good snorkeling on calm days, and breathtaking north-shore sunsets characterize this idyllic beach. To capture a snapshot that will undoubtedly amaze your friends and relatives back home, hike about a half-mile up the **Kalalau Trail**, which begins to the left of the highway.

At the trailhead, you'll also look down upon a stone platform in a grassy area. The upper terrace is **Ke Ahu a Laka Halau Hula** (Lohiau's Dance Pavilion); the lower terrace, paved with flat stones, is **Ka Ulu a Pauoa Heiau** (Inspiration of Pauoa Temple). You can also hike to this *heiau* following a lower trail from Ke'e Beach. Pauoa was a hula master who taught the finest of Hawaii's ancient dancers at Ke'e; the dance pavilion is a shrine to Laka, goddess of hula. *Halaus* (hula schools) still perform at the pavilion and often place floral offerings to Laka on the terraces of the shrine.

Legend says that Pele and her sister, Hiiaka, came to Ke'e while a hula ceremony was in progress, attended by the handsome chief of Kauai, Lohiau. Pele was entranced by Lohiau and decided to marry him, but first she wanted to find a fiery place for them to live. When she dug into Kauai, the caves (at Haena) filled with water. Eventually she and Hiiaka discovered the Halemaumau firepit on the Big Island. Pele sent Hiiaka to bring Lohiau to her, but in his loneliness for the absent Pele, Lohiau had hanged himself. Hiiaka dutifully nursed his spirit back into his body, but in so doing, she inevitably and fatefully fell in love with him herself. When they reached the Big Island safely, she kissed Lohiau.

Pele was so furious she covered Lohiau with molten lava. Hiiaka escaped to return to Haena. Miraculously, Lohiau's brothers again nursed him back to life and brought him home to Kauai, where he and Hiiaka were reunited at the *heiau* at Ke'e Beach.

The 11-mile (18 km) Kalalau Trail is a popular overnight trek for backpackers. Camping permits should be obtained before undertaking the rigorous hike; write to the Division of State Parks, P.O. Box 1671, Lihue, Kauai, HI 96766.

*Right: Trucks piled high with harvested cane are a common sight on Kauai's roads.*

A shorter 2-mile (3 km) hike along the Kalalau Trail leads to **Hanakapiai Beach**. Boulders frame part of the beach along Hanakapiai Stream, which empties into the ocean at the crescent-shaped beach. An additional 1-mile (1,6 km) hike upstream leads past an abandoned homestead, the ruins of an old mill, and eventually to the base of **Hanakapiai Falls**. The remote traces of an earlier civilization are an ironic reminder that people once farmed these rugged valleys, now a tangled, uninhabited jungle.

## NIIHAU

A cloud of obscurity has shrouded **Niihau** since the late nineteenth century, when Elizabeth Sinclair purchased the isle from King Kamehameha IV. Until 1987, few people visited the privately owned island. Mrs Sinclair's descendants, the Robinson family, live just 17 miles (27 km) northeast of Niihau on Kauai's nearest shore, across the Kaulakahi Channel, and they issued few invitations.

But the isolation drifted slightly off-center in 1987 when Bruce Robinson initiated helicopter tours. They were begun in part as a way to fund the operation of the seven-seat, twin-engine helicopter deemed necessary to transport goods and people (in case of medical emergencies) to Kauai.

Variously called "The Forbidden Island" or "The Mystery Island," the mystique of this windswept isle – slumbering in isolation, its estimated 225 residents seemingly caught in an eighteenth-century time warp – was further enhanced by the Robinsons' patriarchal restriction on visitors.

The myths about Niihau originated with the first Polynesian explorers, who came upon the 6-by-18-mile (10-by-29-km) strip of generally arid land. With them, they brought chants telling how Niihau and its tiny islet neighbors, **Lehua**

and **Kaula**, were born as triplet siblings to the ancient gods Papa and Wakea. Another creation chant claims Niihau was the first Hawaiian home of the volcano goddess, Pele. And modern volcanologists seem to agree with the legend that it was indeed the first of the Hawaiian Islands.

The seventh largest island in the Hawaiian chain, Niihau was formed by a shield volcano. Its highest point is only 1,281 ft (390 m). Two large freshwater ponds, **Halulu** and **Halalii**, on the southern part of the upland plain periodically disappear during times of drought.

In 1778, when Captain James Cook made Niihau the second stop (after Kauai) on his voyage of discovery of the Hawaiian islands, he filled the water caskets of the *Resolution* and *Discovery* with fresh water from small streams flowing from the two ponds. In turn, he traded goats and pigs, the seeds of fruits and vegetables, and nails and other bits of iron, to the people of "Oneehow" for fresh produce and salt.

The *Resolution* and *Discovery* returned 14 months later without Cook (who had been killed on the Big Island). They found that, in addition to watermelons and musk melons, the sailors on their previous visit had left venereal disease. Other ships later found Niihau unchanged except for its declining population.

King Kamehameha gained control of Niihau in 1810. In 1864, when Mrs Sinclair paid $10,000 for the island, she also acquired 300 Hawaiian residents.

Elizabeth McHutcheson was born in Scotland in 1800, undoubtedly with a sense of adventure. She married a former navy officer, Francis W. Sinclair, in 1824, and in 1841 they accepted a land grant and took their six children to New Zealand. In 1863, after a shipwreck had killed her husband and eldest son, the widow Sinclair sold her farm and moved to Honolulu. When King Kamehameha IV and Queen Emma offered to sell Niihau, the Sinclairs inspected it – lush after two years of abundant rainfall – and

agreed it would make a good location for a ranch.

After Elizabeth Sinclair died in 1892, a grandson, Aubrey Robinson, became the owner. He bequeathed Niihau to his children. Today it is managed by Aubrey's two grandsons, Keith and Bruce Robinson. They continue to guard Niihau and its people from outside influences so diligently that it has become one of the last true enclaves perpetuating the Hawaiian lifestyle of yesteryear.

Residents speak Hawaiian as their primary language, though English is taught at school. Most homes do not have indoor plumbing, telephones or electricity, though generators power lights and televisions for some residents. No alcohol is allowed. Horses and bicycles are the main modes of transportation. Ironically, Niihau students benefit from the use of four solar-powered computers in the school's three classrooms.

*Above: A rare conch shell caught in the rising sun on a Niihau beach.*

Today, visitors arrive on the island in a Augusta 109 helicopter after a noisy 15-minute flight from Burns Field near Hanapepe, Kauai. The first 20-minute stop is on a cliff above **Keanahaki Bay**, at the southern tip of the island. The second stop is on the northern head of the seal-shaped island at **Puukole Point**.

You're more likely to see a wild ram clatter across the barren lava than you are to see any native people. Tours do not include the western coastline, where the village of Puuwai is located.

The parched lava gives way to bleached sand rimming **Ka'auku'u Bay**, where a barge delivers mail and goods twice a week. The beach is littered not only with sea shells, but also with Spam tins, plastic six-pack holders and empty bottles. Occasionally, half-hidden in the sand, you'll see a green glass fishing ball that has floated in from some Japanese fishing net. Inland, a rustic corral made of gnarled branches waits to hold the next herd of cattle to be loaded onto barges for shipment across the sea to market.

The **Robinson Ranch** covers the entire island. Cattle and sheep roam the range. In addition, income is derived from Niihau Sunset Brand Charcoal, fired in kilns from the abundant island *kiawe* growth. *Kiawe* honey has also improved Niihau's financial outlook, with 60,000 pounds (27,200 kg) produced per year.

But the island is perhaps best known for the intricate necklaces that Niihau's women painstakingly string from tiny shells that wash up on the wave-drenched shores. They've practiced this art since long before Captain Cook's arrival. The miniature turbans, sea snails, sun dials, conch shells, cowries, moon and rock shells, miters and scallops are found in greater abundance on Niihau than on other islands – though even on Niihau, some of the rarest can be collected only in small amounts during specific times of the year. Niihau shell leis can be purchased at jewelry stores throughout Hawaii, and at a number of outlets on Kauai. Prices range from perhaps $100 to many thousands of dollars.

Island visitors are not shown the small, neat homes scattered among gnarled *kiawe* trees, nor the schoolhouse that children may now attend through high school. Neither do guests see the church that is a mainstay of life.

Few visitors have ever had full freedom to roam the island. On December 7, 1941, after the attack on Pearl Harbor, a Japanese plane short of fuel was forced to land a few hundred feet from Puuwai Village. Shigenori Nishikaichi, the Japanese fighter pilot, was at first welcomed by the villagers, who were not aware that Pearl Harbor had been attacked. Eventually, the truth of the matter was revealed, and by December 14, emotions ran high. Nishikaichi escaped confinement, reclaimed his weapons, and went in search of his flight papers. A brawl ensued. Nishikaichi wounded one resident who still had enough strength to bash him into a stone wall and kill him.

In 1944, 42 American servicemen sent in to install a coast guard station compared the remote isle to Alcatraz. The Robinsons had required the military to sign an agreement that alcohol would not be used in the barracks, or elsewhere for that matter and that no social intercourse would be permitted with the people of Niihau. That included attending church. Later, local GIs manned the station, which was abandoned in 1951.

When Hawaii voted on statehood in 1959, Niihau was the only district in the territory to vote "No." In 1981, Governor George Ariyoshi and his wife Jean, accompanied by the first reporter to visit the island in more than 20 years, were invited to spend a day. They were welcomed with shy sincerity, and were impressed by the pride of the islanders.

Since the advent of helicopter tours in 1987, visitors have been cautiously welcomed to Hawaii's most inaccessible major island. For tour information, write to **Niihau Helicopters**, P.O. Box 370, Makaweli, Kauai, Hawaii 96769.

## KAUAI
(All area telephone codes are 808)

### Lihue-Kapaa
#### Accommodation

*LUXURY:* **Aston Kauai Resort,** 3-5921 Kuhio Hwy., Kapaa 96746, Tel: 245-3931, 800-342-1551. **Coco Palms Resort,** 4-241 Kuhio Hwy., Wailua, (P.O. Box 631), Lihue 96766. Tel: 822-4921, 800-338-1338. **Westin Kauai Resort,** Kalapaki Beach, Lihue 96766, Tel: 245-5050, 800-228-3000. *MODERATE:* **Colony's New Kauai Beachboy,** 484 Kuhio Hwy., Kapaa 96746, Tel: 822-3441, 800-367-6046. **Islander on the Beach,** 484 Kuhio Hwy., Kapaa 96746, Tel: 822-7417, 800-367-7052. **Kauai Sands,** 420 Papaloa Rd., Coconut Plantation, Wailua 96746, Tel: 822-4951. *BUDGET:* **Bed and Breakfast-Hawaii,** (P.O. Box 449), Kapaa 96746, Tel: 822-7771, 800-733-1632. **Garden Island Inn,** 3445 Wilcox Rd., Lihue 96766, Tel: 245-7227, 800-648-0154. **Hotel Coral Reef,** 1516 Kuhio Hwy., Kapaa 96746, Tel: 822-4481, 800-843-4659. **Ocean View Hotel,** 3445, Wilcox Rd., Lihue, HI 96760, Tel: 245-6345.

#### Attractions

**Alakoko Fishpond,** Nawiliwili, Lihue. **Fern Grotto,** Wailua River, access by commercial launch. **Grove Farm Homestead,** (P.O. Box 1631), Lihue, Tel: 245-3202, 10am and 1pm Mon, Wed and Thu by reservation. **Kamokila Hawaiian Village,** 6060 Kuamoo Rd., Wailua, Tel: 822-1192, 9am-4pm Mon-Sat. **Kauai Museum,** 4428 Rice St., Lihue, Tel: 245-6931, 9am-4:30pm Mon-Fri, 9am-1pm Sat. **Kilohana,** 3-2087 Kaumualii Hwy., Lihue, Tel: 245-9593. **Lihue Lutheran Church,** Hoomana Rd., Lihue; **Nawiliwili Harbor,** Nawiliwili Rd., Lihue. **Opaekaa Falls,** Hwy. 580, Wailua. **Smith's Tropical Paradise,** Wailua River Rd., Tel: 822-4111, 12-4pm Mon- Fri, 10am-4pm Sat-Sun. **Wailua Falls,** Hwy. 583, Wailua.

#### Restaurants

*AMERICAN:* **Ono Family Restaurant,** 4-1292 Kuhio Hwy., Kapaa, Tel: 822-1710. *CHINESE:* **Wah Kung Chop Suey,** Kinipopo Shopping Village, 4-356-D Kuhio Hwy., Kapaa, Tel: 822-0560. *CONTINENTAL:* **Gaylord's at Kilohana,** 3-2087 Kaumualii Hwy., Lihue, Tel: 245-9593. **Midori,** Kauai Hilton, 4331 Kauai Beach Dr.; Wailua (tel.245-1955). *HAWAIIAN:* **Lagoon Dining Room,** Coco Palms Resort, 4-241 Kuhio Hwy., Wailua, Tel: 822-4921. **Ma's Family Restaurant,** 4277 Halenani St., Lihue, Tel: 245-3142. *ITALIAN:* **Casa Italiana,** Haleko Rd., Hwy. 50 and 56, Lihue, Tel: 245-9586. *JAPANESE:* **Hanamaulu Tea House,** Kuhio Hwy.,

Hanamaulu, Tel: 245-2511. *KOREAN:* **Kun Ja's,** 4252 Rice St., Lihue, Tel: 245-8792. *MEXICAN:* **Rosita's,** Kukui Grove Center, 3-2600 Kaumualii Hwy., Lihue, Tel: 245-8561. *STEAK AND SEAFOOD:* **Buzz's Steak & Lobster,** Coconut Plantation, Kapaa, Tel: 822-7491. *THAI:* **The King and I,** Waipouli Plaza, 4-901 Kuhio Hwy., Kapaa, Tel: 822-4311.

#### Shopping

**Fashion Landing,** Westin Kauai Resort, Kalapaki Beach, Lihue, Tel: 245-5050. **Kapaa Shopping Center,** Kuhio Hwy., Kapaa. **Kauai Village,** Kuhio Hwy., Kapaa. **Kilohana,** 3-2087 Kaumualii Hwy., Puhi, Lihue, Tel: 245-9593. **Kinipopo Shopping Village,** 4-356 Kuhio Hwy., Kapaa. **Kukui Grove Center,** 3-2600 Kaumualii Hwy., Lihue, Tel: 245-7784. **Market Place at Coconut Plantation,** 4-484 Kuhio Hwy., Waipouli, 9am-9pm daily.

#### Tourist Information

**Hawaii Visitors Bureau,** Suite 207, Lihue Plaza Building, 3016 Umi St., Lihue 96766, Tel: 245-3971. **Kauai Visitor Center,** Coconut Plantation, 4-484 Kuhio Hwy., Waipouli, Tel: 822-0987.

### Poipu Beach
#### Accommodation

*LUXURY:* **Hyatt Regency Kauai,** 1571 Poipu Rd., Koloa 96756, Tel: 742-1234, 800-233-1234. **Kiahuna Plantation,** Route 1, Box 73, Koloa 96756, Tel: 742-6411, 800-542-4862. **Stouffer Waiohai Beach Resort,** 2249 Poipu Rd., Koloa 96756, Tel: 742-9511, 800-426-4122. *MODERATE:* **Grantham Resorts,** 2721 Poipu Rd., (P.O. Box 983), Koloa 96756, Tel: 742-7220, 800-325-5701. **Poipu Beach Hotel,** 2251 Poipu Rd., Koloa 96756, Tel: 742- 1681, 800-426-4122. **Sunset Kahili,** 1763 Pe'e Rd., Koloa 96756, Tel: 742-1691, 800-827-64780. *BUDGET:* **Garden Isle Cottages,** 2666 Puuholo Rd., Koloa 96756, Tel: 742-6717. **Gloria's Spouting Horn Bed & Breakfast,** 4464 Lawai Rd., Koloa 96756, Tel: 742-6995.

#### Attractions

**Brennecke's Beach,** bodysurfing, Hoone Rd., Poipu Beach. **C.J.M. Country Stables,** E end Poipu Rd., Poipu Beach, Tel: 742-6096. **National Tropical Botanical Garden,** Allerton Estate, Lawai Kai, Tel: 332-7361, tours Mon-Fri by appointment. **Prince Kuhio Beach Park,** Lawai Rd., Poipu Beach. **Spouting Horn,** near Kukuiula Harbor, Lawai Rd., Poipu Beach. **Tree Tunnel,** Hwy. 52, Maluhia Rd. north of Koloa.

#### Restaurants

*AMERICAN:* **Koloa Broiler,** Old Koloa Town, Koloa, Tel: 742-9122. *CONTINENTAL:* **Planta-**

tion Garden, Kiahuna Plantation, 2253 Poipu Rd., Koloa, Tel: 742-1695. *INTERNATIONAL:* **Mango's,** Old Koloa Town, Koloa, Tel: 742-7377. **Tamarind Room,** Stouffer Waiohai Beach Resort, 2249 Poipu Rd., Poipu Beach, Tel: 742-9511. *ITALIAN:* **Fez's Pizza,** Old Koloa Town, Koloa, Tel: 742-9096. *JAPANESE:* **Naniwa,** Sheraton Kauai Hotel, 2440 Hoonani Rd., Koloa, Tel: 742-1661. *MEXICAN:* **Taqueria Nortenos,** Poipu Plaza, 2827-A Poipu Rd., Poipu Beach, Tel: 742-7222. *STEAKS AND SEAFOOD:* **Brennecke's Beach Broiler,** 2100 Hoone Rd., Poipu Beach, Tel: 742- 7588. **House of Seafood,** Poipu Kai Resort and Racquet Club, 1941 Poipu Rd., Koloa, Tel: 742-6464.

### Shopping

**Hawaiian Trading Post**, Koloa Rd., Lawai. **Kiahuna Shopping Village,** Poipu Rd., Poipu Beach, 9am-9pm Mon-Sat, 9am- 6pm Sun. **Old Koloa Town,** Poipu and Koloa roads, Koloa, 9am-9pm daily. **Poipu Plaza,** Poipu Rd., Poipu Beach.

## Waimea and West Kauai
### Accommodation

*MODERATE:* **Waimea Plantation Cottages,** 9600 Kaumualii Hwy., Suite 367, Waimea 96796, Tel: 245-5050, 800-992- 4632. *BUDGET:* **Classic Vacation Cottages,** 2687 Onu Place, (P.O. Box 901), Kalaheo 96741, Tel: 332-9201.

### Attractions

**Alakai Swamp,** Mount Waialeale, trails from Kokee State Park. **Hanapepe Valley Overlook,** W of Kalaheo on Kaumualii Hwy.. **James Hoyle Gallery,** 3900 Hanapepe Rd., Hanapepe, Tel: 335- 3582. **Kalalau Lookout,** end of Hwy. 55, Kokee State Park. **Kokee Natural History Museum,** Kokee Rd., Kokee State Park, Tel: 335- 6061, 9am-5pm daily. **Kokee State Park,** Kokee Rd., Hwy. 55. **Niihau Helicopter Tours,** Burns Field, Hanapepe. **Old Russian Fort, Fort Elizabeth,** Kaumualii Hwy., Makaweli. **Olu Pua Botanical Garden,** Kaumualii Hwy., Kalaheo, Tel: 332-8182. **Polihale State Park, Barking Sands Beach,** Hwy. 50 past Kekaha. **Salt Pond Beach Park,** Hanapepe. **Waimea Canyon,** Hwy. 55.

### Restaurants

*AMERICAN:* **Camp House Grill,** Kaumualii Hwy., Kalaheo, Tel: 332-9755. **Kokee Lodge,** Kokee State Park, Tel: 335- 6061. *CONTINENTAL:* **Green Garden,** 13749 Kaumualii Hwy., Hanapepe, Tel: 335-5422. *ITALIAN:* **Brick Oven Pizza,** 22555 Kaumualii Hwy., Kalaheo, Tel: 332-8561.

### Shopping

**Eleele Shopping Center,** Kaumualii Hwy., Eleele, near Hanapepe. **Kashuba Fine Arts and Gifts International,** Kaumualii Hwy., Waimea, Tel: 338-1750. **Kauai Pineapple Cannery,** Koloa Rd., Lawai.

## Hanalei and North Kauai
### Accommodation

*LUXURY:* **Colony's Cliffs at Princeville,** (P.O. Box 1005), Hanalei 96714, Tel: 826-6219. **Hanalei Bay Resort,** (P.O. Box 220), Hanalei 96714, Tel: 826-6522, 800-657-7922. **Sheraton Mirage Princeville,** 5520 Ka Haku Rd., (P.O. Box 3069), Princeville 96722, Tel: 826-9644, 800-826-4400. *MODERATE:* **Ka'eo Kai,** 3970 Wylie Rd., (P.O. Box 3099), Princeville 96722, Tel: 826-6549. **Mahi Ko Inn,** Bed & Breakfast, 4481 Malulani St., Kilauea 96754, Tel: 828-1103, 800-458-3444.

### Attractions

**Christ Memorial Episcopal Church,** Kilauea. **Guava Kai Plantation,** Kuawa Rd., Kilauea. **Hanalei National Wildlife Refuge,** Hanalei Valley. **Hawaiian Art Museum and Book Store,** Kolo Rd., Kilauea. **Kalalau Trail,** 11 mi, begins at Ke'e Beach Park, end of Kuhio Hwy., (Hwy. 56). **Kilauea Point National Wildlife Refuge and Lighthouse,** Lighthouse Rd., Kilauea, 10am-4pm Mon-Fri. **Lumahai Beach,** W of Hanalei. **Maniniholo Dry Cave,** Haena Beach Park. **Na Pali Coast Zodiac Tours,** Makua Beach, off Kuhio Hwy., Tel: 826- 6804 or 826-9371. **Native Hawaiian Trading and Cultural Center,** Ching Young Shopping Center, Hanalei. **Waikanaloa and Waikapalae Wet Caves,** Haena Beach Park. **Waioli Mission House,** Kuhio Hwy., Hanalei, Tel: 245-3202, 9am-3pm Tue, Thu and Sat.

### Restaurants

*CONTINENTAL:* **Charo's,** 5-7132 Kuhio Hwy., Haena, Tel: 826-6422. *INTERNATIONAL:* **Bali Hai,** Hanalei Bay Resort, 5380 Honoiki Rd., Princeville, Tel: 826-6522. *ITALIAN:* **Casa di Amici,** Keneke St. and Kilauea Rd., Kilauea, Tel: 828-1388. *SEAFOOD:* **Beamreach,** Pali Ke Kua, 5300 Ka Haku Rd., Princeville, Tel: 826-9131. *STEAKS:* **Chuck's Steak House,** Princeville Center, Kuhio Hwy., Princeville, Tel: 826-6211.

### Shopping

**Ching Young Shopping Center,** Kuhio Hwy., Hanalei. **Kong Lung Store,** Keneke St. at Lighthouse Rd., Kilauea. **Princeville Center,** Kuhio Hwy., Princeville, open 9am-6pm Mon- Sat, 10am-5pm Sun.

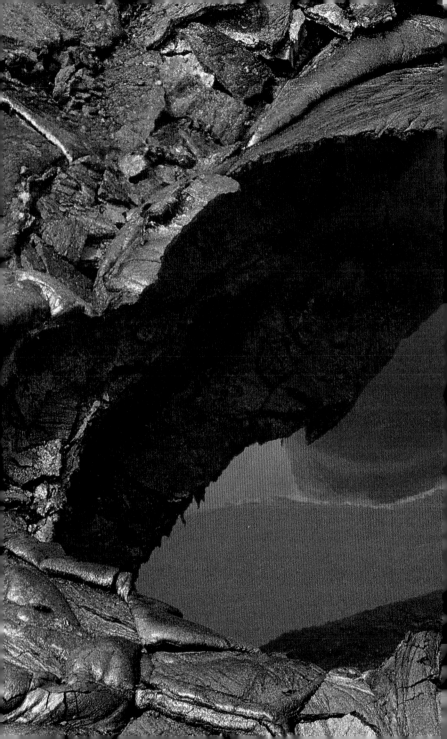

## SHOPPING

Serious shoppers and souvenir collectors alike will find many opportunities to browse and buy throughout the islands.

The distinctive Hawaiian aloha shirts are classics, and during daylight hours, men will find that they're suitable nearly everywhere. Many Hawaiian business executives wear jackets and ties to work, but on "Aloha Friday," it's common practice to finish the week by relaxing in an aloha shirt. Then, too, island women don their favorite *muumuu* or *holoku*, a loose-fitting dress. One can find inexpensive aloha shirts and *muumuus* in many shops and stores. On Oahu, perhaps the largest selection is available at **Hilo Hattie's**, which manufactures more than 80,000 garments a month. Here one will find virtually every color and vivid pattern under the rainbow, along with other resort wear and swimsuits.

More expensive aloha shirts and *muumuus* are available in specialty stores such as **Andrade's** and the island-based **Liberty House** department stores. Branches of these stores are scattered throughout the islands. The main Liberty House store is at **Ala Moana Center** in Honolulu; there's another on Kalakaua Avenue in Waikiki. The clothes by such island designers as Tori Richard are particularly worth taking home. (Only a few hotel and resort restaurants require men to wear jackets and ties.)

Many "typically Hawaiian" products are widely available, and they make excellent gifts and souvenirs. Virtually everywhere, one will see wooden bowls, trays and decorative objects made from monkeypod. Sometimes, they will be stamped "Made in The Philippines."

*Preceding pages: A run on the beach at sunset. A socalled skylight, a cave-in in the hardened crust offers a glimpse of live lava oozing to the sea. Right: Souvenirs on sale at a stand in Waikiki.*

Those who prefer one-of-a-kind hand-carved or hand-turned wooden items, should look to the gift department in Liberty House or in upscale art galleries, not souvenir stores. Many woodworkers specialize in items made from uniquely Hawaiian tropical woods, such as *koa*, which is becoming increasingly rare and expensive.

If one would like to bring home a taste of Hawaii, the choices are nearly endless. Of course, there are delicious, calorie-laden macadamia nuts, expensive but almost irresistible. Such delicacies as Kona coffee, Maui onion mustard, pineapple preserves, tropical blossom honey, mango chutney and macadamia honey butter make a welcome, thoughtful gift for family or friends back home. Some island-made cordials may be interesting for their novelty value; these include pineapple, passion fruit and Kona coffee liqueurs.

### A Wealth of Handcrafts

*Lauhala* (woven leaf) items are among the few indigenous traditional Hawaiian handcrafts. The products are for the most part fairly inexpensive, and one can sometimes see craftspersons fashioning them at Waikiki's **International Market Place**. Works include hats, purses, floor mats and table mats.

Decorative arrangements of wood-rose products are sold almost everywhere. Common as they are in Hawaii, they will take on added distinction back home. Wood roses are actually locally grown seed pods, but they resemble intricate carvings.

Other Hawaiian specialties include perfumes, made from island blossoms, as well as seed or shell necklaces and earrings. More expensive is jewelry made from black, pink or gold Hawaiian coral. (One may also see deep red coral, and it's lovely, but it's Mediterranean in origin.) Prices may vary widely, so it's a good idea to comparison shop. Among the best

known local jewelry producers is **Maui Divers, Ltd.**, which has more than 75 locations throughout the Hawaiian islands. The firm recently opened a visitor attraction, the Maui Divers Jewelry Design Center Tour in Honolulu. It's on Lions Street near Ala Moana Center. Visitors follow multilingual guides through a gallery and exhibit area and enter a video theater to view a nine-minute film. Afterwards, you see goldsmiths and artisans cutting and polishing coral and setting jewelry with diamonds or pearls.

Dedicated shoppers will find distractions at every turn. The vast Ala Moana Center has more than 180 shops and restaurants, including one of the world's largest food courts.

Side by side on Ala Moana Boulevard, two contemporary style centers offer some excellent shopping options. **Ward Warehouse** includes 75 shops and restaurants. **The Arts Guild**, representing some of Hawaii's most notable artists and craftsfolk, has an excellent inventory that changes almost daily, depending upon the artists who are represented. Look for wood-block prints, ceramics, scrimshaw (ivory carving), silk-screen works, furniture, and woodcarvings. All works must meet the guild's high standards of craftsmanship.

If you want to sample fresh island fruits and vegetables, as well as local color, stroll to the rear of Ward Warehouse to the **Ala Moana Farmers Market** on Auahi Street.

### The Shops of Waikiki

You may want to start your Waikiki Beach shopping expedition at the Hilton Hawaiian Village's **Rainbow Bazaar**. There, you'll find many excellent gem stores and galleries specializing in Far Eastern fine art and antiquities. The Bazaar's "name" stores include Adrienne Villadine, Esprit, Whaler's General Store, and Bernard Hurtig II, a fine jewelry shop. **China Treasures** showcases a splendid selection of Asian furniture. There's also a small, well-stocked branch

jewelry, carved temple images, *koa* wood boxes and carvings, and locally made fine jewelry.

Somewhat smaller than the Royal Hawaiian Shopping Center is the **Waikiki Shopping Plaza** at Kalakaua and Seaside avenues. Its five-story water sculpture is an area landmark. Fast-food stands on the lower floor are topped by five levels of shops and specialty restaurants. The Plaza includes branches of such Ala Moana boutiques as Villa Roma, and several national chains, including Waldenbooks.

Nearby, at Kuhio and Seaside avenues, is the **Waikiki Trade Center**. Many visitors miss it, but it's worth the short stroll off Kalakaua to browse amid the two-story **Circle Gallery**. A branch of the world's largest fine graphics house, it showcases lithographs by Hawaiian artists. International artists are represented here as well.

of Liberty House. And aloha shirt devotees shouldn't miss **Kula Bay**, which has brought back some of the original classic designs in aloha shirts, fashioning them in soft cottons.

In the heart of Waikiki, the handsome **Royal Hawaiian Shopping Center** fronts several blocks of Kalakaua Avenue before the Royal Hawaiian Hotel. It is made up of three handsome four-story structures, their interior façades adorned with tropical flowers and vines. Atriums are alive with native Hawaiian trees. In the center's charming waterfall courtyard, entertainers from the Polynesian Cultural Center sometimes perform, and craftspersons demonstrate *lauhala* weaving, lei- and quilt-making, and other traditional skills. The 12-story shopping center includes some of Waikiki's most exclusive shops. Its **Little Hawaiian Craft Shop** offers rare Niihau shell

Back on Kalakaua Avenue, the renowned **International Market Place**, with wooden and thatched structures sprawling beneath and around a huge banyan tree, reflects a certain South Pacific ambience. Most stalls and stores are open-fronted, displaying a variety of trinkets and souvenirs culled from the world over. One shouldn't overlook nearby **Kuhio Mall**, across Kuhio Avenue to the *mauka* (mountain) side. It's an attractive Polynesian-style complex wrapped around a central courtyard. Shops include **The Butterfly Gallery** and **Hawaii Farms**, specializing in local agricultural products.

At **King's Village** (formerly King's Alley) across from the Princess Kaiulani Hotel, one will find branches of Andrade's and **Crazy Shirts**. Nearby, the **Hemmeter Center** shops – in the Hyatt Regency Waikiki – have some of Waikiki's highest-caliber emporiums, including Gucci, House of Jade, The Coral Grotto, and Chapman's, a menswear store that is very fashionable.

*Above: Photo session with a mackaw in Lahaina, Maui. Right: Peddling Polynesian wares at Waikiki's International Market.*

### Neighbor Island Shopping

On the Neighbor Islands, shopping remains diverse and delightful. Many resorts and hotels have branches of Liberty House, Andrade's and other well-known island stores.

A number of the state's best-known artists and craftspeople live and work in Maui's upcountry. Some artisans welcome visitors to their studios with advance notice. To find out more about this kind of visit, inquire locally at the Maui Visitors Bureau.

In Lahaina, the prestigious **Lahaina Galleries** display and sell the works of such internationally known Maui artists as Guy Buffet, Robert Lyn Nelson and David Lee. **Lahaina Printsellers**, both in Lahaina and Kaanapali's **Whalers Village**, feature rare maps, engravings, paintings and prints of Hawaiian wildlife and other bits of ephemera. Also in Whalers Village, **Ka Hono Gift Gallery** has notable selections of South Pacific wood carvings and batiks.

Those who take the drive to Hana, might stop at the **Maui Crafts Guild** in Paia. It has excellent selections of ceramics, silks, bamboo and Hawaiian woods.

On the Big Island of Hawaii, **Alihi Creations Scrimshaw** (ivory carving) in Waimea's **Parker Ranch Shopping Center** showcases works of local craftsmen who work in precious metals and feathers. One can also watch some of the few remaining scrimshanders working. Nearby **Nikko Gallery** features work of some of the state's best artists. Here one will find jewelry, glass, ceramics, woodwork and Japanese antiques.

In Hilo, there are one-of-a-kind bowls crafted from exotic native hardwoods. They're made by **Dan Deluz**, who operates his own gallery. More *koa* bowls and other Hawaiian crafts are sold at **The Most Irresistible Shop in Hilo**.

On Kauai, the **Kong Lung Company** in Kilauea features island-made crafts and fine aloha wear. And in Hanalei, both the **Artists Guild of Kauai** and **Ola's** exhibit works by artisans resident on Kauai.

## THE LEI

The loveliest things in life are often the most perishable. Fragile flowers that bloom and are gone even as we hold them symbolize both the poignancy of our passings and the elixir of our great moments.

Native Hawaiians cannot imagine an occasion without a lei of flowers to mark it. They marry in leis of *maile* and *ilima,* dance draped in ferns and *ohia lehua*, and bury their dead beneath mounds of delicate *pikake* leis. Birthdays, graduations, weddings, arrivals, departures, achievements, even funerals and disappointments, are all celebrated or regretted with leis. A lei speaks more eloquently than words, which might stumble.

The first thing a jet-dazed traveler can expect to receive upon landing in Hawaii is usually a lei. The crowded baggage claim area at Honolulu International Air-

*Above: The lei endows a Hawaiian wahine (woman) with a particulary exotic look.*

port tends to look like the finish of a Kentucky Derby won by a mob, with every victor draped in garlands of flowers. Moreover, the dizzying mixture of smells adds its power to the experience.

The lei has come to symbolize Hawaii, and along with the hula is one of the few authentic aspects of Hawaiian culture to have survived Western contact. It is such a treasured icon that the word "lei" is often used to mean "child."

The exact origins of the lei are unknown. With such a short shelf life, there were never any around for archaeologists to uncover. It may very well be that early man performed his first aesthetic act when he looked around the jungle and decided to upgrade his image by decorating himself in its flora.

The stringing of flowers into garlands was first ritualized on the Asian continent. From there the custom was carried by migrating people eastward into Polynesia. The *maile* lei, similar to laurel, is considered to be the oldest lei. Its use, in related botanical forms, is prevalent throughout Polynesia and extends to Malaysia. The fragrant ginger lei was such a favorite that the plant was carried by the Polynesians on all their oceanic wanderings.

It was in Hawaii that lei-making really blossomed. Early visitors were overwhelmed by the beauty and artistry of the garlands. Intrepid traveler Isabella Lucy Bird wrote a letter home to her sister in Scotland in 1873 describing King Lunalilo of Hawaii, whom she had met at a reception: "He was almost concealed by wreaths of *ohia* blossoms and festoons of *maile*, some almost two yards long, which had been thrown over him."

She went on to describe others at the party: "All wore two, three, four or even six beautiful leis, besides festoons of the fragrant *maile*. Leis of crimson *ohia* blossoms were universal, but besides these, there were leis of small red and white double roses, *pohas*, yellow amaranth, cane tassels like frosted silver, the orange pandanus, and delicious gardenia, and a very few orange blossoms, and the great grandilla or passion flower."

## May Day is Lei Day

In recognition of its cultural importance, an official Lei Day was established in 1929. Princess Abigail Kekaulike Kawananakoa, one of the true remnants of Hawaiian royalty, crowned the first Lei Day Queen in the lobby of the Bank of Hawaii Building in downtown Honolulu. It's now celebrated annually on the first of May.

While much of the rest of the world is parading its nuclear hardware, Hawaii affirms flower power. There are lei-making contests, hula and song pageants – and every school has a May Day pageant, usually with a king and queen. In spite of its slightly compromised beginnings, Lei Day is probably the one holiday Hawaiians celebrate more for themselves than for tourism. Lei stands are set up on street

corners. Leis are worn to the office and bestowed on friends. Banks and stores are dressed up in leis. Children spend weeks preparing for school pageants, learning their hula and song and finally fashioning their own leis. Lei Day is when the seeds of the culture are sown in the next generation.

Leis have taken on associations. Politicians prefer hefty "power" leis of red carnations. Brides and grooms insist on *maile, ilima* and *pikake*. If high-school and college graduates aren't up to their mortarboards in garlands of flowers, it means they were wallflowers. Consequently, caring, sensitive parents give their offspring double-carnation leis for bulk, home-grown plumeria leis for quantity and strands of whatever-is-on-special-at-the-lei-vendor's-stall just for variety.

No one spends a lot of money for an esoteric lei for a first-time tourist, simply because the visitors don't know what they're getting. Newcomers are typically greeted with orchids and tube-rose, the latter for fragrance (they always sniff it first) and the former because it absolutely astounds them to have a whole string of orchids around their necks. It's called the "Wow, Mabel" effect.

A lei can be made of almost anything: flowers, fruit, leaves and vines. Permanent leis are crafted of feathers, *kukui* nuts, shells, seeds, and (in more hostile times) human hair. Contemporary innovations include leis of candy and bubblegum (for departing children) or of airline-sized liquor bottles (for elderly men), and are regarded as the ultimate in tropical tackiness.

Although every lei is treasured, a subtle floral hierarchy exists. Plumeria is the most common lei; pansy is one of the most expensive. Most appreciated are leis of flowers picked from the giver's garden – such as *pikake*, a tiny pearl-like jasmine blossom, divinely scented; tiare Tahiti, the Polynesian gardenia; pink carnation;

stephanotis; lantana; *ilima*, a small, bright-orange native flower; plumeria, also known as frangipani, and ferns.

Leis for hula dancers are the hardest to create. To find the fragrant *palapalai* fern, the pink-berried *pu kiawe* and the scarlet *ohia lehua*, sacred to the fire goddess Pele, it is necessary to hike into the forest. When the gathering is done, it's appropriate to drape a lei around a tree branch in gratitude for what the forest has yielded.

The neighborhood florist is a "last resort" when little is blooming or, more likely, when time is limited.

### Master Lei Makers

Some leis are prized because of the reputation of the lei maker. Sisters Marie McDonald and Irmalee Pomroy have devoted more than 30 years to lei

*Above: Keikis (children) learn to string leis at the Mauna Kea Beach Hotel on Big Island. Right: The flowery spirit of aloha.*

making. McDonald has written the definitive book on the subject: *Ka Lei*.

Barbara Meheula is famous for her use of native Hawaiian plant material. Before making a customer's lei, Meheula meditates on the name of the recipient in order to match the flowers to the personality. "I've never missed," she says. "I can't explain it. I'm doing leis for a big Merrill Lynch (stockbrokers) convention. They send me the names and a budget and I begin meditating."

Leis are not immune to trends. The *maunaloa* lei and Micronesian ginger lei, both intricately crafted floral necklaces, are currently popular because they complement high fashion clothing. The no-frills, tight and tailored *lei pua kika*, commonly called the "cigar flower lei," in shades of rust and orange, is a masculine favorite. So is the new braided *ti* leaf lei, which also has the advantage of being low-priced. To make the *ti* leaves supple, they are placed in a microwave.

A little more traditional are the two most common lei-making techniques.

The *kui* method is simply stringing the flowers together with needle and thread. *Haku* calls for a braided base of ferns to which other materials are attached by cord. Purists use softened banana fiber and call the *haku* a *wili* lei. Cheaters use dental floss.

In its many forms, the lei is a link to Hawaii's past, stretching back through time and across oceans. It is the tangible expression of the philosophy of aloha, the recognition of the sacredness of life. It is always given in love. The sentiment is poetically expressed in the song, *Ka Moa'e*:

*E lei aku 'oe ku'u aloha*
*I ko'olua nou i kahi mehameha.*
That means:
*Wear my love as a lei*
*And as your companion in lonely places.*

The sad fact is, that with more than 6 million tourists annually, the state of Hawaii would be bankrupt if it provided leis for everyone. If you have booked a tour or are being met by a friend, you can expect a lei. Otherwise, you will not get one.

To surprise your traveling companion(s) and delight yourself with a lei, you may contact **Greeters of Hawaii**, Alohaland Delights, P.O. Box 29638, Honolulu, HI 96820. There are toll-free numbers from the United States – 800/367-2669 – and from Canada – 800/423-8733. Prices range from $14.95 for a tube-rose and orchid lei to $42.95 for a *haku* lei. The greeter will also assist with baggage handling and transport.

To have a custom lei designed by a master lei maker, expect to pay from $15 to $100. These can be shipped anywhere, but the further the leis travel, the greater the risk of perishability.

In downtown Honolulu, Maunakea Street is lined with lei shops. Local people shop here for variety and price.

At Honolulu International Airport, a well-marked area with convenient parking is set aside for a lineup of lei stands. You'll pay slightly more than you would in town, but the selection is profuse.

217

## HAWAIIAN QUILT

The stitching of a Hawaiian quilt is more than an art. It is even more than an expression of culture. Above all, a Hawaiian quilt embodies the aloha, the love, of those who make it.

Generation upon generation of islanders have treasured their family quilts, passing them down as heirlooms. Quilts were usually made to commemorate special occasions such as the birth of a grandchild or a visit to a faraway place. They were often given as farewell gifts to friends or relatives who were leaving Hawaii. Usually, these family quilts are kept clean, neatly folded and stored away, out of sight, and brought to light only on special occasions or for viewing by special people.

Under such circumstances, without exposure, the art of Hawaiian quilting was little known by outsiders and had become

*Above: A tutu (grandmother) making a Hawaiian quilt. Right: A typical pattern.*

an almost extinct medium, practiced by a few Hawaiian women who had learned the technique from their grandmothers. In 1965, developer Laurance Rockefeller gave the art its biggest boost when he commissioned 30 quilts to decorate the walls of his new **Mauna Kea Beach Hotel** on the Big Island.

Since that time, Hawaiian quilts have gained an international following, won awards in prestigious national shows, and were featured in the Great American Quilt Festival at New York's Museum of American Folk Art in 1986. In January 1989, a royal Hawaiian flag quilt sewn in 1899 fetched $44,000 at an auction at Christie's in New York. It is believed to be the highest price ever paid for a Hawaiian quilt.

The woman credited with reviving popular interest in the Hawaiian quilt is Mealii Kalama, the master quilter commissioned by Rockefeller for the Mauna Kea Beach Hotel. Rockefeller first consulted the Rev. Abraham Akaka, then minister of Honolulu's **Kawaiahao Church**. When asked who might be able to contribute Hawaiian folk art for the hotel's open corridors, Akaka suggested that Kalama, a lay minister at his church, create a series of quilts with Hawaiian themes. The catch: It would take a miracle to complete the project by opening day, only six months away. It normally takes about 1,000 hours to do a single Hawaiian quilt, and that time usually is spread out over a period of months and even years. But Kalama immediately designed the 30 individual quilts around four themes inspired by Hawaii's flora – the breadfruit, *kukui* nut, coconut tree, and flower leis. She added one motif created for the occasion, an abstract pattern that she named "Pumehana Ke Aloha o Mauna Kea" ("Mauna Kea Welcomes All Who Visit Her"). She then mobilized the students in her quilting class at the church. Together, they sewed 60 million stitches with 30,000 yards (27,400 m) of

thread and brought Hawaiian quilting out of the closet. Miraculously, they had their quilts in place on opening day.

In 1985, Kalama's quilting achievements were recognized nationally when she was honored by the National Endowment for the Arts as one of America's "living treasures."

## Characteristics of Kapa Lau

Several characteristics distinguish Hawaiian quilts – called *kapa lau* – from other American quilts. Instead of being pieced together patchwork-style, from many swatches of fabric, the *kapa lau* is composed of a design (*lau*) cut into a single piece of fabric, then appliqued over another large piece (*kahua*) that forms the basis of the quilt. The two pieces are usually, but not always, solid colors of contrasting hue.

The design is achieved by folding the upper fabric into eighths and cutting it out in the manner of cutting snowflakes in paper. Once the design is appliqued onto the base, the stitching is done in the echo or contour style that suggests an undulating wave. In this manner, it radiates out from the center (*piko*) to the border (*ho' opaepae*) and through a layer of batting and a cloth backing (*pili*).

Stitches are smaller than in American quilts, averaging between 6 and 10 to an inch (three or four per cm), with rows of stitching a half-inch (about 1 cm) apart. The quilting frame consists of two 12-ft (3.6 m) pieces of lumber affixed by dowels to two wooden horses.

Traditionally, quilt designs were based on themes from nature: flower, fruit, leaf or lei. They also represented volcanic fire, ocean waves and a variety of royal motifs, such as the royal coat of arms, crowns, calabashes and *kahili*, the feathered standards of nobility.

Some quilters refused to be confined by norms and took their inspirations from Spanish combs, ivory fans, electric-light chandeliers, and even Halley's Comet.

When the Hawaiian monarchy was overthrown in 1893 and flying the

Hawaiian flag became an act of treason, families quilted their banners onto the canopies of their four-poster beds, so they could sleep under their beloved flag and hold it in a place of honor, above their heads. This gave rise to a whole genre of Hawaiian flag quilts. Among Hawaiian families, they are still the most treasured, and still surrounded by an air of secrecy. They are rarely displayed by their owners.

### The Origin of Hawaiian Quilting

Mystery surrounds the origin of the Hawaiian quilt just as it veils the beginnings of all things Hawaiian – even the people themselves. There are many stories about how quilting came to the islands and how it developed into its distinctive style. Some are more believable than others.

*Above: A master quilt-maker holds up a sample of her work. Right: Strong colors are distinctive in Hawaii.*

The most popular tale claims the Hawaiian quilt was born when a woman drying bedsheets on her lawn noticed the shadow cast upon her fabric by a breadfruit tree. She was so inspired by the dramatic outline that she cut it out, pasted it on another piece of material, and stitched the first Hawaiian quilt.

Many believe, on the other hand, that the first Christian missionaries were responsible for introducing the art of quilting to Hawaii.

In fact, stitchery predates the missionaries by many years. As early as 1809, one Archibald Campbell noted that native tailors did their work as perfectly as Europeans. The Russian explorer V.M. Golovnin recorded in 1817 that Hawaiian women were wearing robe-like calico dresses, a statement that challenges the widespread belief that missionaries first draped the *wahine* in the *muumuu*.

Prior to contact with the Western world in 1778, the Hawaiians had a history of sewing with *olona* plant fiber and needles made from bone. They also had a taste for fine bedding and made beautiful sheets from the bark of trees. They then dyed them and applied designs.

The quilt is a synthesis of many of the island arts. Its design concept features the creative boldness of fine *tapa* cloth art. Like the hula, it both tells a story and conveys a message. Most importantly, the Hawaiian quilt is a celebration of beauty and an expression of the basic philosophy of aloha, love.

### Where to Find Quilts

Here are some places where Hawaiian quilts can be seen and/or purchased:

On Oahu, the **Bishop Museum**, 1525 Bernice St., Honolulu (tel. 847-3511), has a collection that includes the oldest-known Hawaiian quilt, an 1840 flag quilt. Quilting classes are conducted by master quilter Deborah Kakalia.

In the Hyatt Regency Waikiki, 2424 Kalakaua Ave., Honolulu (tel. 923-1234), **Hyatt's Hawaii** is a showcase of Hawaiian arts and crafts, including quilters. The unique store is operated by quilter Malia Solomon.

The **Mission Houses Museum,** 553 S. King St., Honolulu (tel. 531-0481), displays heirloom quilts in the New England-style homes of the first Christian missionaries to Hawaii. The museum also mounts an annual quilt show in June.

New and old quilts are on display and for sale at **Quilts Hawaii**, 2338 S. King St., Honolulu (tel. 942-3195).

On the Big Island, the exhibit at the **Mauna Kea Beach Hotel**, Kohala Coast (tel. 882-7222), is the largest standing display of Hawaiian quilts. Guidebooks and walking tours explain the quilts and other fine pieces of Asian and Pacific art.

The **Lyman House Museum**, 276 Haili St., Hilo (tel. 935-5021), is an old missionary home that incorporated old quilts into the house's furnishings.

On Maui, the **Baldwin Mission House**, Front Street, Lahaina (tel. 661-

3262) is an oasis of serenity that displays a few old quilts amid its nineteenth-century objects and furniture, relics of old Hawaii.

Quilts are part of the extensive art collection at the **Hyatt Regency Maui**, Kaanapali Resort (tel. 661-1234). Ask for the self-guided walking tour. Several quilts are also on display in the lobby of the **Maui Marriott Hotel** at Kaanapali (tel. 667-1200).

The **Hana Cultural Center** in Hana (tel. 248-8622) is a small museum with a big Hawaiian flag quilt at its entrance. There are other quilts among the interesting cultural artifacts.

On Kauai, the **Kauai Museum**, 4428 Rice St., Lihue (tel. 245-6931) displays some of the finest old quilts from this lush island.

A tour of the **Grove Farm Homestead**, Lihue (tel. 245-3202), one of the island's first sugar plantations, includes the historic home of the Wilcox family with its elegant furnishings, *koa* wood floors and Hawaiian quilts.

## HAWAII'S FRIENDLY VOLCANOES

When a volcano erupts in most parts of the world, people flee in terror. But when one erupts on the Island of Hawaii, people flock to the crater rim from all over the world to watch the show, knowing they will be safe. Like the balmy weather, sandy beaches and friendly people of the islands, **Kilauea** – the volcano that has been erupting almost continually since 1980 – is a gentle giant. Its eruptions are mild and are almost never an immediate threat to people.

The lava Kilauea produces is another matter. It flows over the rim in a fire river slow enough for everyone on the island to know its exact location. Unfortunately nobody has found a way to stop lava once it begins flowing into neighborhoods and the unlucky few in the lava's path may

*Above: A fiery eruption along Kilauea Volcano's East Rift Zone. Right: A portion of highway covered by lava.*

have only hours to move their belongings while others have been able to dismantle their houses and move everything they owned before the lava arrived.

Otherwise, volcano-watching is such a popular activity on Hawaii that when Kilauea and **Mauna Loa** were uncharacteristically quiet in the early 1980s, the tourism industry was afraid the volcanoes had gone dormant, and some scientists speculated that an earthquake might have sealed the lava vents. But fears vanished when eruptions ended a 30-month lull in spectacular fashion.

Since then an entire community, **Kalapana Gardens**, has been destroyed by the lava. The latest count was 181 structures – 178 of them homes – engulfed by the lava. This latest flow has added approximately 300 acres (120 hectares) of contorted lava to the island, including a remarkable black-sand beach to replace an older one covered by the flow.

The entire volcano area, from Mauna Loa to the newer Kilauea and on down to the sea, is enclosed in the 230,000-acre

(93,000 hectare) **Hawaii Volcanoes National Park** that was established in 1916. The park is on Highway 11, which runs between Hilo and the Kona-Kohala Coast. From Hilo, one will drive through tropical forests, often through rain, mist and overcast weather. The Kona Coast is also wet but the Kohala Coast to the north is almost an exact opposite, with its desert environment and thousands of square miles of lava wasteland caused by numerous lava flows over the centuries.

Kilauea is the only active volcano in Hawaii now, and is the third most important one on the island of Hawaii. **Mauna Kea** founded the island, so to speak, then **Mauna Loa** appeared. Mauna Kea has been classified as dormant for many years, and its 13,796-ft (4,205 m) summit is often covered with enough snow to attract diehard skiers. It is also the site of five major astronomical observatories.

Since detailed records of volcanic activity were begun in 1927, Kilauea has erupted at least once every other year. The most spectacular series began in February 1969 and continued off and on for more than two years. Lava flowed down the slopes and through the forests, setting several fires, and occasionally went all the way to the ocean, increasing the island's shoreline by several square miles.

## A World-class Attraction

Since the eruptions are usually nonexplosive, the crater rim becomes a genuine tourist attraction. People from other islands, the mainland and various parts of the world gather. Many of them are scientists studying the volcano, but most are just people fascinated by these kinds of natural spectacles.

The National Park Service always closes the park and evacuates visitors until it can be determined how violent the eruption will be. The service also considers which way the lava will flow, as it has a habit of crossing the park's paved roads; this could strand visitors between rivers of molten rock. The park is sometimes kept closed to private vehicles, thus

compelling visitors to travel only in con-·
cessionaires' buses.

As the island is so large and has so
many hotels, both in Hilo and along the
Kona and Kohala coasts, getting rooms is
seldom a problem. One exception is the
**Volcano House**. This small (37-room)
hotel is perched on the rim of the Kilauea
caldera with a sweeping view across the
vast volcano that seems to be always
steaming, even when it isn't erupting.
The hotel has been there in one form or
another since 1846, when a local planter
erected a grass shack on the site.

One can charter planes and helicopters
in Hilo or Kona to take flights around the
rim. The Federal Aviation Administration
has set up rigid flight rules during eruptions with specific air corridors for all aircraft. This allows good views of the
craters but keeps the small aircraft out of
each others' way.

*Above: A lonely creature on a cold flow.*
*Right: Ferns are amongst the first plants to*
*take root following lava flows.*

Whether a spectacular eruption is
under way or not, taking an hour-long
helicopter ride through Hawaii Volcanoes
National Park has become the highlight
of many vacations. All the volcanoes,
dormant and active, can be seen, and the
pilot will show one the crater from which
the river of lava flows. He will take one
down the route of the lava flow, which is
only occasionally seen as usually it flows
through tubes created beneath the crust
formed as the lava cools. However, holes
that occur in the crust create "skylights"
where you can see the fiery lava flowing
swiftly to the sea. One will also see sub-
divisions and farms covered by the lava,
including street signs and stop signs almost drowned in the molten rock. And
one will see cars flooded by the fiery
flow that in no time reduces them to
twisted, scorched metal.

Unless a pyrotechnic eruption is in
progress, the most dramatic part of the
eruption to watch is the lava pouring into
the ocean – acres and acres of it, hour
after hour. The molten rock hitting the

Pacific creates an enormous cloud of white steam against the dark tropical sky, that shoots constantly skyward, much like a factory smokestack. The lava enters the ocean near the **Crater Rim Drive**. Visitors can walk out to an overlook to watch the show.

The Kilauea caldera is encircled by the 11-mile (18 km) Crater Rim Drive, which runs clockwise from park headquarters past several old craters and numerous overlooks with signs explaining the scene below. A few spur roads dead-end where lava flows recently crept across the pavement or deposited mountains of lava where campgrounds once stood.

### A New Observatory

The National Park Service recently opened a new observatory that looks out over the rim of the caldera and gives tourists the most stunning views of the volcano yet. Originally built as a scientific laboratory, it was recently replaced by a new laboratory with more modern equipment. The observatory has numerous scientific instruments that monitor the volcano activity. This equipment is so accurate, and the volcano so predictable, that eruptions can be prognosticated almost to the hour.

Hawaii is the only island in the chain that is still growing through volcanic action. Scientists are convinced that the entire Hawaiian chain was formed by a single volcanic vent in the earth's surface. According to the continental drift theory, the Pacific Plate of the earth's crust slowly migrates northwest past a volcanic "hot spot", which remains stationary. As the plate moves northwest, the volcano keeps creating new islands or – as it is doing now – increasing an island's size. Midway Island, far to the northwest, was the first of the chain to be created. The long string of islets and reefs between Midway and Kauai are islands of varying sizes that have eroded back into

the ocean. The oldest inhabited island now is Kauai; the spectacular Waimea Canyon is evidence of the constant erosion process that gradually washes the soil of the island back to sea.

There is ample evidence to support the plate theory. In 1964, a geologist measured the ages of rocks on each of the islands, and found that those collected on Kauai were from 3 to 5 million years old. The rocks became progressively younger as the geologist sampled them on down the chain, through Oahu, Molokai, Maui, Lanai and finally the Big Island, Hawaii.

A few miles off the southeast coast of Hawaii, another island is in the making. Now only a seamount called Loihi, it will eventually rise above the surface of the ocean. Perhaps in 10,000 years it will develop its own soil and become an inhabitable island.

For general information on Hawaii Volcanoes National Park, telephone 808/967-7643. For information on eruptions only, call the eruptions hotline: 808/967-7977.

## HAWAIIAN FOOD

Hawaii is the culinary crossroads of the Pacific. Its cuisine is a rainbow of all its races. These ethnic groups invite the visitor to *hele mai aha'aina* – to come join the feast, a feast as diverse as the peoples themselves.

The first meager table was set by immigrating islanders more than 1,000 years ago, after they landed in the double-hulled canoes that carried them from central Polynesia. Cages were built into canoe hulls to hold chickens, dogs and pigs for breeding stock. Plants were carefully tended with the precious fresh water they carried in lengths of bamboo and in oiled gourds. Dried fish, bananas, *taro*, coconuts, yams and breadfruit sustained them en route, and were the first crops they planted after arriving. The ocean was a treasure trove of edible seaweed

*Above: Farmers harvest taro in Kauai's Hanalei Valley. Right: Poi is traditionally scooped to the mouth with one's fingers.*

and 600 species of tropical fish. Fish and *poi* – a paste of ground *taro* root – were the two staple foods in the diet. Fishermen and farmers exchanged their bounty, resulting in a good diet for both.

The early language had many words for "food" and "eating," but none for "time." Isolated from the rest of the world, the early islanders prayed to their gods and shared with each other. From the earliest times, each bountiful harvest was followed by a *luau*, a traditional feast in praise of the gods.

The people remained blissfully unaware of the world until British explorer Captain James Cook accidentally rediscovered the islands in 1778. Since then, Hawaii was transformed from a collection of simple people living in primitive fashion on subtropical islands to the home of polyracial peoples of the atomic age. A flood of foreign traders and adventurers came in ships loaded with new livestock, fruit trees and garden vegetables. Fortunately, they also brought cook pots and exotic tastes!

Puritan missionaries followed God's call to "convert the childlike heathens." Along with fire and brimstone, the missionaries and sailors brought ingredients for puddings, pies, dumplings, gravies and roasts. They added coconut cake to the smorgasbord. Whalers introduced rum and concocted *lomi lomi*, salmon marinated with tomatoes and onions.

**The Ethnic Cornucopia**

In the twentieth century, the rapid mechanization and development of Hawaii's two great crops – sugar and pineapple – led to big changes in the ethnic and culinary diversity of the islands. Neither crop was suited to the small farmer, but called for big business. The Polynesians refused to work on the *haoles'* (white men's) plantations. Poor Asians were hired as contract laborers beginning in the mid 1800s.

The first wave was Chinese. Many left the plantations as soon as their contracts of indenture had expired. With the money they saved, they opened restaurants or started farms where they raised chickens and ducks, and cultivated new vegetables with seeds brought all the way from China. Water chestnuts, *litchi* (lychee), mandarin oranges, mustard cabbage and delectable dwarf bananas were among their contributions. Chinese cooperatives grew coffee, peanuts and bananas. They added their own spices to the culinary mix, as well as setting a trend that resulted in rice becoming a staple instead of bread. Today, Honolulu's Chinatown has some interesting older markets, and Chinese restaurants are everywhere throughout the islands.

When the Chinese left the plantations, Japanese tenant farmers were brought in. The Japanese also preserved their traditions and saved money for a better life. Some worked an extra half-hour a day in exchange for the use of a quarter-acre of land to grow some of their favorite crops:

soybeans, daikon (radishes), turnips, eggplant and cabbage. On the plantations, as in Japan, there were no ovens. Food was boiled, broiled, fried or steamed. *Shoyu* (soy sauce), made of soybeans, barley and salt, was the principle seasoning.

Authentic Japanese food is easy to find in Hawaii today, at **Woolworth's** on Kalakaua Avenue, for example, or at the Ala Moana Shopping Center. There's a *sushi* bar and *bento* lunch boxes, with *tsukemono* (pickled cucumber), *sashimi* (sliced raw fish), *tempura* (foods deep-fried in a light egg-and-flour batter), and *miso* soup (a clear broth made with soybean paste). *Sukiyaki* is a combination of vegetables, meat and *tofu* (pressed soybean) prepared in a boiling stock.

On Kauai, **Hanamaula Restaurant and Tea House** has a lovely Japanese garden, along with delicious Chinese and Japanese food. In Wailua, **Restaurant Kintaro** serves outstanding Japanese cuisine. If you're in Hilo, on the Big Island, visit the **Nihon Cultural Center** for a taste of Japan.

Or go to one of the islands' many *saimin* shops for a hearty bowl of noodles, broth, vegetables and meat, chicken or fish. *Saimin* is a word unique to Hawaii – like so much else here, it's a blend of two Japanese words for noodle soups, *soba* and *ramen*.

Koreans came as contract laborers at the turn of the twentieth century. Even though they comprise less than 1 % of Hawaii's population, they have left their culinary mark in the ubiquitous *kim chee*: garlicky, pickled cabbage with red peppers. It's served all over, especially with wieners as "*kim chee* dogs" at beach stands in Waikiki. Seoul food takes many other delicious forms, from spicy noodle soups to *kalbi*, barbecued short ribs. Other sumptuous treats include *bulgoki*, marinated beef and vegetables grilled over an open fire; and *pibimbap*, rice smothered with a mix of chicken, beef and vegetables.

*Above: Yellow-fin tuna, one of the most prolific catches from Hawaii's offshore waters.*

After Hawaii was annexed as a U.S. territory in 1900 and Asians could no longer become naturalized citizens under U.S. law, plantation owners looked to the Portuguese from Madeira and the Azores. Their contribution to the communal table was more than just Portuguese bean soup; *pao dulce*, or sweet bread; and *malasadas*, sugared holeless doughnuts. The Portuguese introduced a Mediterranean influence that pervades much of Hawaii's cuisine.

Filipinos comprised the last large migration to the sugar fields. Their culinary traditions added yet another flavor to the foods of Hawaii with *adobos* – stews of fish, meat or chicken, usually in a rich vinegar and garlic sauce, with exotic spices – as well as *lumpia* (flaky spring rolls), *pancit* (variations of noodles made into ravioli-like bundles, stuffed with pork or other meat), *lechon* (whole suckling pig, stuffed and roasted), *siopao* (a steamed dough ball filled with chicken and various other tidbits), and *halo halo* (a rich confection of shaved ice, smothered in preserved fruits and some canned milk).

## Indigenous Cuisine

Sadly, Hawaiian food itself is fast becoming an anomaly in its own land. Only a few restaurants still serve it: **People's Café** in Waikiki, **Helen's** in Kalihi, **Ono Hawaiian Food** in Kapahulu. Typical is the *luau*. Though many of the large hotels stage them for tourists, true *luaus* are private affairs, held by Hawaiian families to celebrate important events of life.

Guests sit on grass mats. They are given a bowl of *poi* and a plate of *pipikaula* (a mixture of beef jerky, chili peppers, Hawaiian rock salt and a green onion). *Poke* (raw seasoned seafood), *opihi* (small limpets harvested from rocks at low tide), raw crab and other seafood might be included. A piece of sweet potato comes on a *ti* leaf. *Haupia* (coconut pudding) or *kulolo* (*taro* pudding), coconut cake and whole pineapples are placed in the middle of the table for all to share. The main dishes include *lomi lomi*, chicken or squid *luau*, chicken long rice, *kalua* pig and other *laulau* (side dishes). The drama begins when the pig is uncovered and taken out of the *imu*, the earthen pit where the *luau* food is cooked. The pit is dug and lined with *kiawe* wood and (if available) hot lava rocks; these impart a flavor that can't be duplicated with standard ovens.

Cold beer, soft drinks and *mai tais* are the usual beverages. *Mai tais* are a mixture of light and dark rum, orange curacao liqueur, orange and almond flavoring, and lemon juice. These and other colorful island drinks look innocent when served in pineapples, coconuts or frosted glasses. Fruit and rum are combined in other popular drinks such as the *chi chi* (vodka, pineapple juice and coconut syrup), *Blue Hawaiian* (vodka and blue curacao) and *planter's punch* (light rum, Grenadine, bitters and lemon juice).

Although Hawaii has had a broad range of ethnic foods, it has never been known as a gastronomic haven – that is, until a handful of young chefs began to realize its potential. Hawaii's modern culinary identity began to take form in the early 1980s, when American-trained chefs began replacing European-schooled chefs in the resort dining rooms. Young mainlanders were flabbergasted to find that in the island setting, frozen fish – shipped from California or Alaska – was the norm.

Hawaii became more than merely a tourist's paradise: it was the land of culinary opportunity. The chefs began working with local farmers to grow premier produce. Alliances were formed, promoting the aqua-farming of fish and the raising of local lamb.

Beyond the contemporary, a second regional cuisine is developing, taking its example from the spirit of the islands itself. Creative chefs combine Asian and Western ingredients in dishes using both European and Oriental cooking techniques. This Eurasian or Pacific Rim approach is magic in the hands of a creative chef who is in tune with the harmony of the two worlds of food.

At the **Avalon** restaurant in Lahaina, Maui, Mark Ellman brings some of the best elements of Pacific Rim food together in a dish of deep-fried local fish, transformed by a garlicky black-bean sauce.

Hawaii's fresh fish and perfectly ripened exotic fruits and vegetables are a national treasure, and they taste best in their natural setting. A casual walk through island markets, big or small, will give you a real education in island foods. Sweet Maui onions, Manoa bib lettuce, fern shoots, burdock, *cherimoya* (custard apples), passion fruit, Kona oranges, pineapples with lots of perfume. With Hawaii's everlasting summer, the list is endless. If you're lucky, you might even find homemade mango bread!

## ETHNIC TENSIONS

Race relations in Hawaii can be described with two antithetical images.

(1) The islands are a benign, progressive rainbow of races, working together and soaking up each others' cultures while enjoying the soothing sunshine.

(2) The islands are small pools of tension, where racial exclusiveness, if not outright hostility, stays just beneath the surface because members of various races or ethnic groups have been too downtrodden and underpoliticized over the past decades to protest.

The lack of a majority culture (Anglo-Americans or *haoles* comprise little more than one-fourth of the population) and the importation in the last century of immigrant laborers have kept the racial pattern so diverse that Hawaii is no Detroit. More than 60% of the marriages are

*Above: Relaxing in genuine Hawaiian style in Hanapepe, Kauai. Right: African Americans also contribute to Hawaii's ethnic mix.*

cross-ethnic. But while economic class may be the real issue, when resentment is voiced, it's in racial terms, especially as the state's economy polarizes.

Since the first white contact in the second half of the eighteenth century, Anglo-Americans developed and ran the "Big Five" agricultural concerns. Other ethnic groups – Chinese, Japanese, Koreans, Filipinos, Puerto Ricans and Portuguese – were brought in as plantation workers in successive waves, living in cottage "camps" segregated according to home country.

After World War II, the Japanese minority – now a quarter of the state's population – rose to fill key positions in the state's educational system and territorial bureaucracy, areas they have continued to monopolize up to the present.

By the 1960s, the infant state was almost totally democratic (with a big and little "d") and fiercely proud of its liberalism and racial tolerance. Now Anglo-Americans may still dominate the top corporate landscape, with local Chinese-

American and Japanese-American contributions, but its internal makeup is far more internationalized, with Japanese nationals owning nearly all major hotels.

At the small business level, Vietnamese and Laotian refugees have turned Chinatown into Indochina-ville; Koreans own many small stores and innumerable "hostess" bars. Filipinos continue to immigrate, filling service and landscaping jobs.

### Hawaiians: The Big Losers

The unfortunates during this 200-year history of human immigration and rapid development have been the native Polynesians who were in Hawaii 1,300 years before Captain James Cook arrived in 1778. They lived harmoniously with the environment.

After tens of thousands succumbed to various white-borne diseases in the early nineteenth century, the 200,000 Hawaiians and part-Hawaiians remaining in Hawaii continue to suffer higher mortality rates than any other ethnic group in the islands. Their lung cancer incidence is the highest in the United States. They also populate Hawaii's prisons and welfare rolls disproportionately.

(For purposes of inventory, a "Hawaiian" is anyone who says he is. A trace of Hawaiian blood is required for someone to vote in the Office of Hawaiian Affairs elections. But to be eligible for trust money earmarked exclusively for Hawaiians, one's ancestry must be at least 50% Hawaiian.)

Americans – businessmen, sugar cane growers and their military protectors – overthrew the Hawaiian monarchy in 1893, annexing the islands as a territory five years later. In 1959, Hawaii became a state. Despite the mass jubilation, a small group of Hawaiians has continuously fought the illegal occupation of the islands.

In the last five years, a sovereignty movement has grown into several groups with memberships in the thousands. Whether to go for a nation-within-a-na-

231

tion status or full independence frames some of the arguments that continue to divide the leadership.

Without the land base to which native Americans were banished, Hawaiians have had trouble giving form to a Hawaiian nation on the model of more than 300 native American "nations," most of them focused on designated reservations. Nearly 200,000 acres (80,000 hectares) of land too marginal for agriculture have been held as Hawaiian homelands, but the allocation of house lots has been a painfully slow process encumbered by sloppy bureaucracy. Revenues from nearly 2 million acres (806,500 hectares) that the monarchy "ceded" in 1898 to the U.S. government were to benefit the native Hawaiians, but although 1.35 million acres (about 550,000 hectares) were returned to the state, the lands are still being inventoried and the definition

*Above: Watching the world go by on Lahaina's Front Street. Right: Charo performs at the Hilton Hawaiian Village.*

of "revenues" being somewhat massaged. The state Office of Hawaiian Affairs, set up to spend the income, has been rejected by activist Hawaiians as inherently corrupt and compromised by its relationship with the state government.

One of the largest landowners, the Bishop Estate, set up by a Hawaiian princess to benefit her people, pays its trustees high six-figure salaries and sustains a Hawaiians-only private school that has turned out more firefighters than financiers.

### The 'White Supremacy' Issue

Politically, Hawaiians seek to rid the islands of "white supremacy": they want land, reparations and an apology. But on the streets, part-Hawaiians also resent the climb from poverty that Orientals – the ethnic Japanese, Chinese and Koreans – have accomplished. Although having a part-Hawaiian governor is a source of symbolic pride, many Hawaiians reserve special scorn for Governor John Waihee

who has seemed to do little to better their lot so far during his time in office.

Every year or so, a land issue will erupt into protest that rallies Hawaiians and their sympathizers. From 1989 to 1991, a geothermal development project on Hawaiian lands on a Big Island became a bone of contention. The state traded the 27,000 acres (10,900 hectares) to the private Campbell Estate, which needed acreage suitable for steam exploration. Although drilling has begun in the Wao Kele o Puna rainforest, protest and economic questions have delayed the project, which aimed to pipe power 150 miles (240 km) underwater to the island of Oahu.

Another ongoing fight has been that of Hawaiian activists attempting to stop U.S. military bombing practice on the uninhabited island of Kahoolawe. In a transparent move to get fellow Republican Patricia Saiki elected to the U.S. Senate, President George Bush vowed to stop the bombing on the eve of the November 1990 elections. Since Saiki's election loss, the federal government has backpedaled, assigning Kahoolawe's fate to a commission, a delaying act well known to the Hawaiians.

Race relations exploded on the normally peaceful University of Hawaii campus in the fall of 1990 in a non-violent, almost pensive Hawaii style. Part-Hawaiian professor Haunani Kay Trask attacked a white student in the university newspaper, causing a storm of debate on and off the commuter campus in the Manoa valley.

Young people began to argue the prevalence of racism, while the university philosophy department called for Trask's censure. Caught in a veritable limbo in this argument are the majority of students who are of Asian-American ancestry.

The year 1993 marks the 100th anniversary of the monarchy's overthrow. Observers expect a more vocal and focused sovereignty movement in the 1990s, bringing increased tensions due to the extremely high cost of living and low service wages.

233

## HAWAII'S ECONOMY

As the 1980s became the 1990s and the U.S. economy hurtled toward recession, Hawaii's economy continued to look bright, despite a few warning signals on the horizon.

Fueled heavily by overseas investment, particularly by Japanese businesses, Hawaii has been able to circumvent the rapidly growing problems of other states facing massive unemployment, plummeting real-estate prices and – in the most extreme cases – bankruptcy.

But for all its successes, Hawaii has paid a price. Economists are divided as to what the future will hold for the island paradise.

A vivid illustration of Hawaii's economic wealth can be seen in the 1990 Gross State Product: It reached U.S. $26.9 billion, a 12% increase from 1989.

A drive around any of the major islands, especially Oahu, reveals a booming construction industry. Highrises, once strictly confined to Waikiki and downtown Honolulu, are spreading across the landscape at such a rapid rate, the local joke is that the construction crane should be designated Hawaii's official state bird.

The skyrocketing value of Hawaii's real estate, and the related problem of a serious shortage of affordable housing for Hawaii's residents, are volatile issues. As the rest of the United States fell into a housing slump in 1990, Hawaii's housing prices continued to increase in value – by a staggering 30% annually. This meant that those fortunate enough to already own something even as modest as a single-family dwelling, even a wooden plantation-era cottage on a wallet-sized parcel of land, could sell their property and make a financial killing.

Unfortunately, most soon discovered that their profit, no matter how great, was

*Right: The Pioneer Mill in Lahaina, Maui, is one of many that still operate in Hawaii.*

not enough to buy another house in Hawaii. Today, as land prices continue to soar and Hawaii's population keeps growing, the shortage of housing is becoming more acute. Those houses that are available are unaffordable to the average wage-earner.

As the gap between the haves and the have-nots widens, and state and local governments continue their debate on how best to alleviate the problem, the situation has reached catastrophic proportions with no clear answer in sight. Although Hawaii can boast an unemployment rate of just 2.8%, one of the lowest in the nation, local wages are far below those on the mainland – while the cost of living in Hawaii is the highest in the United States.

In recent years, many local residents have voted with their feet and left the islands for the mainland's better wage structure and lower cost of living.

Tourism, Hawaii's biggest and most lucrative industry, continues to grow, accounting for U.S. $10.9 billion in 1989. During that year, 6.6 million people visited the islands. Approximately 64% of these visitors were westbound from the U.S., while visitors from Asia accounted for approximately 22.3%. European visitors, a market expected to increase in the 1990s, made up 3.1%.

Hawaii's other industries are presently going through periods of change and redefinition. Agriculture and related manufacturing, mainly sugar and pineapple production, were once the mainstays of Hawaii's economy. Today, the industry continues to stagnate, contributing just U.S. $564 million in 1989.

Despite recent federal cuts in military spending, Hawaii remains a major outpost for American armed forces, an industry that brought about U. S. $2 billion into the state in 1989. Local economists are divided as to how and if the recession already underway in the rest of the United States will affect Hawaii. So far,

widespread Japanese investment has acted as a buffer against the ills affecting mainland states. Of course, if recession affects tourists' solvency, Hawaii could indirectly suffer.

Hawaii's growth is expected to continue, albeit more slowly than in recent years. While the recession will probably result in a decrease in visitors from the U.S. mainland, the steady influx of eastbound Asian visitors is expected to increase by 11% in the next year.

Hawaii's economy in the 1990s is characterized by cautious optimism, but the state remains vulnerable to the economic mood swings of Asia, particularly Japan, as well as those of the United States.

### Japanese Investment

Situated in the middle of the vast Pacific Ocean like rocks in a Zen garden, the Hawaiian Islands have long been stepping stones for the Japanese people and culture. In 1860, Honolulu was a brief stop for diplomats heading to Washington for their first tentative attempts at negotiating trade relations with America. Travelers from the Far East have been stopping in Hawaii ever since.

In the last century, many of these visitors have lingered, become residents, borne children, and have uniquely shaped the islands. The Japanese soon came to refer to Hawaii as "Tenjiku" – "the heavenly place." Plantation workers and immigrant laborers in the late nineteenth century formed the base of a Japanese population which today comprises about one-quarter of Hawaii's people. The influence of this group – and that of overseas Japanese visitors – has permeated almost every sphere of island life.

While words such as *sushi* and *sashimi* have only recently entered the vernacular of mainland Americans, the people of the islands have long been comfortable with sleeping on a *futon*, soaking in an *ofuro*, and sipping *sake*. Replicas of Japanese structures abound, from a scaled-down version of Kamakura's giant Buddha

(Jodo Mission, Maui) to Kochi Castle (Makiki Christian Church, Honolulu), to Kyoto's Golden Pavilion (Honolulu Memorial Park).

The analogy of the Zen garden may be appropriate in reference to Japan-Hawaii business relations. Japanese gardens are designed as microcosms of a larger, more chaotic world. They are places where the gardener can plant, develop, prune, or expand his visions, all in a controlled environment. For the most part, Hawaii has been a fertile and friendly plot for traditionally insular and conservative Japanese businesses to plant seeds and develop their foreign-investment landscape.

The first Japanese companies to invest in Hawaii (the Yokohama Specie and Sumitomo banks) were open for business in 1892. Except for a brief period during and after World War II, the yen has been at work in Hawaii ever since.

*Above: Beachfront at Waikiki. Right: The Dole Cannery in Honolulu, where fresh fruit is sliced, diced and put into cans.*

Mainlanders may be shocked by recent Japanese acquisitions of large properties, including entertainment conglomerates, in North America. But the people of Hawaii have solicited, albeit with some trepidation, large-scale investment for several decades. By the mid-1960s, three Sheraton hotels were sold to Japanese interests, including one of Waikiki's historic landmarks, the Moana. The next decade saw the transfer of two more Sheratons, as well as the grand old "pink palace" – the Royal Hawaiian Hotel – to Japanese hands. The same period saw Japanese investors become braver and begin their own construction on undeveloped properties, including the building of commercial retail space, most notably the Mitsukoshi department store and offices.

For the most part, overseas investment has been seen as beneficial and even essential to the life and economy of Hawaii. As long as hotels and other developments were being built and not only acquired, as long as jobs were being created and

workers were not simply receiving pay packets from new hands, outside capital was welcomed. This general acceptance of friendly foreign investment persisted throughout the 1970s and early 1980s, with only a few dissenters beginning to express concerns about the virtually unrestricted deployment of foreign capital.

The realignment of international exchange rates in 1985, however, triggered a *tsunami*, or tidal wave, of new investment on the part of the Japanese. In March of that year, the yen traded in the 260-to-\$1 range. Within three years, it was in the 120-to-\$1 range. The "Hang Loose" T-shirt which cost \$6 in Waikiki in early 1985 could be had in 1988 for the equivalent of \$2, after currency was exchanged. Undoubtedly, the same economic equations were motivating bigtime investors, whether they were contemplating the acquisition of shopping centers or homes in Honolulu's desirable Kahala district.

Suddenly, Hawaii has been put up for sale, at what amounts to bargain-basement prices. Some people refer to Hawaii as Japan's "48th prefecture (province)." Many of the residents who promoted unrestricted investment opportunities in the past, in the face of perceived speculation and rising prices, are beginning to call for guidelines that would limit the ways in which outside capital could be used. In a poll at the end of the 1980s, fully 60% of Hawaii residents said they were now somewhat or strongly opposed to Japanese investment.

Interestingly enough, while Japanese property investment in the U.S. has always been primarily concentrated in the Aloha State, figures since 1988 indicate that at least three mainland states now attract more Japanese money than Hawaii. It seems that, among other factors, a successful experience over the years in the islands has led many Japanese businesses to take that great big step beyond "the heavenly place." Just as elements of the Japanese vocabulary are moving past Hawaii onto new shores, so, too, the migration of the yen is proceeding.

## ENVIRONMENTAL ISSUES

Visitors to Hawaii are often shocked at the concrete density in what had been advertised as a natural paradise. Meanwhile, local environmentalists and planners are struggling to maintain some kind of balance between the urban facts of life and the increasingly rare presence of what is native.

The true native forest, birds and insects are found more and more only in the high centers of each island. Hawaii loses more native species each year than any other state in the United States. However, the numbers of indigenous species are also high, because of the myriad tiny ecosystems created by volcanic activity and the islands' isolation.

Scientists have called the Hawaiian Islands one of the greatest natural labora-

*Above and right: Urbanization and industrialization have cost the lives of numerous species in Hawaii. What remains is generally found in the higher elevations.*

tories in the world for the study of evolution. The colonizing species that traveled thousands of miles from larger land masses to the islands spun off strange new lineages, adapted at times to just the tiny circumference of a single volcanic nodule (or *kipuka*).

98% of Hawaii's birds, 93% of its flowering plants and almost every one of its invertebrates are found nowhere else on the planet. These species lack natural defenses, until recently having known few predators. Now, exotic competitors from abroad have invaded almost every place below 1,000 m elevation, finding little resistance to a complete takeover.

Most of the native world is unknown and unseen by residents, let alone visitors. The resort-lobby flora and fauna that tourists experience is not Hawaiian, but is imported from other tropical regions. Few of the state's 1 million residents have ever been in a true Hawaiian rainforest, but turn to the coastline for recreation. The Hawaiian phrase *aloha aina*, "love of the land," is increasingly given

mere lip-service as high rise buildings, manicured fantasy resorts, costly golf courses and pork-barrel highways are given political precedence by government officials.

But Hawaii residents do hold their environment dear. They have recently embraced recycling, beach cleanups and saving a real if invisible rainforest from further destruction.

Native forest is preserved by the federal government on the Big Island in Hawaii Volcanoes National Park and the Hakalau Wildlife Refuge, normally closed to visitors. The state maintains a Natural Area Reserve System of about 200,000 acres (80,000 hectares) throughout the islands. But until recently, this program has lacked resources to fence off and clean up the forests from feral pig and human depredations.

The nonprofit and private Nature Conservancy also holds a significant acreage of preservation land, and is restoring the land as much as possible to its natural state. Botanical gardens also nurture native species and may be the best places for visitors to observe them, particularly the Pacific Botanical Center on Kauai and the Lyon Arboretum on Oahu.

The state boasts a questionable commitment to alternative and non-polluting energy. With the perpetual sunshine here, solar energy has been surprisingly underutilized. About 10% of the dwellings have rooftop water heaters. Wind power supplies 3% of the electrical power of the Big Island. And sugar cane residue, or bagasse, is burned to contribute 7% of Hawaii's electricity. Still, all alternative sources together make up only about 13 % of the state's power sources.

The island of Oahu is also building two modern coal-burning plants and recently completed a 50-megawatt garbage-to-energy burner. Plans are in the works for a massive geothermal project on the Big Island that would supply 500 megawatts of electricity to the island of Oahu by an undersea cable. This project has been highly controversial and is opposed by many environmental organizations.

239

# Nelles Maps ...the maps, that get you going.

- Afghanistan
- Australia
- Bangkok
- Burma
- Caribbean Islands 1 /
  Bermuda, Bahamas,
  Greater Antilles
- Caribbean Islands 2 /
  Lesser Antilles
- China 1 /
  North-Eastern China
- China 2 /
  Northern China
- China 3 /
  Central China
- China 4 /
  Southern China
- Crete
- Egypt
- Hawaiian Islands
- Hawaiian Islands 1 / Kauai

## Nelles Maps

- Hawaiian Islands 2 /
  Honolulu, Oahu
- Hawaiian Islands 3 /
  Maui, Molokai, Lanai
- Hawaiian Islands 4 / Hawaii
- Himalaya
- Hong Kong
- Indian Subcontinent
- India 1 / Northern India
- India 2 / Western India
- India 3 / Eastern India
- India 4 / Southern India
- India 5 / North-Eastern India
- Indonesia
- Indonesia 1 / Sumatra
- Indonesia 2 /
  Java + Nusa Tenggara
- Indonesia 3 / Bali
- Indonesia 4 / Kalimantan

- Indonesia 5 / Java + Bali
- Indonesia 6 / Sulawesi
- Indonesia 7 /
  Irian Jaya + Maluku
- Jakarta
- Japan
- Kenya
- Korea
- Malaysia
- West Malaysia
- Nepal
- New Zealand
- Pakistan
- Philippines
- Singapore
- South East Asia
- Sri Lanka
- Taiwan
- Thailand
- Vietnam, Laos
  Kampuchea

**HAWAII**
©Nelles Verlag GmbH, München 45
All rights reserved
ISBN 3-88618-376-9

First Edition 1992
Co-Publisher for U.K.:
Robertson McCarta, London
ISBN 1-85365-241-5 (for U.K.)

| | | | |
|---|---|---|---|
| **Publisher:** | Günter Nelles | **DTP-Exposure:** | Printshop Schimann, Ingolstadt |
| **Chief Editor:** | Dr. Heinz Vestner | | |
| **Project Editor:** | John Gottberg | **Color** | |
| **Editor in Charge:** | Dr. Bernd Peyer Ellen Knutson | **Separation:** | Scannerstudio Schaller, München |
| **Cartography:** | Nelles Verlag GmbH, München | **Printed by:** | Gorenjski Tisk, Kranj, Yugoslavia |

- 01 -

## *TRAVEL INFORMATION*

## PREPARATION

### Arrival Formalities

If you're traveling to Hawaii from Asia, Australia, or other Pacific islands, you'll clear customs and immigration at Honolulu airport. Coming from Europe, you must complete formalities at the first point of arrival in the United States, even though it may be only an intermediate stop en route. For example, if you're flying from London via New York and Los Angeles, customs and immigration procedures will take place in New York. Baggage will be put back on the plane and delivered in Honolulu at baggage carousels.

### Immigration/Visas

Hawaii is an integral part of the United States. As such, a valid passport and U.S. visitor visa are required for entry. Consult the U.S. embassy or consulate nearest you for specific requirements and application procedures from your country.

### Customs

Visitors to the United States are allowed to bring with them duty-free: 300 cigarettes, 50 cigars and one quart (0,946 liter) of wine or other alcoholic beverages. Remember that items such as cigars from Cuba are prohibited from entering the U.S.A., even though some customs officials don't seem to take much notice of the brand you smoke.

All produce, plant materials and wild animals are subject to border inspection by the State Department of Food and Agriculture, to determine their admissibility and quarantine laws. Fresh fruits and meats typically are forbidden entry. Dogs and cats must have been certified as vaccinated against rabies within the previous year.

### Climate

Geographically located between 19 and 22 degrees north latitude, Hawaii has a balmy tropical climate with no marked distinction between seasons. During the summer months, April-October, temperatures range from 75° to 90° F (24° to 32° C); in "winter", the range is 65° to 85° F (18° to 29° C). Except in the higher elevations, it's rare for the temperature to drop below 60° (15° C). Northeasterly trade winds keep humidity to a minimum most of the year.

Light afternoon showers frequently roll shoreward from the island's mountains, release a not-unpleasant, cooling sprinkling, and then retreat. Truly rainy days are infrequent in most parts of the state, except on some windward slopes. Mount Waialeale in the center of Kauai is recorded as the wettest place on earth, with an average annual rainfall of 486 in (12,344 mm).

On the other hand, the Ka'u Desert, on the south side of the Big Island, is extremely arid. The community of Puako averages 9.5 in (241 mm). Average annual rainfall in Honolulu is 24 in (610 mm); in Hilo, it's a hefty 134 in (3,403 mm).

For weather information, call 836-2102 on Oahu; 877-5111 on Maui; 961-5582 on the Big Island; or 245-6001 on Kauai.

### Clothing

As long as you're staying in the beach resorts, you can keep apparel to a minimum. You'll want beachwear, of course, including open-toed sandals. Evening wear is casual but "trendy;" Some of the fancier establishments and resort restaurants may require formal evening dress, so it is wise, just in case, to pack a jacket and tie.

Many visitors "go local," with men buying colorful, floral aloha shirts and women opting for free-flowing muumuus.

The occasional cool night is possible, even on Hawaii, so remember to pack a sweater. If you're going to Maui's Haleakala or the Big Island's Volcano House, you'll need the sweater, and perhaps a jacket as well. Don't forget a pair of good walking shoes with thick, wool socks if you're a hiker.

### Currency and Exchange

Most banks are open from 10 am to 3 pm Monday to Thursday, and 10 am to 5.30 pm Friday.

Major banks and independent currency exchange bureaus will trade in major foreign currencies during banking hours. Honolulu International Airport has a currency exchange office, with extended hours of operation to serve travelers.

Few hotels or shops will accept foreign currency. Travelers checks in U.S. dollars offer the greatest convenience and safety for travelers.

Plastic money, i.e. credit cards, are among the most common ways of paying and are highly respected, especially American Express, Master Card, Visa, and JCB (Japan Credit Bank). It is even possible to charge phone calls to your card: Dial "0" for the operator.

## TRAVELING TO HAWAII

**Air**: Major airlines of the United States, Canada, and many Asian and Pacific countries arrive and depart on a regular basis from Honolulu International Airport. Among the carriers are Air New Zealand, American Airlines, Canadian, Cathay Pacific, China, Continental Airlines, Delta, Hawaiian, Japan Airlines, Korean Airlines, Northwest, Philippine, Qantas, Singapore, Thai and United Airlines.

There are also direct flights between the U.S. mainland and Hilo, Kailua-Kona, and Maui, and one-stop connections to Kauai.

**Sea**: Major international cruise liners frequently stop in Honolulu and other Hawaiian ports-of-call.

## TRAVELING IN HAWAII

### Inter-Island Travel

**Air**: Aloha, Hawaiian, and Mid-Pacific airlines serve the islands of the archipelago with frequent daily flights. These major carriers land in Honolulu, Kahului (Maui), Lihue (Kauai), and Kona and Hilo (Hawaii).

Associated commuter airlines serve smaller communities, including Kaanapali and Hana; Hoolehua and Kalaupapa, Molokai; Lanai City, Lanai; Kamuela/-Waimea, Hawaii; and Princeville/Hanalei, Kauai, as well as Honolulu.

In-state fights are handled by several major carriers such as *United* and *American*. Any travel agent will have more information concerning their services. The great price wars of the past years have driven serveral of Hawaii's smaller airlines out of business. Of the surviving ones are:

*Aloha Airlines,* P.O. Box 30028, Honolulu, HI 96820, Tel: 836-1111.

*Hawaiian Airlines,* 1164 Bishop Street, (P.O. Box 30008), Honolulu, HI 96820, Tel: 537-5100.

To give you an idea of air fare prices, Hawaiian Airlines charges for all inter-island flights: US$ 65,95 *each way* for non-island residents, US$ 57,95 for islanders, US$ 49,95 for all travelers over 60 years of age.

It is also worth keeping an eye out for special deals (such as Hawaiian Airlines' day's first-and-last flight to most islands from Honolulu.) If in a hurry, you can always book a flight at one of the ticket offices at the inter-island terminal of Honolulu airport. Visit-America passes are honored by the airlines.

**Sea**: Small cruise ships, such as the *S.S. Monterey*, offer sailings of three to seven days around the islands. Travel agents or the Hawaii Visitors Bureau have details. There are currently no commuter lines between islands.

### Local Land Transportation

**Taxis**: In cities and resort areas, taxis can usually be hailed from the street or found waiting outside major hotels and attractions. Otherwise, it may be necessary to call in advance for pick-up. Hotels and restaurants can do this for you. Taxis are reasonably priced for short distances, expensive for longer distances. Then, it's wise to take a bus or rent a car.

**Buses**: In Honolulu, the mass transit system is known simply as The Bus. The bright yellow-and-white-striped vehicles serve the entire island of Oahu, with round-the-island fares reasonably priced. (Call 531-1611 for information). Maui, Kauai and the Big Island (Tel: 935-8241) all have their own bus systems.

**Car Rental**: You can't miss the agents' booths at any of the island's major airports. There are always a handful of them facing the baggage carousels. Agencies are also located in resort communities.

Rates typically start around $40 a day. Travel sections of major newspapers often advertise very inexpensive specials. Drivers must be at least 21 years old, often 25, for insurance purposes. Drivers require a license valid in any country signator to the 1949 Geneva Agreement. Drivers also should carry a major credit card or be able to post a cash deposit (sometimes $600 or more).

Agencies with rental offices on each major island include Alamo, Avis, Budget, Dollar, Hertz, Roberts, and Tropical.

## PRACTICAL TIPS

### Accommodation

Hawaii has a wide range of accommodation in moderate and deluxe price categories, a more limited range at the budget level. Oahu, Maui, Kauai and Big Island each have a large number of world-class luxury hotels. Elsewhere on the islands are lower-priced hotels and bed-and-breakfast inns, youth hostels and campgrounds.

Because of the islands' popularity, it's important to book well in advance.

The top resort properties charge $200 per night and more for standard rooms. More moderately priced hotels often cost $100 per night and upwards, with economy units in the $50 range. One possibility sometimes offered by hotels and travel agents are packages including round-trip airfare, or packages for stays on several islands.

Increasingly popular among visitors, especially those planning to stay for two weeks or longer, are condominiums and apartment hotels. These are endowed with kitchen facilities, enabling guests to prepare their own meals and save on restaurant costs. Rates are typically $100 or more per night. Vacation homes can also be rented for a much higher price, but it might pay for a family or small group.

Bed-and-breakfasts (B&Bs) are growing in number in Hawaii. Most charge between $50 and $100 per night. Statewide reservation services and booking agencies include All Islands B&B, 823 Kainui Dr., Kailua, HI 96734; Bed & Breakfast-Hawaii, P.O. Box 449, Kapaa, HI 96746; Bed and Breakfast Honolulu, 3242 Kaohinani Dr., Honolulu, HI 96817; and Bed & Breakfast Pacific Hawaii, 970 N. Kalaheo Ave., #A218, Kailua, HI 96734.

Campgrounds in the islands are located in national parks, state parks, and city and county properties. It's advisable to reserve space well ahead of your visit. Write to the specific national park, or to the **Division of State Parks** on Oahu (1151 Punchbowl St., Honolulu 96813); Maui (P.O. Box 1049, Wailuku 96793); Molokai (P.O. Box 153, Kaunakakai 96748); Hawaii (P.O. Box 936, Hilo 96720); and Kauai (P.O. Box 1671, Lihue 96766).

The addresses of **City and County Parks** are: Oahu, 650 S. King St., Honolulu 96813; Maui, 1580 Kaahumanu Ave., Wailuku 96793; Molokai, Dept. of Parks and Recreation, Kaunakakai 96784; Hawaii, 25 Aupuni St., Hilo 96720; and Kauai, 4396 Rice St., Lihue 96766.

## Alcohol

The legal drinking age is 21, so don't forget your legal identification (ID) when out for a drink. Alcohol can be purchased by the package in licensed stores, or by the drink in licensed restaurants, taverns or lounges.

## Electricity

Electric current, standard across the United States, is 110-115 volts, 60 AC. Most hotels do *not* have direct-current converters.

## Festivals and Annual Events

**January**: *2nd week*, International Bodyboard Championships, Makapuu Beach, Oahu. *3rd week*, Hawaiian Open Golf Tournament, Honolulu. *3rd Saturday*, Hula Bowl (college football), Honolulu. *Mid-month* to *mid-Feb*, Narcissus Festival, Chinatown, Honolulu, and other islands. **February**: 1st Sunday, Pro Bowl (National Football League), Honolulu. *2nd, 3rd, 4th weekends*, Big Board Surfing Classic, Makaha, Oahu. *Presidents' Day weekend*, Hawaii Ski Cup, Mauna Kea, Hawaii; Great Aloha Run, Honolulu. *4th weekend*, Captain Cook Festival, Waimea, Kauai.

**March**: *1st week*, Hawaii Sport Kite Championships, Kapiolani Park, Honolulu. *2nd Saturday*, Kamehameha Schools Ho'olaule'a, Honolulu. *2nd Sunday*, Maui Marathon, Kahului to Kaanapali; Hawaiian Song Festival, Waikiki. *17*, St. Patrick's Day Parade, Waikiki. *Last week,* Prince Kuhio Festival, statewide. *Last Saturday,* Great Hawaiian Rubber Duckie Race, Honolulu. *Late month to early April*, Cherry Blossom Festival, all islands.

**April**: *First week*, Merrie Monarch Festival, Hilo, Hawaii. *First Sunday,* Buddha Day, statewide; East-West Center International Fair, University of Hawaii, Honolulu. *2nd Saturday,* Carole Kai International Bed Race and Parade, Waikiki. *2nd Sunday,* Miss Korea Hawaii Pageant, Honolulu. *Last week,* Lei Day competition, statewide.

**May**: 1. May Day/Lei Day, statewide. *2nd and 3rd weeks,* World Cup of Windsurfing, Hookipa Beach, Maui. *2nd full week,* Military Week, Honolulu. *3rd weekend to 2nd weekend of June,* Hawaiian Body Surfing Championships, Point Panic, Oahu. *3rd full week*, Western Week, Honokaa, Hawaii. *4th weekend,* Barrio Festival, Wailuku, Maui; Hanalei Stampede, Hanalei, Kaiai. *4th Saturday,* Ke Ola Hou Hawaiian Spring Festival, Hanapepe, Kauai. *4th Sunday,* Keauhou-Kona Triathlon, Hawaii. *Last week to mid-June,* 50th State Fair, Honolulu.

**June**: Fiesta Filipina, statewide; Hawaii Pacific Games. *1st two weeks,* Festival of the Pacific, Honolulu. *2nd week,* Mission Houses Fancy Fair, Honolulu. *2nd week,* King Kamehameha Day celebrations, statewide; Aloha State Games, Oahu. *2nd and 3rd weekends,* Kapalua Music Festival, Kapalua, Maui. *3rd weekend,* Renaissance Faire, Lihue, Kauai. *Last weekend,* State Horticultural Show, Hilo, Hawaii. *Last Saturday to 2nd Sunday of June,* Trans-Pacific Yacht Race, Diamond Head to Long Beach, California.

**July**: 4, Independence Day celebrations, statewide. *1st weekend,* Parker Ranch Rodeo, Kamuela, Hawaii. *1st Saturday,* Lantern Boat Ceremony and Bon Dance, Lahaina, Maui. *2nd weekend,* Pacific Handcrafters Guild Fair, Honolulu. *3rd week,* International Fesival of the Pacific, Hilo, Hawaii. *3rd Saturday,* Prince Lot Hula Festival, Honolulu. *Last Saturday,* Plantation Days, Koloa, Kauai. *Last Sunday,* Ukulele Festival, Waikiki.

**August**: *All month,* Bon Odori, statewide. *1st Saturday,* State Outrigger Canoe Championships, Hilo, Hawaii. *1st three Sundays,* Na Hula O Hawaii,

Waikiki. *2nd and 3rd weeks,* International Billfish Tournament, Kailua-Kona, Hawaii. *15,* Toro nagashi (Floating Lantern Ceremony), Honolulu. *3rd weekend,* Tahitian Dance Festival, Kapa'a, Kauai. *3rd Saturday,* Hari Boat Festival, Hilo, Hawaii. *3rd Sunday,* South Pacific Chili Cookoff, Honolulu; Gabby Pahinui/Atta Isaacs Slack Key Guitar Festival, Honolulu. *4th weekend,* International Ocean Challenge, Oahu. *4th Sunday,* Haleakala Run to the Sun, Kahului, Maui. *Last weekend,* Kauai County Farm Fair, Lihue, Kauai; Okinawan Festival, Honolulu.

**September**: Miss Hawaiian Islands Pageant, Honolulu. *1st weekend,* Queen Liliuokalani Long Distance Canoe Racing Championships, Oahu. *2nd full week,* Hawaii County Fair, Hilo, Hawaii. *Last 3 weekends,* Parade of Homes, Oahu. *4th Sunday,* Chinese Moon Festival, statewide. *Last week,* Aloha Week, statewide..

**October**: *1st Thursday to Sunday,* Maui County Fair, Wailuku, Maui. *1st weekend,* Waimea Falls Park Makahiki, Oahu. *2nd weekend,* Kanikapila music festival, Honolulu. *2nd Sunday,,* Molokai Hoe (canoe race), Molokai-Waikiki. *3rd week,* World Invitational Rugby Tournament, Waikiki. *3rd weekend,* Hawaiian Canoe & Kayak Championships, Waikiki. *3rd Saturday,* Ironman World Triathlon Championships, Kailua-Kona, Hawaii. *4th Sunday,* Macadamia Nut Festival, Hilo, Hawaii.

**November:** Na Mele O Maui, Kaanapali, Maui; Top Gun Hydrofest, Pearl Harbor, Oahu. *3rd Week,* Kona Coffee Cultural Festival, Kailua-Kona, Hawaii. *3rd weekend,* Sid Fernandez Celebrity Golf Classic, Honolulu. *3rd Sunday,* King Kalakaua Regatta, Honolulu. *Mid-month to mid-December,* Triple Crown of Surfing, North Shore, Oahu. *Last weekend,* Ultraman Endurance Challenge, around Hawaii island.

**December**: Festival of Trees, Honolulu; *Early,* Christmas Parade and Festival, Kapa'a, Kauai. *First weekend,* Mission Houses Museum Christmas Fair, Honolulu. *First week,* International Film Festival, Honolulu. *1st Saturday,* Kaneohe Christmas Parade, Kaneohe, Oahu. *7,* Pearl Harbor Day ceremonies, Oahu. *2nd Sunday,* Bodhi Day, statewide. *3rd Sunday,* Honolulu Marathon, Honolulu. *25,* Aloha Bowl (college football), Honolulu.

## Health

There is no compulsory or government health plan in the United States. Therefore, travelers should purchase travel and health insurance to cover them in the event of any emergency. By the way, health care is perfectly adequate on the Hawaiian Islands.

Major hospitals have 24-hour emergency rooms. Large resort hotels normally have doctors on call. Pharmacies may be open until 9 pm or later. In case of a medical emergency, contact your hotel desk or phone 911 and request an ambulance. The water on the islands is safe to drink.

## Holidays

Hawaii observes all the usual U.S. national holidays and several unique state holidays. Government offices and banks are closed on these days. If a holiday falls on a Saturday, the preceding Friday is a holiday. If a holiday falls on a Sunday, the following Monday is celebrated. The exceptions are Independence Day, Easter, Christmas and New Year's Day, which are held on the actual holiday dates. For the others you will have to consult your calendar, and count up the weeks in the month in which the holliday falls.

The following are the combined Hawaiian and American holidays:

*New Year's Day,* Januar 1.
*Martin Luther King's Birthday,* on the second Monday in January.
*Presidents Day,* on the third Monday in February.

*Prince Kuhio Day,* on March 26 (celebrations take place on the nearest weekend).
*Good Friday.*
*Easter.*
*Memorial Day,* on the last Monday in May.
*Kamehameha Day,* June 11.
*Independence Day,* July 4.
*Admission Day,* August 16.
*Labor Day,* on the first Monday in September.
*Columbus Day,* on the second Monday in October.
*Veterans Day,* November 11
*Thanksgiving,* on the fourth Thursday in November.
Dec. 25, *Christmas.*

### Hospitals and Medical Centers

**Oahu:** Castle Medical Center, Kailua (Tel: 263-5500); Kaiser Medical Center, Waikiki (Tel: 834-5333); Kapiolani Medical Center, Honolulu (Tel: 947-8511); Kuakini Medical Center, Honolulu (Tel: 536-2236); Queen's Medical Center, Honolulu (Tel: 538-9011); St. Francis Medical Center, Honolulu (Tel: 547-6011); Straub Clinic and Hospital, Honolulu (Tel: 522-4000).

**Maui:** Wailuku/Kahului (Tel: 244-9056).

**Big Island:** Hilo (Tel: 969-4111); Kona (Tel: 322-9311).

**Kauai:** Wilcox General Hospital, Lihue (Tel: 245-1100).

### Information

For visitor information, contact the Hawaii Visitors Bureau in Honolulu, Kahului (Maui), Lihue (Kauai), Hilo or Kailua-Kona (Big Island). See addresses under "Tourist Offices," below.

### Newspapers

The state's major newspapers are the two Honolulu dailies: the *Honolulu Advertiser* (morning) and The *Honolulu Star-Bulletin* (afternoon). On the Big Island, most people read the *Hawaii-News-Tribune,* published in Hilo, and on Maui, the *Maui News* is a daily published in Kahului.

### Photography

Photography is, of course, permitted almost everywhere on the islands except in restricted military installations and certain places of worship. When in doubt, ask. Film is readily available and reasonably priced.

### Postal Services

Mail service is very reliable; your hotel desk may even sell stamps and be able to mail your letters and postcards for you. General delivery service (poste restante) is available at central city post offices.

Postage rates were increased in early 1991. Domestic postage is now 29 cents for the first ounce; 23 cents for each additional ounce, and 19 cents for a postcard. Postage to most foreign countries is 50 cents per half-ounce. (It's 40 cents per ounce to Canada).

Most post offices are open 8am to 4pm Monday to Friday, 9am to 12 noon Saturday, closed Sunday.

### Restaurants

Every resort community has a wide choice of wonderful international foods, and some regional creations known collectively as "Pacific Rim cuisine." Less expensive local food is readily available away from the resort strips.

### Shopping

Stores catering to tourists are generally open seven days a week, 12 hours a day (9 am to 9 pm). Downtown businesses may have more conventional hours: 9 am to 5.30 pm Monday to Friday.

### Statistics on Hawaii

*Area:* 6,471 sq mi (16,760 sq km). Includes Hawaii, 4,034 sq mi (10,448 sq km); Maui, 729 sq mi (1,888 sq km); Oahu, 594 sq mi (1,538 sq km); Kauai,

549 sq mi (1,422 sq km); Molokai, 261 sq mi (676 sq km); Lanai, 140 sq mi (363 sq km); Niihau, 70 sq mi (181 sq km); Kahoolawe, 45 sq mi (116 sq km).

*Population:* (1989 estimate) Total 1,112,100. Includes Oahu 841,600, Hawaii 122,300, Maui 88,100, Kauai 50,700, Molokai 6,900, Lanai 2,200, Niihau 210. *Capital:* Honolulu (ca. 450,000).

*Highest points:* Mauna Kea, Hawaii, 13,796 ft (4,205 m); Haleakala, Maui, 10,023 ft (3,055 m); Kawaikini, Kauai, 5,243 ft (1,598 m); Kamakou, Molokai, 4,961 ft (1,512 m); Kaala, Oahu, 4,017 ft (1,224 m); Lanaihale, Lanai, 3,370 ft (1,027 m); Pu'u Moa'ulanui.

*Distances between islands:* Oahu-Kauai, 72 miles (116 km); Kauai- Niihau, 17 mi (27 km); Oahu-Molokai, 26 mi (42 km); Maui-Molokai, 9 mi (14,5 km); Maui-Lanai, 9 mi (14,5 km); Maui-Kahoolawe, 7 mi (11 km); Maui-Hawaii, 30 mi (48 km).

*Nickname:* The Aloha State. *Motto:* Ua mau ke ea o ka aina i ka pono, " The life of the land is perpetuated in righteousness." *State flag:* Eight stripes of white, red and blue represent the major islands. The design in the upper left resembles the Union Jack of Great Britain. *State flower:* Hibiscus Brackenbridgei. *State tree:* Kukui (candlenut). *State bird:* Nene (Hawaiian goose). *State fish:* Humuhumunukunukuapua'a (rectangular triggerfish). *State animal:* Humpback whale.

## Time

Hawaii Standard Time is 10 hours earlier than Greenwich Mean Time; two hours earlier than the U.S. West Coast. When its 6 am in Hawaii, it's 8 am in Los Angeles, 11 am in New York, and 4 pm in London.

When daylight savings time is in effect (October to April) on the U.S. mainland, Hawaii time is unchanged and there's a three-hour difference between the islands and the West Coast.

## Tipping

Tipping is an American custom so deeply ingrained in the hospitality industry that it is considered rude not to tip. A minimum of 15 per cent of the bill is normally paid to restaurant waitpersons. Bar tenders, taxi drivers, barbers, hair dressers, and other service industry people expect similar tips. Airport porters and hotel bellmen should be paid at least 50 cents a bag; valets should get no less than $1 for retrieving your car from a parking lot. Chambermaids should be tipped $1 a day.

## Tourist Offices

The **Hawaii Visitors Bureau** has five island locations:

**Oahu**: Suite 801, Waikiki Business Plaza, 2270 Kalakaua Ave., Honolulu 96815 (Tel: 923-1811).

**Maui**: Suite 112, 111 Hana Hwy., Kahului 96732 (Tel: 871-8691).

**Kauai**: Suite 207, Lihue Plaza Building, 3016 Umi St., Lihue 96766 (Tel: 245-3971).

**Big Island**: Suite 105, Hilo Plaza, 180 Kinoole St., Hilo 96720 (Tel. 961-5797), and 75-5719 W. Alii Dr., Kailua-Kona 96740 (Tel. 329-7787).

## Weights and Measures

Hawaii has yet to convert to the metric system of measurement. Thus:

1 inch = 2.54 centimeters
12 inches = 1 foot = 0.3048 meter
5.280 feet = 1 mile = 1.609 kilometers
3, 560 sq ft = 1 acre = 0.4047 hectare
640 acres = 1 sq mile = 2.59 sq km
2 pints = 1 quart = 0.9463 liters
4 quarts = 1 gallon = 3.7853 liters
1 ounce = 28.3495 grams
16 ounces = 1 pound = 453.59 grams

As in the entire USA, temperatures are measured in Fahrenheit. To get the Celsius value, use the following formula: F - 32 x 5/9 = ° C. The following chart lists approximate Celsius values:

32°F . . . . . . . . . . . . . . . 0°C

| | | |
|---|---|---|
| 50°F | . . . . . . . . . . . . . . | 10°C |
| 68°F | . . . . . . . . . . . . . . | 20°C |
| 75°F | . . . . . . . . . . . . . . | 24°C |
| 90°F | . . . . . . . . . . . . . . | 32°C |

## ADDRESSES

(**Please note**: All toll-free numbers (beginning with 800...) listed in this book may only be used when calling from the United States.)

### Important Telephone Numbers

**Oahu:** Emergency (police-fire-ambulance), 911. Mayor's office, 523-4385. Governor's office, 548-6222. Airport manager, 836-6533. Consumer protection department, 548-2540. Surf report, 531-7873.

**Hawaii:** Police, 935-3311 (Hilo), 323-2645 (Kona). Fire and ambulance, 961-6022. Mayor's office, 961-8211. Governor's representative, 961-7293. Airport manager, 935-0809 (Hilo), 329-2484 (Kona).

**Maui:** Emergency (police-fire-ambulance), 911. Mayor's office, 245-3385. Governor's representative, 245-4460. Airport manager, 246-1400. Consumer protection office, 245-4365.

**Kauai:** Emergency (police-fire-ambulance), 911. Mayor's office, 244-7855. Governor's representative, 244-4398. Airport office, 877-0078 (Kahului), 669-0228 (West Maui). Consumer affairs office, 244-4387.

### Foreign Representation in Honolulu

**Australia**: 1000 Bishop St., Honolulu (Tel: 524-5050).

**Austria**: 2895 Kalakaua Ave. (Tel:923-8585).

**Belgium**: Financial Plaza of the Pacific, Honolulu (Tel: 524- 1191).

**China**: 2746 Pali Hwy. (Tel: 595-6347).

**Denmark**: Suite 311, 444 Hobron Lane (Tel: 955-1001).

**Finland**: 605 Kapiolani Blvd. (Tel: 525-8000).

**France**: Room 706, 130 Merchant St. (Tel: 533-7378).

**Germany**: 916 Kaaahi Place (Tel: 847-4411).

**Indonesia**: Suite 924, Davies Pacific Center (Tel: 524-4300).

**Italy**: 11 Hanapepe Place (Tel: 523-3622).

**Japan**: 1742 Nuuanu Ave., (Tel: 536-2226).

**Korea**: 2756 Pali Hwy. (Tel: 595-6109).

**Netherlands**: Suite 1100, 2222 Kalakaua Ave. (Tel: 923-3344).

**New Zealand**: Suite 1707, 2270 Kalakaua Ave. (Tel: 922-3853).

**Norway**: 536 Ulukou St. (Tel: 732-6009).

**Philippines**: 2433 Pali Hwy. (Tel: 595-6316).

**Portugal**: 20th Floor, 1441 Kapiolani Blvd. (Tel: 946-8080).

**Sweden**: 1856 Kalakaua Ave. (Tel: 941-1477).

**Switzerland**: 1060 Kealaolu Ave. (Tel: 737-5297).

**Thailand**: Suite 305, 735 Bishop St. (Tel: 524-3888).

**Western Samoa**: 1720 Ala Moana Blvd. (Tel: 941-9418).

### Hawaii Visitors Bureaus Abroad

**California**: Room 502, Central Plaza, 3440 Wilshire Blvd., Los Angeles, CA 90010, (Tel: 213-385-5301); and Suite 450, 50 California St., San Francisco, CA 94111, (Tel: 415-392-8173).

**District of Columbia**: Suite 519, 511 K St., N.W., Washington, DC 20005, (Tel: 202-393-6752).

**Illinois**: Suite 1031, 180 N. Michigan Ave., Chicago, IL 60601, (Tel: 312-236-0632).

**New York**: Suite 1003, 441 Lexington Ave., New York, NY 10017, (Tel: 212-986-9203).

**Canada**: 205-1624 56th St., Delta, B.C. V4L 2B1, (Tel: 604-943- 8555).

**Australia**: Walshes World, 8th Floor,

92 Pitt St., Sydney, N.S.W. 2001 (Tel: 02-235-0194).

**Britain**: First Public Relations, Ltd., 2 Cinnamon Row, York Place, London SW11 3TW (Tel: 71-924-3999).

**Germany**: Hans Regh & Associates, Elbinger Str. 1, D-6000 Frankfurt/Main 90 (Tel: 49-69-704-013-1415).

**Hong Kong**: Suite 3702A, West Tower, Bond Centre, Queensway, Hong Kong (Tel: 05-260-387).

**New Zealand**: Walshes World, 2nd Floor, 87 Queen St., Auckland 1 (Tel: 09-793-708).

## GLOSSARY

A form of Pidgin English is spoken on Hawaii that includes genuine Hawaiian and English words, frequently in combination.

As you will notice glancing at the following list, some words are, barring somewhat different enunciation, recognizable as English.

### Hawaiian and Pidgin Words

akamai . . . . . . . sophisticated, "hip"
aloha . . . . . . . hello, farewell, love
aloha nui loa . . . . . . very much love
auwe alas . . . . . . . . . . . . . oh!
da kine . . universal pidgin expression, used anywhere, anytime, any way
E komo mai . . . . . . . . welcome
gecko
. . local lizard, friendly and good luck
geev'um . . . . . . . . . . . go for it!
hana . . . . . . . . . . . . . . . work
hana hou . . . . . . . . . . do it again
haole . . . . . . . . . white foreigner, often applied to any Caucasian
hapa . . . . . . half, or mixed ethnicity (as in hapa-haole)
hapai . . . . . . . . . . . . . pregnant
Hauoli la hanau . . . . happy birthday
Hauoli Makahiki Hou   Happy New Year
heiau . . . . . . . ancient rock temple
hele . . . . . . . . . . . on get moving

howzit . . . . . . "How's it?" Greeting
huhu . . . . . . . . . . . angry, upset
hui . . . . . . . . . group, association
imu . . . . . . . . . . earthen pit oven
kahuna . . . traditional Hawaiian priest, medical practitioner, and/or spiritual adviser
kai . . . . . . . . . . . . . . . . ocean
kalua . . . . . pig great luau delicacy
kamaaina . . . . . . long-time resident
kane . . . . . . . . . . man, husband
kapu . . . . . . . . . sacred, forbidden
kaukau . . . . . . . . . . . . . . food
keiki . . . . . . . . . . . . baby, child
kokua . . . . . . . . help, assistance
kuleana . . . responsibility, jurisdiction
laulau   individually wrapped servings of meat and/or fish
lolo . . . . . . . . . . . . . . . . stupid
luau . . . . . traditional Hawaiian feast
mahalo . . . . . . . . . . . thank you
mahalo nui loa . . thank-you very much
makai . . . . . . . toward the ocean
make (pronounced "mah-kay" dead
makule . . . . . . . . . . . . . . . old
malihini . . . . . . . . . . newcomer
mauka . . inland, toward the mountains
Mele Kalikimaka . . Merry Christmas
moke . . . . . local tough guy, juvenile delinquent
momona . . . . . . . . . . . . . . fat
mo'bettah . . . . . . . . . . . better
niele . . . . . . . . . . . . . . . nosy
okole . . . . . . . . . . . . . buttocks
ono . . . . . . . . . . . . . . delicious
opu . . . . . . . . . . . . . . stomach
pau . . . . . . . . . . . . . . finished
pau hana . . . . . . . done with work
pilau . . . . . . . . . . . . . . dirty
puka . . . . . . . . . . . . . . . hole
pupu . . . . . . . . . . . . . appetizer
pupule . . . . . . . . . . . . . . crazy
shaka . . oustanding! Also, a hand signal with thumb and small finger extended
s'koshi . . . . . . . . . . . a little bit
tita . . . . . . . . . . tough local girl
tutu . . . . . . Hawaiian grandmother
wahine . . . . . . . . . . woman, wife
wikiwiki . . . . . . . quickly, in a hurry

## AUTHORS

**John Gottberg**, project editor of this book, is a freelance travel writer based in Seattle. He has lived and worked many years in Hawaii as a reporter for *The Honolulu Advertiser* and an academic fellow at the University of Hawaii.

**Allan Seiden**, the book's principal photographer and writer on history, has written and photographed ten books of Hawaii. He makes his home in Honolulu.

**Jeri Bostwick**, former Pacific bureau chief for Travel Age Publications and *Travel Management Daily,* has contributed to eight other books on the state of Hawaii.

**Edgar** and **Patricia Cheatham** are two-time winners of the Society of American Travel Writers' Lowell Thomas award. Their work is published in *Travel & Leisure, Travel Holiday, The New York Times* and *International Herald Tribune.*

**Thelma Chang** is a freelance writer who lives in Honolulu. Her work has been widely published in the islands and on the U.S. mainland.

**Betty Fullard-Leo** is the editor of *Pacific Art & Travel* magazine, and a former editor at *Aloha* magazine. She lives in Kailua, on Oahu.

**Rita Ariyoshi**, author/photographer of *Maui on My Mind* and frequent articles in *Islands, Travel & Leisure* and *The Los Angeles Times,* has been honored for her writing and photos numerous times by the society of American Travel Writers and the Pacific Area Travel Association. She is a resident of Honolulu.

**Peggy Rahn** is a staff writer for the *Pasadena Star.* Rahn has traveled around the world to research stories on food and wine for a variety of publications.

**Archie Satterfield** is the author of four books and a contributor to newspapers and magazines throughout the United States and Canada.

**Susan Manuel** is a reporter for *The Honolulu Star-Bulletin* and a former

holder of the prestigious Gannett Fellowship.

**Bill Nikolai**, a multifaceted talent, is a writer/photographer and actor now based in Vancouver, Canada. A former resident of Honolulu, he frequently travels to the islands.

**Carol Khewhok** is director of public relations for the Honolulu Art Academy and a graduate of the University of Hawaii.

## PHOTOGRAPHERS

# INDEX